"Intimate Allies *penetrates to the heart of the pattern of love and marriage imaged by God throughout Scripture. God's passionate courtship of his beloved, flawed, yet believing church is an immensely powerful metaphor. This heavenly marriage model enhances and informs the human union of husband and wife, and the human relationship, in turn, gives a kind of earthy reality to our understanding of God's ardent pursuit of us, his bride.*

"True Christian marriage is God's way of reversing the broken-ness of a spoiled Eden, of mending our torn, fragmented world, of healing our deepest wounds. The precepts and prescriptions in Intimate Allies *bring potent, healing medicine to today's troubled marriages."*

LUCI SHAW
writer in residence, Regent College
author of *God in the Dark* and *Writing the River*

"Allender and Longman combine scholarship *and storytelling to intrigue us once again, this time with a refreshing new look at marriage and marriage roles. Though engagingly practical,* Intimate Allies *is unique in pointing spouses beyond material survival or even mutual happiness to the possibility of reflecting more accurately who God is and what he is like. Thus the ordinary pleasures and struggles of married life are infused with eternal significance and tastes of deep joy—a vision much longed for and full of hope for us all."*

NANCY GROOM
author of *Heart to Heart about Men:
Encouraging Words for Women of Integrity*

"Once again Allender and Longman have merged their minds and skills to give us an eloquent book packed with biblical wisdom. Intimate Allies shows us marriage as God intended it to be—a taste of heavenly realities. This book is for every husband and wife who long to become true soul mates."

DRS. LES AND LESLIE PARROTT
codirectors, Center for Relationship Development,
Seattle Pacific University
authors of *Saving Your Marriage Before It Starts*

"When I read Intimate Allies, I got caught up in the five stories; I even shed some tears over one story. I could see the couples, sometimes as clearly as I can see people who sit across from me in my office. The struggles the couples face are real, and Allender and Longman don't flinch from addressing the issues head-on.

"Intimate Allies touched me in deep places. Not since I read Mike Mason's Gold Medallion-winning book, The Mystery of Marriage, have I been so affected by a marriage book. You may not agree with all of the things that Allender and Longman say in this book, but this book will make you think and feel deeply about real issues and struggles in marriage. It will touch your soul."

DR. EVERETT L. WORTHINGTON JR.
founding editor, *Marriage and Family: A Christian Journal*
author of *Hope for Troubled Marriages*

"Biblical, relevant, realistic, sensitive, practical, stimulating—these words all describe the authors' fresh look at marriage as God intended it to be and as it can be, even in these times of change and uncertainty."

DR. GARY R. COLLINS
president, American Association of Christian Counselors
author of *Family Shock: Keeping Families Strong in the Midst of Earthshaking Change*

"Intimate Allies *will challenge your paradigms and change your life. If you're looking for a stimulating book that will widen your perspective of your spouse and deepen your understanding, then this is it.*"

DENNIS RAINEY
executive director, FamilyLife
host of *Family Life Today*

"*The authors map flaws in modern middle-class marriages with vivid realism and offer Bible-based wisdom to repair the damages. This is a book to take to heart and work with. Struggling couples who do so will gain great help from it. In the midst of confusion and clamor about marriage, this book is something of a landmark.*"

JAMES I. PACKER
Sangwoo Yotuong Chee professor of theology, Regent College
author of *Knowing God*

INTIMATE ALLIES

INTIMATE
ALLIES

TYNDALE HOUSE PUBLISHERS, INC. WHEATON, ILLINOIS

DAN B. ALLENDER
TREMPER LONGMAN III

Library of Congress Cataloging-in-Publication Data

Allender, Dan B.
  Intimate allies : rediscovering God's design for marriage and
becoming soul mates for life / Dan Allender and Tremper Longman III.
    p.   cm.
  Includes bibliographical references.
  ISBN 0-8423-1802-X (alk. paper)
  1. Marriage—Religious aspects—Christianity. 2. Marriage—
Biblical teaching. I. Longman, Tremper. II. Title.
BV835.A455 1995
248.8′44—dc20   95-24136

To our wives, Rebecca and Alice,
for their passion for glory

CONTENTS

PART FOUR

*How Do We Experience the Deepest,
Most Profound Intimacy of Body and Soul?*

PART FIVE

*How Do We, Two Sinners, Learn to Live
with Each Other?*

ACKNOWLEDGMENTS

Each book seems like a child we offer to the world, not knowing how she will serve the good of our God. Our fondest dream is that our voices will draw a few to the high calling of living out in their marriage the mystery of the goodness of God. We are grateful to the many people who have made it possible for us to give birth.

To Ray Dillard, whose wisdom and passion was sorely missed on this project—we long to live in a way that honors your life.

To Tyndale House Publishers, particularly Ron Beers—your willingness to risk the wild evolution of this project from a study Bible took great faith and courage. Thank you. To Ken Petersen, who shepherded us through the conceptual twists, and to Lynn Vanderzalm, who graciously and persistently refined our verbiage to make it more readable—we are so grateful.

To our friends who read the manuscripts, prayed with us, and nourished us during odd, dark struggles—we would never have finished this work without your belief in us.

Last and most important, to our wives, Rebecca and Alice—our labor is and will remain the quiet gift you offer to the reader. We would be beggars without your tender and tenacious pursuit of us and your God. No words or gestures could say any more than "We love you."

INTRODUCTION

Marriages are under assault. Some suffer the tragedy of affairs, abuse, and divorce. Others endure the tedium of a relationship that is an institution and not a romance. Most of us who are husbands and wives feel an exhaustion that comes from the frenetic pace required to honor the competing loyalties of family, work, church, community, parents, friends, neighbors, and more.

Under the weight of competing priorities, we often feel like passing couriers who can only wave and wish the other well. We do not like the growing distance, but we endure it as a reasonable necessity to get through the "busy" time. We hope to patch over the slow loss of passion and purpose by taking an evening out, a weekend away, or a summer vacation. We hope that somehow life tomorrow will enable us to do what we cannot do today. But for many of us, the hope of tomorrow evaporates, and the foundation of our relationship slowly erodes.

No one plans on having an affair. No one plans at the beginning of their marriage to divorce. No one thinks they will be stuck in the doldrums of a passionless, convenient business arrangement that hides a bankrupt relationship.

But it happens.

Many couples who walk into a Sunday-morning church service are merely existing, not thriving in their marriages. Some spouses feel lonely, bored, empty, angry, afraid, or confused. They may look as if they know what to do and how to do it, but appearances are often deceiving, especially in marriage.

What is not seen in many cases is what happened on the way to church—the words that were spoken or not spoken, the accusations that were lobbed, the anger that made the children see their parents' pious veneer as hypocrisy.

Many of these couples live with an underlying contempt for each other. Their smiles hide a quiet hatred for the other. Others live with an unstated and largely ignored distance that robs them of any real hope for change. Others are happy because of a naïve, eager hopefulness that somehow, in some way, all things are going to be fine if they can just listen, learn, and do what the pastor says.

Our marriages *can* grow. They can escape the cycle of boredom, emptiness, anger, and fear, but not without honest assessment. Something is wrong in every heart: We are sinners. Consequently, when two sinners join together in marriage, something will always be wrong in our hearts and in our marriages.

But let's not be pessimistic. We have choices. We can either learn to live with what is wrong—leading to contempt, distance or naïveté—or learn to fight, struggle, honestly seek, ask, and knock.

The language of a battle may disturb many readers, but life is a war. And marriage, at times, requires war if the battle of life is to be fought well. But are our spouses noncombatants, people disengaged from the real battles of our life? Or worse, are our spouses enemies whom we fight daily?

God's intention is for our spouses to be our allies—intimate friends, lovers, warriors in the spiritual war against the forces of the evil one. We are to draw strength, nourishment, and courage to fight well from that one person who most deeply supports and joins us in the war—our soul mate for life. Husbands and wives are intimate allies.

This book invites all of us to learn to struggle according to biblical principles of what God intends marriage to be, what is wrong with our marriages, and how we can honor our spouses in the midst of the struggle and become soul mates for life. We will do this by looking at the Bible to rediscover God's design for marriage and by looking at several marriages in which husbands and wives struggle to live according to God's design.

The Bible is neither a marriage manual nor a systematic statement of how to live. It is a love story, revealing the intimate relationship between God and his people. This divine-human marriage begins with fresh romance, devolves into a divorce, and then ends with a wedding. The Bible's love story illumines the heart of our divine Lover, exposes our spiritual adultery, and woos us with the wonder of our Bridegroom's persistent, unending love.

The Bible is a love story that is intended to encompass the story of our lives here on earth. It is, therefore, the frame that is to hold the picture of our marriage.

Most couples display their wedding pictures, which remind them of the moment they exchanged vows and became husband and wife. They moved from being two separate human beings into a one-flesh relationship, a new unity of soul and body before God.

Becky and I (Dan) hung our wedding picture on the wall opposite our bed. It is the last photograph I see before I retire in the evening and the first when I rise in the morning. I don't think we thought much about it when we first placed the picture there, but I am grateful for its location. It reminds me that I am first and last a man linked to one woman, with one commitment that is to last a lifetime.

My relationship to Becky is one of a kind. I have not made that kind of exclusive commitment to any other person— parent, child, friend, or neighbor. I am bonded to one person only, and that has to guide me from my rising in the morning to my retiring in the evening. It must shape every moment of my life, because it is the one relationship I am to honor if I want to adorn the gospel.

Marriage is not merely a convenience to overcome loneliness or an expedient arrangement to propagate the race. First and foremost, marriage is a mirror of the divine-human relationship. Every marriage is meant to represent God: his perfect relationship with himself—Father, Son, and Holy Spirit—as well as his relationship with his people.

But as the Bible recounts the divine-human relationship, we see that it is not a pretty picture. God's people have affairs with other gods; they abandon him, their first love. The Bible uses marriage imagery—love, bride, Bridegroom, redemption, sacrifice, and even prostitution, adultery, and divorce—to describe God's relationship to his people.

And the Bible, though not a how-to book of marital skills and principles, is nevertheless the guiding story of what God intended for our marriages, what went wrong, and how we can restore that intimacy. The Bible reveals to us the marriage story that is to shape our marriages.

For this reason, we have made the biblical data our top priority in this book. Most of the passages considered are relevant to relationships as a whole, but no relationship bears more importance to culture or to the church than marriage. The study of marriage can profoundly affect our heart, our pursuit of God, and the living out of the gospel in our godless day. Struggling with our relationships with our spouses can lead not only to significant growth and healing as couples but also to a foundation that will allow us to move into a secular culture with the good news of the gospel.

Of course, a book is biblical not because it quotes the Bible a lot but because it is able to apply the biblical text to modern issues and problems with insight and integrity. We are not the ones to evaluate our success in this, but our previous joint projects, *Bold Love* and *Cry of the Soul,* have also combined our distinct expertise in biblical studies and counseling for this same purpose: making the ancient biblical text speak to our modern needs and problems. This book is not a book of Bible exposition, but behind our comments stands serious exegesis.

Further, we do not labor under the illusion that our marriages are perfect or that any one model of marriage is perfect or exclusively biblical. We have read books and attended seminars where a particular cultural model has been baptized with biblical texts and christened the "biblical model" of marriage. On the one hand, as we will see, we receive much divine guidance in biblical principles of marriage, but these principles can take many shapes in how married partners relate to one another.

We also feel that the people who write books about marriage should admit something of the ups and downs of married life. We have wonderful, yet sinful wives; we know we have many faults as husbands. Perhaps the most important lesson we learned before getting married was something Jay Adams used to say: "When you join two sinners in holy matrimony, you don't get a perfect couple." Anticipating problems in marriage keeps all of us from expecting the impossible.

What is the purpose of this book if a perfect marriage is beyond the realm of possibility? We believe that the Bible cuts through our defensiveness, our deceit, our pretense, our busyness and restores the vitality and excitement of all our relationships. The Bible helps us understand ourselves better, our spouses better, and God better. It is only through our study of the Bible that we will have God-pleasing and enjoyable marriages.

We believe it is possible to glimpse joy now in our marriages, but not in an obvious way. The Bible will guide us on a route to joy that seems as insane and absurd as giving up one's life in order to find it.

This book has an order that may be helpful to know before you plunge into the text. We address five basic questions that are foundational to our lives as Christians:

- Who are we?
- What are we to do?
- How are we to do it?
- What will be the fruit of our labor?
- What is wrong with us and our world?

When we translate these questions into the marriage relationship, the questions look like this:

- Who are we as husbands and wives?
- What are our roles as husbands and wives?
- How will we work together as husbands and wives?
- How do we experience the deepest, most profound intimacy of body and soul?
- How do we, two sinners, learn to live with each other?

This book will address each of these five questions in three ways. First, each of the five parts of the book will begin with a vignette, a slice-of-life story that gives a glimpse of a married couple struggling with one of the questions. The stories are not case studies meant to explain the problem or the solution; instead, they are intended to draw you into thinking about your marriage. While you may differ from the couples in the stories in many ways, we hope you see the issues portrayed as universal.

A second chapter in each part will explore what the Creation story tells us about God's design for marriage. What do the first husband and wife teach us about those five questions? Questions at the end of the chapter will help you reflect on the meaning of the chapter for your marriage relationship.

A third chapter in each part will expand the Creation principle by examining other biblical passages and biblical marriages. Questions at the end of the chapter will help you integrate the biblical principles into your marriage.

The final chapter in each section returns to the slice-of-life story and shows how the couple moves toward wholeness in their relationship as husband and wife begin to understand the biblical principle and its impact on their marriage. These stories are not happily-ever-after stories as much as they are glimpses of the beginnings of change.

We are excited that you have chosen to join us in this exploration of God's design for marriage. We pray that your marriage will be strengthened, enriched, and deeply changed by your interaction with the biblical passages in this book. If your marriage is to gain the maximum growth from this book, we invite you to pray for these three things:

First, be willing to struggle rather than demand a quick fix. You may find answers to your problems, and you may experience hope for change. But those answers and that hope do not come when we expect them to or in the form we expect. Growth in our marriages involves far more than doing something right; it involves an openness to think and pray, to ask and search the Bible for truth about ourselves and our marriages.

It is clear that God blesses those who hunger and thirst for righteousness, not those who want to use him as a magician. The passages we look at are not quick fixes for change, magical incantations that if memorized and practiced will lead to good results. They are more like a treasure map that will guide our search.

Second, be willing to talk with your spouse about the issues of your marriage. Reading this book together will open up important discussions that will lead to growth in your marriage. This book will confront you with the unsettling truth about yourself and God's design for marriage. No one fully faces what is true—it would be too difficult—but are you willing to talk honestly and directly with your spouse about your marriage? Many of you may find that the issues raised in this book will stir up deep emotions. Discussing them may be one of the more difficult experiences in your relationship. On the other hand, honest involvement not only is the route for a changed marriage but also opens up a new path for needing and knowing God. Commit yourself to praying for each other and for your marriage as you discuss these things together.

However, it is possible that your spouse may not read and talk with you about your marriage because of either busyness or lack of interest. You may have to discover other ways to communicate with your spouse about the biblical principles you will discover about your marriage. If your spouse will not read this book with you, find someone—perhaps a close friend of the same gender—who will interact with you and be a mirror to reflect what he or she sees in your life. You will internalize the material in the chapters more effectively if you read it and discuss it with someone else.

You may find the questions that appear at the end of some of the chapters helpful in guiding your discussions.

Third, be willing to dream rather than to live with expectations that are far less than God's design. Many spouses refuse to hope after years of disappointment. They stop dreaming and praying. We pray that you will set your sights high. Be willing to dream, even when it is painful and appears fruitless.

Why did you originally marry your spouse? What are the highest goals for your marriage now? For many people their highest goal is little more than survival; for others it is the ideal of mutual happiness. A marriage will never rise above its highest purpose. We want you to dream of a marriage that goes well beyond what most of us allow ourselves to desire. We pray that you will dream of becoming a couple whose marriage has such intimacy that it mirrors the love of the Father and the Son (John 17:21-23). We want you to dream of developing a marriage that points people to the extravagant love of God.

Our desire is to see each of us humble and hungry for what God intended for our marriages. Our marriages have the opportunity and privilege of being living pictures of the Trinity. We can reveal God by the way we love our spouses.

We desire to see God lift us to a taste of his marvelous plan for our marriages. If you wish to move to the kind of joy that requires wisdom and courage, then we invite you to join us on this journey.

Part One

WHO ARE WE AS HUSBANDS AND WIVES?

JACOB AND LYNN:
THE COUPLE WHO DIDN'T
KNOW WHO THEY WERE

Lynn dressed with no thought about her appearance. She didn't need to; she always looked unusually natural and classy. Other women often wondered how she achieved such an effortless look. She wondered why anyone noticed. She knew she was pretty, but she never considered herself a knockout.

But her husband did. After nineteen years of marriage, Jacob still caught himself gazing at Lynn, lost in thought. Jacob turned away from watching Lynn dress and looked in the mirror.

He didn't like what he saw. He was a middle-aged man with thinning hair. His face was creased with the numbering years, and his skin seemed both sallow and puffy. He put his hands on his face and pushed his cheeks against the bone, but when he released his hands, his skin looked no less pale or soft. He said to himself, *Of all times, why do we need to see a counselor now?*

Lynn had insisted they see a counselor. Their marriage had bogged down in frustration and boredom. She had begun to ask if she could remain married when the marriage for her seemed oppressive. Jacob had agreed several months ago, but he had never thought she would test his sincerity. He was a sincere man, but he seldom found it necessary to back up his claims with action. He would never hurt her or betray her for all the wealth in the world. He loved her. If anything, he loved her to the point of driving her mad with frustration and confusion.

They met in college at a Christian ministry gathering. She was innocent and beautiful. He was two years older, had a car, and knew his way around the town and the university. He was surprised at her interest and warmth the first time they talked. After a few meetings, he finally worked up the nerve to ask this goddess out for a date, and to his utter delight, she said yes.

Lynn had dated many other men that year, but of all the men she met, Jacob was the most consistent, caring, and available. He seemed to love the Lord, and she liked the attention Jacob gave her. The years passed, and after Jacob graduated, he turned down a good job to stay in the area to keep their relationship alive. Lynn felt honored but uncomfortable with his decision. Lynn had a difficult time understanding her reaction; she was aware only of the fact that at times she felt suffocated when she was with Jacob. She didn't know how to vocalize her concern, but before the fall semester ended, she broke off the relationship.

Jacob had eventually returned to the East and gotten a good job in a marketing firm as a junior accountant. He was good with numbers and a successful prognosticator of market trends. He loved research and predicting twists and turns in the economy. His own portfolio burgeoned, and his reputation as a shrewd businessman increased; but he was lonely and consumed with thoughts about Lynn.

He had tried unsuccessfully to restart the relationship many times. His repeated efforts in letters and phone calls were rebuffed. Lynn eventually asked him to not contact her again. He complied.

After almost eight months of no contact, Jacob found a card from Lynn in his mailbox on Valentine's Day. It said, "I know this is a surprise, but I didn't want you to think that I hated you or no longer cared. It has been a hard time for you. It makes me sad to think about how I have hurt you, but I think it was necessary for me to get to know the Lord better. I hope someday we can at least be friends. Happy Valentine's Day, my friend." He read the words over so many times that he could repeat them and hear her voice. He called her the next day.

Now, nearly twenty years since that note had been written, he was about to talk with a stranger about a problem that he could neither name nor understand. The best Lynn could say was that she felt cold toward him, smothered by him, and very, very lonely in their marriage. It made no more sense to him than when they had broken up more than two decades earlier.

As Lynn moved to go down to the kitchen, she said: "We will need to leave in about fifteen minutes." She hated telling him when they had to leave. Why wouldn't he know that? Why did she have to tell him that it was time to pick up their son at the soccer match? Why did she need to remind him to cut the lawn? It seemed so small, so petty, but she hated his sincere concern that hardly ever materialized in self-initiated movement. Even sexually, she had to "tell" him when it was an acceptable time to act. He loved her beyond words, but he

5

seldom offered much more than words to speak of his love. She was sick of being adored; she was disgusted with his "love."

How many times had she heard her friends talk about Jacob? Two close friends had husbands who would no more do what they had asked them to do than give up their season tickets to the Broncos games. They envied Lynn. They wanted husbands who would pay attention to them, work around the house, and sit for hours talking about a movie. Jacob did that without thinking twice. Lynn felt crazy for not being grateful, crazy for wanting something that seemed like the very thing she already enjoyed—a husband who really loved her.

Fifteen minutes passed. Lynn stood in the kitchen trembling with anger. Should she wait and risk being late to their first counseling session? Or should she call up to Jacob to remind him that they had to leave? Moments passed, and she caved in to her anger. She walked to the stairs and yelled: "We're late. I'm going now. If you're going to go, then come now." She felt a cacophony of pity and rage when he walked out of the bedroom, seconds after she had yelled, smiling and ready to go.

An hour later, Jacob and Lynn were sitting together on a couch, in the middle of a conversation that might either ruin or redeem their marriage. The words were painful on all fronts.

Lynn: "I feel trapped by Jacob's sincere but empty enjoyment of me. I know he loves me, but I feel it's an empty love. I feel that Jacob looks at me to fill something in him rather than to enjoy me."

Jacob: "Honey, I *love* you. I do my best, but I know I am failing in some way. If I understood what I am doing wrong, then I would change. I don't want to hurt you or offend you."

Lynn: "That's my point. You would do anything for me, but it feels as if you do it more for yourself than for me."

Jacob: "I am doing it for you. But only because I love you. Am I wrong to want to please you?"

Lynn: "I don't know. All I know is I want to get away from you. It feels strange to say that, because most people think you are the greatest guy in the world."

Counselor: "Jacob, do you find anything undesirable in your wife now or in most encounters like this? Or let me put it more directly: When do you experience your wife to be awful, despicable?"

Jacob: "I don't find her undesirable or despicable. I think she is a beautiful, godly, loving woman. I know she could be more patient and be less irritated, but most of the time she's right to be upset."

Lynn: "Stop it, Jacob. Do you think I am God? Do you think I am sinless? You treat me like a goddess that can give or take away life. I hate the power. I hate the position you put me in."

Counselor: "Lynn and Jacob, we have three possible directions to take. One is to assume that Jacob is a godly husband and that Lynn simply needs to relax and enjoy his love. But that route doesn't take into account the fact that Lynn feels smothered. Am I in the ballpark, Lynn?"

Lynn: "Yes. I feel pursued by Jacob, but it's a pursuit that makes me feel like a meal, not a woman."

Counselor: "On the other hand, Jacob, the first approach—assuming Lynn simply needs to realize you love her and then relax in your pursuit—does not take into account that she is a sinful woman with significant struggles with God and with you. For some reason, you simply don't want to face what kind of woman she is, and so your

7

enjoyment of her is not like God's. He sees her heart at its depth and still pursues her. Jacob, you love your wife in a way that will not admit or grapple with her sin; therefore your wife does not feel loved. She seems to feel cheapened by your unrealistic adoration."

Jacob: "OK, but I don't see her as some terrible person. I love her, and I really don't understand what she means by the idea of a 'meal.'"

Counselor: "A second option is to assume that Lynn has been a doormat to your demands, Jacob. Somehow she has bought into a false view of submission and has relegated her life to pleasing you. The route to change then is for Lynn to build more appropriate boundaries and to limit her involvement with you, Jacob. And you, Jacob, need to develop your own interests outside of the marriage. If you both build more intact, separate worlds, then eventually you will be able to come back together without using one another."

Lynn: "So far that seems more true than the first option."

Counselor: "I agree. This approach assumes the problem really is an empty self. But frankly, it makes God little more than a servant who exists to fill your emptiness and guide you in self-discovery. This is the god of the self-help generation, not the God of the Bible."

Lynn: "I will be honest to say that I thought the second option would be the one you would recommend. It still seems more true than the first."

Jacob: "I really don't know what to think. I know my wife is unhappy. I may be empty, but I do love her. I don't want to hurt her, and I am willing to do whatever is required to make my marriage happy. So what is the third option?"

Counselor: "I wish this route was simple and could easily be described. I fear it is so obvious that it can be quickly dismissed. Most couples marry because they fit like a lock and key. They find in each other qualities that offer a taste of life that they have not experienced with anyone else. Those qualities—like Jacob's consuming obsession with you, Lynn—at one time made you happier than anything else in life. Now they repulse you. Lynn, Jacob's pursuit of you once touched your heart, but now it has become something that disgusts you."

Lynn: "That's painful to hear, but I know it is true. For a long time, Jacob's obsession with me felt wonderful. I bragged about how much he lived his life for me. And now it is awful."

Counselor: "Lynn, it's not my desire to point a bony finger at you, but what you are acknowledging is not merely a marriage driven by emptiness but a marriage that has defiled you both. You each have made the other into an idol, a god that you depend on more than the true God."

Jacob: "I don't know. How can love be wrong?"

Counselor: "Jacob, your delight in your wife lacks true sincerity, true depth because you refuse to face her sin—her deep hard-heartedness—and you equally refuse to see your own demandingness. In fact, you may deeply believe you delight in her, but you don't delight in her the way God delights in us; God delights in us but also fully sees our sin. You both have been living a life outside of God's desire. You both have chosen to ignore in yourself and in the other realities that could, in fact, drive your hearts back to a deeper relationship with God, and thus with each other. I know the third option is not clear or real attractive, but it is the one I want to take with you two."

Jacob: "I don't know. It sounds harder than merely learning to communicate better. Honestly, it scares me."

Lynn: "Yeah. I don't know either. You seem to understand how I feel, but I really thought we would go a different direction. I think this option will require more of me than the second option. I think you are right, but I don't know what will be required of me if we go in the third direction."

Counselor: "I don't know either. The path I am talking about will take us all into the valley of the shadow of death. But I believe it is the place you will meet God and grow together in a different, and far more passionate, real marriage."

THREE WEEKS LATER.   Jacob slammed the door when he came in from work. It was the first time in nearly twenty years that Lynn could remember Jacob coming home clearly angry. He barked at Lynn: "When I come home from work, I at least want someone to get the bikes out of the driveway so I can get in the garage without getting out of the car! Is that clear?"

Lynn smiled. She felt frightened at his outburst, but it was different from any other homecoming. Jacob was normally either very kind or preoccupied and distant. But even in his distance he was almost always generous. Finally, he was more obviously sinful, more clearly demanding, and more tragically human than ever before.

Lynn felt for the first time that there might be an honesty, a joint struggle, and a potential for delight in their marriage.

2

RE-ENTERING EDEN:

SEEING GOD IN OUR SPOUSE

Marriage is the soil for growing glory. We must see our spouses in light of what they are meant to become, without turning bitter or complacent about who they are. Marriage requires a radical commitment to love our spouses as they are, while longing for them to become what they are not yet. Every marriage moves either toward enhancing one another's glory or toward degrading each other.

Spouses degrade each other when they show a contemptuous, shaming, judgmental spirit. Degradation can also come when one spouse makes the other into a false god. Jacob degraded Lynn by seeing her as near perfect rather than seeing her as lovely, but capable of being even more godly.

Jacob argued with great passion: "I love her just as she is," yet he adored her with an energy that felt demeaning to Lynn. The reason is that Jacob not only refused to acknowledge his own disappointment in the marriage but also refused to face either his own sin or Lynn's sin.

Many married couples take a "Pollyanna" view of relationships and seem happy and satisfied, but they lack the capacity for honest engagement. Other couples are merely comfortable with life as it is. They refuse to consider how God intends to transform the heart of both husband and wife in every marriage.

Lynn learned over the years to remain numb and guilty. She felt as if she should be thrilled with a husband who utterly adored her. Her discomfort and suspicion about Jacob's reluctance to struggle with their marriage, to face honestly how the marriage could grow, was suppressed with doubt-inducing self-contempt.

Lynn was aware that something was blocking both of them from becoming what God intended for them to be, and her disappointment finally drew her to ask hard questions and put the marriage into a necessary tailspin. Jacob and Lynn will never have a marriage pleasing to God until they comprehend who they are and who they are meant to become. To understand themselves, they must begin to comprehend the wonder of what it means to be made in the image of God.

We all know our marriages have problems. If we are so fooled to think we have escaped problems, then we have an *enormous* problem. But Jacob and Lynn lived for nearly two decades avoiding a serious problem in their marriage—false glorification. Jacob adored Lynn, but Lynn didn't feel enjoyed. At least part of the problem was their unwillingness to ask tough questions about their marriage and about each other. They both refused to "feel" the effects of their sin: Lynn refused to admit her unhappiness and ignored Jacob's failure; Jacob refused to see Lynn's sin and ignored his cowardice. They lived in a cocoon of comfortability, and because they "got along," they presumed all was well. Life and marriage are neither so simple nor easy.

I know life is complicated. I know life's problems are not easily solved, and answers are not simple or easily found. I learned that in first grade. But I need a picture that will help me grasp the simple themes of the problem so that I can keep my eyes on the North Star as I navigate the disturbing waters of life.

How could Jacob and Lynn have faced their problem more quickly and accurately? How might they have saved years of unnecessary sin and suffering? They needed a clearer picture of God's plan for their marriage, a "North Star" to guide them through the dangers in marriage.

The first three chapters of Genesis provide the picture. They offer not only a perspective on the problem but also the cure. If I want to know God's design for my marriage, I must begin at the ground floor of the Bible to understand the foundational perspectives that guide my passage through life.

The first three chapters of the Bible tell a dramatic story. It is the story of a perfect creation, the offer of inconceivable joy, the wild meeting of two people—who were once one, who became two, and who then longed to join again in union—a devastating fall into evil, a divine rescue, and provision for restoration. This story tells me all I ultimately need to know to grasp the simplicity and complexity of life. It sets the tone and direction of the entire Bible.

These chapters are not abstract philosophy; they contain gripping narrative that addresses us in the concreteness and dailyness of our lives. Within the context of the cosmic drama, they answer our most basic questions. These questions and their answers, then, form what we will call the five Creation foundations:

- Who are we?
- What are we to do?

- How are we to do it?
- What will be the fruit of our labor?
- What is wrong with us and our world?

The Bible does not see us as isolated individuals. We are relational beings, and the first three chapters of Genesis also speak to our relationships, first with God, then with one another. In terms of our relationship to one another, surely the most important and the most complex relationship is our marriage. We are not surprised to discover that Genesis 1–3 establishes crucial principles that are to shape our marriages. This story tells us all we ultimately need to know about marriage. When the questions that form the five Creation foundations are translated into our marriage relationships, they look like this:

- Who are we as husbands and wives?
- What are our roles as husbands and wives?
- How will we work together as husbands and wives?
- How do we experience the deepest, most profound intimacy of body and soul?
- How do we, two sinners, learn to live with each other?

We will begin our exploration of marriage in the Bible by delving into five key passages in Genesis 1–3, each dealing with one of the five questions listed above. From this pivotal teaching flows the rest of the biblical teaching on marriage and sexuality.

WHO ARE WE AS HUSBANDS AND WIVES?

Then God said, "Let us make man in our image, in our likeness, and let them rule over the fish of the sea and the birds of the air, over the livestock, over all the earth, and over all the creatures that move along the ground."

So God created man in his own image, in the image of

14

God he created him; male and female he created them.
GENESIS 1:26-27

Who are we? Where do we fit? What is our relationship to others?

We struggle with our identity. We struggle with who we are in relation to what we are to be to others.

The twentieth century asks these questions with angry intensity. Many of the traditional answers and social conventions of the past have disappeared, leaving us vulnerable to new doubts.

One area that has unsettled our generation more than earlier generations is the relationship of the sexes. What, besides the obvious, is the difference between a man and a woman? Do they have the same roles and abilities? Do men and women think, feel, and act identically?

These issues trouble relationships. They have led to deep divisions in our culture and in our homes.

The Bible has been used to justify everything from radical feminism to a severe male dominance. Can we learn anything about the nature of gender and the relationship between the sexes from the pages of God's Word? In this chapter we'll explore the first three chapters of Genesis, and the next chapter will examine other significant passages throughout Scripture.

Made in His Image

We begin at the beginning. Genesis 1 presents a powerful picture of God, the Creator of all things. This foundational chapter narrates how everything in the universe came into existence through the power of God's word alone. He commanded, and the cosmos sprang into being. He is our Creator; he is our Owner. The nature of creation clearly orders us as dependent on the Creator; we serve him. We are not the result of either chance or our own creation. We are not merely the result of his creation—we are the delight of his glory.

We are made in his image. Think about it: We are made in the image of the God of the universe. That truth ought to take our breath away.

Think of how God created the cosmos. God could have ordered the universe into being in a microsecond, but he didn't. The Creation took place over a period of time described as six days. At the end of each creation day, he apparently gazed at his labor and said: "It is good." This was no anemic utterance, no mere "Nice job!" "It is good" is a shout of exultation that cries out: "What I have done is *beautiful!*"

He created and savored. He did not rush or hurry existence. Consider why he took six days. We cannot say with absolute certainty, but it seems his response to each day's labor is an indication. After each day he delighted in his labor. He looked at his artwork and said: "It couldn't be better. I am delighted! It is spectacular." He thoroughly enjoyed and relished his creation.

God's Delight in Glory

God looks at his own handiwork and beams with delight. It is not hard to get a picture of that kind of joy if we have spent time with a young child. The joy of creation radiates over a child's face as he or she shouts: "Look! Look at what I made. Isn't it beautiful?" The shout of joy is an echo of God's delight in standing back and gazing at his own art.

The glory of God radiates. It dazzles. And it compels a response of delight and awe. In other words, God's glory seen in creation compels us to worship—that is, to be staggered by the grandeur of the Creator and moved to gratitude for his kindness in offering us a picture of his character. Creation is a reflection of the very character of God.

Creation reflects God's glory. But what is glory? The

Scriptures never attempt to define or explain glory; they assume we intuitively know something about it.

The spectacle of a sunset—with brilliant shades of purple, orange, and pink silhouetted by clouds that let the final rays of the sun pierce through their dark forms with a mysterious iridescence—leaves us speechless and hungry to thank someone, to applaud the artist who shaped beauty into such an inconceivable form. It is the same, or at least it was meant to be, when a friend labors to comprehend my heart and puts words to dimensions of my life that elicit a "Yes, you know my struggle, and you see what I was meant to be."

CREATION IS A REFLECTION OF THE VERY CHARACTER OF GOD. CREATION REFLECTS GOD'S GLORY.

Any moment of beauty—any moment that gives me a glimpse of the character of God—offers a vista of glory. Glory is mysterious and inexplicable; it is also simple and transparent. It is beauty enfleshed in sensuous form that allures my heart to desire and anticipate seeing the essence of beauty, which is the presence of God. And what we learn from Genesis 1 is that I am the pinnacle of God's revelation of glory in creation. I am actually more impressive and lovely than any sunset, any Grand Canyon, or any created being. I uniquely reveal something about the glory of God.

The Revelation of Glory: Mankind
The climactic day of Creation was the sixth and final day: God fills the realm of the dry land first with livestock and wild animals and then finally with the creation of the first human couple.

17

Genesis 1 presents humanity as the apex of the whole creative process. Humanity is the last and best part of Creation. That crowning touch is so important that it will be the focus of a retelling of the Creation in Genesis 2. It is also signaled by the status that God gives humanity as ruler over the rest of creation (Gen. 1:26, 28).

But perhaps the most startling revelation of this incredible account of our creation is that we are made in the image of God. Human beings are distinguished from the rest of creation by their unique status as the image bearers of God. Further, and more to the point of our issue, Genesis 1:27 goes out of its way to say that *both* sexes are created in the image of God. Both men and women are the image of God! In the world of the Old Testament and the ancient Near East, this teaching was revolutionary. Further, it has tremendous foundational implications for the relationship between the sexes.

What does it mean to be created in the image of God? As we transport ourselves in our imaginations back to the time when Genesis was first written and ask ourselves what the word *image* meant, we get help in our understanding. Ancient kings of the Near East, who ruled vast territories, knew that they could not be physically present everywhere in their kingdoms, so they commissioned statues of themselves to be placed in all the major cities of their realms. When people looked at these statues, they were reminded of the authority of the king who ruled them. The statue was not the same as the king, but it represented the king and was due the same glory and honor. To dishonor the statue of the king was sacrilege, treason.

Humanity was to function in the same way. We are dim reflections, rough analogues of the Creator in ways that his other creatures are not. The startling truth behind the image of God is that we reflect the glory of our heavenly Father:

When I consider your heavens,
the work of your fingers,
the moon and the stars,
which you have set in place,
what is man that you are mindful of him,
the son of man that you care for him?
You made him a little lower than the heavenly beings
and crowned him with glory and honor.
You made him ruler over the works of your hands;
you put everything under his feet:
all flocks and herds,
and the beasts of the field,
the birds of the air,
and the fish of the sea,
all that swim the paths of the seas.
O Lord, our Lord,
how majestic is your name in all the earth! PSALM 8:3-9

We, as human beings, are like God—certainly not exactly, but we dimly reflect him. God is a person; we are persons. He desires; we desire. He thinks; we think. He feels, wills, and acts; we feel, will, and act.

BOTH SEXES REFLECT GOD'S GLORY. What an awesome privilege—to reflect, as finite beings, the infinite, perfect beauty of God. And we are able to do so only in the complexity and distinctiveness of both sexes. Both men and women are made in the image of God. Both are necessary to reflect God; one alone is not only incomplete but also inadequate to reflect his glory. This alone implies that men and women reflect different features of God.

This foundational teaching about gender emphasizes an important truth right from the beginning. Men and women, though different, are equal in the eyes of God. Neither is closer to God; they are both his image.

In other words, sexuality is a part of the creation, not a part of the Creator. God is a person, but he is not a sexual being. God is neither male nor female—but both sexes are necessary to reflect the rich glory of God.

Of course, God represents himself to us throughout Scripture with human metaphors. He is our father, a king, a warrior, a shepherd. But he is also a mother and a wise woman (Ps. 131; Isa. 66; Prov. 8–9).

Men and women are equal before God. Together they are distinguished from the rest of creation by their unique status as the image bearers of God. Both male and female are in essence and status undifferentiated; each is equally and fully the image of God. It is important to insist on this fundamental equality, a fact reiterated in the New Testament when Paul tells us that in Christ "there is neither . . . male nor female" (Gal. 3:28).

BOTH MALE AND FEMALE ARE IN ESSENCE AND STATUS UNDIFFERENTIATED; EACH IS EQUALLY AND FULLY THE IMAGE OF GOD.

This equality has tremendous impact on how we relate to one another. In the first place, we must treat one another with the utmost honor and awe. In marriage and elsewhere we are called to delight as God delights in one another's glory and labor to grow what is lovely to be even more splendid.

WILL WE GLORIFY OR DEGRADE OTHERS?   Our only option in all encounters is to glorify or to degrade. We degrade when we violate the other person's glory or when we use the other's glory for our own purpose. Violation of glory involves any form of emotional, physical, or sexual harm. When a husband verbally demeans his wife or when a wife withdraws from involvement with her spouse, they violate each other, degrade one another.

Degradation can also be more subtle. Jacob degraded Lynn's glory by *using* her glory. Jacob was an empty man who was deeply convinced that he loved, cherished, and honored his wife. In fact, he consumed her. He did not enhance Lynn's glory; he sapped it.

OUR ONLY OPTION IN ALL ENCOUNTERS IS TO GLORIFY OR TO DEGRADE.

If Jacob had more honestly faced Lynn's failure as a woman (and his own as a man) and had been willing to love her in spite of her sin—loving her so that she could become an even brighter reflection of God's glory—then he would not have depended on her to take away his emptiness. He would have lived far less for easy peace and far more for life-enhancing, godly change in each of them.

Men and women must treat each other as who we are: God's representatives on earth. If we degrade, abuse, or neglect one another, we insult the very glory of God. Like the psalmist we should be on the edge of wonder as we consider other people. We will see this to be true even in the light of later passages that suggest distinctive roles for the sexes.

What implications does this truth have for our lives and our marriages? While Psalm 8 does not speak directly of marriage, it certainly outlines the core attitude that must govern every interaction with another human reflection of divine glory. In view of the cosmic status of each individual as a reflection of

God's image, we cannot view our spouse as an object to be tolerated, used, or despised. To do so is to scorn the very glory of God.

What does this say about the nature and purpose of marriage? Simply, the goal of marriage is twofold: to reveal the glory of God and to enhance the glory of one's spouse. If I am to love my spouse as God intended, I will recognize her as an image bearer of God and will live to enhance her beauty, her glory, in order to live out the glory of God. How is that done? What will that look like? Part 2 will give us a clearer idea of our task as husbands and wives and will clarify what we are to do in living out glory.

THE GOAL OF MARRIAGE IS TWOFOLD:
TO REVEAL THE GLORY OF GOD
AND TO ENHANCE THE GLORY
OF ONE'S SPOUSE.

Summary for Marriage: Our spouses are representatives of God. We are called to delight in and to enhance one another's already present glory to the glory of God. Our only option in responding to our spouses is either to glorify or to degrade them.

QUESTIONS FOR REFLECTION AND CONVERSATION
1. Discuss specific situations in which you felt your spouse treated you as an equal partner. What surprised you most about the experience and your response to your spouse?
2. Life often feels so routine. It is more than often busy and mundane. When do you find yourself seeing your spouse as full of glory—a reflection of God? How does that perception change your attitude or behavior toward your spouse?

3. What prevents you from seeing your spouse as a unique reflection of God's glory? What can you change in your marriage to enable this glimpse to occur more often?

4. How does your spouse enhance your glory as a person created in God's image? Every marriage has room for improvement here. How would you be different if your spouse more consistently treated you as a reflection of God's glory?

3

ENHANCING OUR SPOUSE'S

GLORY

For the bride and the groom, their wedding day
borders on the indescribable. It is nearly unreal. They are the
center of attention. Many people have worked hard and incurred considerable expense to make the day special.

As the groom steps out with his best man and ushers, he is
dressed magnificently. His hair is combed perfectly, his cum-
merbund straight, and his smile radiant as he awaits his
beloved.

Then she appears with her father at the back of the church.
The music begins, and she starts her queenly walk toward him.
She is dressed like royalty with her veil and long white train as
she elegantly marches on the unfurled white carpet.

The day before the wedding, both the bride and groom may have been dressed in jeans and T-shirts, and they may have argued. But today their appearance radiates majesty and beauty.

Dressing up for a wedding is a tradition, but it is a tradition that has meaning. The dignified look of the groom and the radiant appearance of the bride emphasize that the day is unlike any other day of their lives. Ordinary days call for ordinary clothes; a wedding day demands far more. The clothes reflect the unparalleled uniqueness of the day. The clothes mirror the beauty, splendor, and glory that are to come from the union of two who will become one. In a sense, this day signals a new creation, and the ambience of the day is to draw forth awe, acclaim, and wonder. Who can resist standing as the bride begins her march? The response is related to what we feel in worship.

MARRIAGE IS A PARADIGM OF GOD'S PURSUIT, PASSION, AND PURPOSE IN CREATING AND REDEEMING HIS PEOPLE.

Marriage provides a lens into the nature of God's relationship with his people. Marriage is a paradigm of God's pursuit, passion, and purpose in creating and redeeming his people. Of course, there are many other pictures, but rarely do we hear God's heart ache so deeply as when he says "I hate divorce" (Mal. 2:16). It is God's desire for our marriages to reflect his character and his involvement with his people. Often, that is not the fruit of marriage.

The wedding splendor at the beginning of married life contrasts sharply with what the pollsters and cultural analysts tell us about the condition of the institution of marriage at the end of the twentieth century. As the young bride and groom meet at the altar, exchange vows, and kiss, some jaundiced, "experienced" onlookers are likely saying to themselves, *Little do they know!*

Anyone who reads newspapers and magazines or watches television and movies knows that marriage is often portrayed as boring, mundane, predictable, aggravating, tiresome at best, and at worst a nightmare. In real life, it falls far short of God's purpose.

But the insight we have gained from Genesis 1:26-27 is that the wedding ceremony is not as unreal as it appears. While marriage brings together two sinners (see part 5), it also unites two glorious image bearers. Losing sight of this fundamental truth leads to mutual degradation rather than glorification between marriage partners.

Indeed, relationships exert powerful influences on people. The closer the relationship is, the more powerful the impact. Of all human relationships, the marriage relationship is the most powerful. Marriage partners will either enhance (give) the glory of the other or degrade (steal) the glory of the other.

MARRIAGE PARTNERS WILL EITHER ENHANCE OR DEGRADE THE GLORY OF THEIR SPOUSE.

To degrade our spouses means to treat them as less than they are, less (or perhaps more) than human. It is to "put them down" and treat them as objects created to serve our own needs and desires. The natural consequence of degrading our spouses is to push them away from us, at least emotionally. It creates a tremendous relational distance.

Our selfishness wants to diminish the glory of our spouses so that our own glory is exalted with no competition. But this is a false hope because our own glory is enhanced as we enhance the glory of our spouses. But nonetheless we persist in our struggle to steal glory rather than give it. We may try to use our spouses' glory for our own purposes or else destroy it so their glory no longer compels our involvement.

As we will see, mutual degradation can take place in more than one way. Indeed there is a paradox here. We can degrade our spouses by treating them as less than an equal person. We can squash and demean our spouses to the point that they feel less than human. But we can also degrade by treating our spouses as an "ideal," making them into something they are not. When we make our spouses to be either our object of vengeance or our hope of redemption, we violate them.

We make our spouses our saviors when we place them on a pedestal and virtually deify them. This imbues them with powers and qualities they cannot offer because it assumes they have passed beyond their own struggles with sin. To *deify* is to set up our spouses to feel used and eventually to topple from their lofty perch. We are called to relate to our spouses as they really are—both a glorious image of God and a sinful, failing human being.

To expand on these thoughts, we will explore several biblical passages that help us understand the meaning of glory, the source of glory, and its relationship to marriage. We will also explore passages that illustrate the opposite of glory, degradation. This chapter will conclude with the story of Ruth and Boaz, who treated each other with appropriate respect and notable love.

GLORY: THE MAJESTIC BEAUTY OF GOD

In the previous chapter we claimed that a fundamental goal of marriage is to enhance the glory of the husband and wife in order to reveal the glorious character of God. The only other option for them is to degrade one another, to make the other person less beautiful rather than more glorious.

The glory of a person is grounded in the fact that every human being is created in the image of God. As a divine image bearer, every human being reflects God's glory. In marriage two glorious creatures are brought together.

This all sounds very nice, positive, and warm and fuzzy, but what does it mean? Glory is an incredibly heavy concept to comprehend. If we want to enhance our spouse's glory, we need to come to some understanding of what it is. Let's first look at passages that describe God's glory, the source of all glory.

The first passage comes from the account of the giving of the Ten Commandments. The Israelites, under the leadership of Moses, expressed their agreement to obey the law, which God had just given them. In response God revealed himself to the leaders. The passage says that the leaders, including Moses, saw something remarkable—they saw God himself. "When Moses went up on the mountain, the cloud covered it, and the glory of the Lord settled on Mount Sinai. For six days the cloud covered the mountain, and on the seventh day the Lord called to Moses from within the cloud. To the Israelites the glory of the Lord looked like a consuming fire on top of the mountain. Then Moses entered the cloud as he went up on the mountain. And he stayed on the mountain forty days and forty nights" (Exod. 24:15-18).

When the Israelites looked up to the top of Mount Sinai, they saw that it was enveloped in a cloud. From the cloud emanated fire, possibly a storm cloud with lightning or a volcano. This cloud was identified with God's glory, and from this cloud he spoke to Moses.

The top of Mount Sinai smoked with fire for the forty days Moses was with God. The people at first stood amazed, but as time went on, they gave up on Moses and on God as well. The powerful display of God's presence on the top of the mountain was not enough for them, so they traded in divine glory for human shame. With their own hands they built a god to worship. With the approval of Aaron, the Israelites built a golden calf idol and worshiped it while Moses was receiving the Ten Commandments.

When Moses returned, he was outraged at the people. He shattered the stone tablets with the Ten Commandments on them. Moses finally prayed, asking God to forgive the people.

In this passage, Moses expresses his need for divine assurance. He needs the Lord to confirm his presence with him. Moses asks God to show him his glory.

God warns Moses that no one can look directly at him and live. He instructs Moses to go stand on a rock. Then God will put his hand over him, not removing it until he has passed Moses. Moses will be able to see only God's back.

> Moses said to the Lord, "You have been telling me, 'Lead these people,' but you have not let me know whom you will send with me. You have said, 'I know you by name and you have found favor with me.' If you are pleased with me, teach me your ways so I may know you and continue to find favor with you. Remember that this nation is your people."
>
> The Lord replied, "My Presence will go with you, and I will give you rest."
>
> Then Moses said to him, "If your Presence does not go with us, do not send us up from here. How will anyone know that you are pleased with me and with your people unless you go with us? What else will distinguish me and your people from all the other people on the face of the earth?"
>
> And the Lord said to Moses, "I will do the very thing you have asked, because I am pleased with you and I know you by name."
>
> Then Moses said, "Now show me your glory."

And the Lord said, "I will cause all my goodness to pass in front of you, and I will proclaim my name, the Lord, in your presence. I will have mercy on whom I will have mercy, and I will have compassion on whom I will have compassion. But," he said, "you cannot see my face, for no one may see me and live."

Then the Lord said, "There is a place near me where you may stand on a rock. When my glory passes by, I will put you in a cleft in the rock and cover you with my hand until I have passed by. Then I will remove my hand and you will see my back; but my face must not be seen." EXODUS 33:12-23

The description of this scene strikes us as strange. It raises questions. Does God have a real hand, a real back? What's the difference between seeing his face or his back?

God is clearly speaking to Moses in a language that he can understand. God does not have a body like ours; he is, after all, a spiritual being. What God is saying to Moses is, "My glory would simply overwhelm you. My beauty is so great it would burn your eyes out of their sockets. I have to protect you from seeing the fullness of my glory because you as a sinner simply cannot tolerate it. I will encourage you with a glimpse of my glory, but anything more would kill you."

A third passage gives us another description of God's glory. Hundreds of years after Moses lived, God called Isaiah to become a prophet. God transported Isaiah into heaven itself in order to ordain him as a prophet. Isaiah describes this as he walks into the very throne room of God in heaven. It is a magnificent scene. As God sits on his throne, seraphs, powerful angelic figures, sing.

In the year that King Uzziah died, I saw the Lord seated on a throne, high and exalted, and the train of his robe filled the temple. Above him were seraphs, each with six wings: With two wings they covered their faces, with two they

covered their feet, and with two they were flying. And they
were calling to one another:
"Holy, holy, holy is the Lord Almighty;
the whole earth is full of his glory."
At the sound of their voices the doorposts and thresholds
shook and the temple was filled with smoke.
"Woe to me!" I cried. "I am ruined! For I am a man of
unclean lips, and I live among a people of unclean lips, and
my eyes have seen the King, the Lord Almighty." ISAIAH 6:1-5

Their singing was accompanied by the rumbling of the
building and the cloudlike smoke we often see in descriptions
of God's glory. In Exodus God's glory was described as local
and veiled. Here the heavenly voices announce that the entire
world reflects his glory.

Glory and Uniqueness

Glory is equated with the presence of God himself, meaning
that glory describes the nature and attributes of God. But the
word itself highlights certain aspects of God. In the first place,
a glorious God is a God like no other. He is a God of
distinction. And when we remember that people in the ancient
Near East believed in thousands of gods, this is no meaningless
fact. God is unique.

God's uniqueness has so many facets that we will not be able
to list them all here. The gods of the Near East were specialists.
There was a god of the earth, of heaven, of war, of love, of rain,
of mountains, and on and on. But the glorious God of the
Bible is the God of everything, of the heaven and the earth.
His importance is tied to his greatness and power.

The gods of the Near East created human beings so that the
humans would serve them. And when men and women died,
the gods had no further use for them. The God of the Bible,
though, was a God who loved his people. He helped them in

their troubles, and when they died, God took them to himself (Ps. 49:15).

The gods of the Near East did not really have high ethical standards for their people; after all, they were a little shady themselves, having many of the weaknesses that we recognize in human beings. But the God of the Bible is holy and demands holiness from his people.

What does this mean for my marriage? In simple terms, I am to see my spouse as a unique reflection of God. She is a woman like no other. Each person, in creation, reflects a unique part of God. As a spouse, it is my privilege to enjoy the reflection of God's glory in my wife; it is my honor to further enhance the power and beauty of that glory in her. No one on the face of the earth has the same access or opportunity both to enjoy and to shape the glory of another person as does a marriage partner.

TO VIEW OUR SPOUSES FROM THE LENS OF GLORY IS TO BE OVERWHELMED BY THE PRIVILEGE OF BEING FACE-TO-FACE WITH A CREATURE WHO MIRRORS GOD.

Do we see our spouses as reflecting the face of God? Or are we captured more by their imperfections and our own disappointment? To view our spouses from the lens of glory is to be overwhelmed by the privilege of being face-to-face with a creature who mirrors God. Consequently, as partners, we will feel more overwhelmed with gratitude than disappointment; we will experience more joy than bitterness. Glory requires a submission to mystery; it demands our heart, soul, mind, and energy.

Glory and Mystery

God's glory, his distinctiveness and importance, is revealed in the Scriptures as cloud and fire. The fire represents his purity, holiness, majesty, and power. Fire both attracts us and scares us. It is both compelling and dangerous. Similarly, glory both allures us and unnerves us. We desire to approach, but we do so only with our shoes off—aware that we are in the presence of the holy, the mysterious, the all-beautiful, all-encompassing essence of existence.

The cloud, on the other hand, veils; it shields and hides the divine glory. It reminds us that no Old Testament saints ever looked directly at the divine glory. If they had, the brilliance of the glory would have destroyed them. It also reminds us that God is powerful and majestic, never fully seen without dire consequences. Seeing divine glory would be analogous to staring directly at the sun during an eclipse.

The cloud does more than shield; it also intrigues us. How often we want to look at the eclipse. But since we know we cannot without great harm, we construct little reflecting boxes in order to see it indirectly, to get a taste of what it is all about.

To delight in and enhance the glory of our spouses, we must equally be drawn to their mystery and in awe of their hearts. Too often we assume after a few years of marriage that we know our spouses; we think we have explored their hearts and mapped all the territory. Nothing could be more untrue and more destructive to glory.

One's spouse is a mystery—a terrain that each year will reveal more depth and beauty than could have been imagined when we walked out of the church as husband and wife. We should approach each other with a sense of eager anticipation, as if we are exploring an uncharted island paradise. The fruit is delicious and ample, the terrain beautiful and overwhelming. The foliage is dense and demanding but opens to waterfalls, vistas, and Edenic beauty. An entire lifetime will not provide ample time to explore the depths of uniqueness found in this one embodiment of God's image.

When we glory in our spouses, we approach the mystery with circumspection and awe. I am not to approach the soul of my wife with a familiarity that forgets that nothing on earth more clearly reveals the holiness and mercy of God than she does. I am to talk with her, make love to her, shop with her, plan a vacation with her in ways that reflect an awe of her being; otherwise, I will approach the holy fire in her with my shoes on, cavalier and ignorant of a hidden but enticing beauty that beckons me to praise and gratitude.

Glory and Worship

God reveals his glory in all created things. He refuses to be hidden away in insignificance, ignored by his creation. God's glory highlights his importance. He is majestic, carrying the greatness, power, majesty, and dignity of a king. The Old Testament gives us hints that behind the cloud is a scene of God on his throne, surrounded by his angelic council. He rules the universe from behind the cloud, and his angels do his bidding. The royal nature of his glory is important as we later explore the nature of human glory.

Because God has glory, he deserves respect, honor, and esteem. And this is the essence of worship: giving God the honor that belongs to him. The passages in Exodus and Isaiah show that the proper response to a revelation of God's glory is to worship him. When we glorify God, we simply desire to acknowledge his importance, distinction, majesty, power, and beauty.

If we are to enhance the glory in our spouses, does this mean we are to worship our spouses? No, but catching a glimpse of the glory of God in the face of our spouses ought to lead to something quite similar. Worship is offering God praise for his glorious, awesome being and gratitude for his kindness on our behalf. I am not to bow my knee to anyone except God; but loving my wife parallels loving God. My spouse's beauty, which is a reflection of God's glory, fills me with awe. If I am not in awe and if I am not caught up in delight, I will not enhance my spouse's glory and I will not reveal a taste of God's goodness to a world blind to glory.

How is this different from Jacob's infatuation and idolatrous deification of Lynn? Jacob did not allow himself to feel the sorrow of his wife's sin, and he had no desire for a deeper, more intimate relationship. He was satisfied with their status of intimacy; he grew comfortable with the relationship as it was. He settled for what *is* rather than allowing Lynn's beauty to transport him to an even greater vision of what she was meant to be. In one sense, to be caught up in the delight of a person's glory is also to grieve at what they are not and to envision what they could become. Jacob should have grieved at her distance and coldness, but instead he encouraged it by placing her on a pedestal. When we refuse to grieve and desire more, we are blind to the effects of sin. We must see both in our spouses if we are to love them well.

Glory is an elusive concept. It is difficult to make it concrete in our minds. It is especially hard to see how God's glory fills a sinful, evil world. Fortunately, God did not leave us to wallow in darkness. He did something that surpassed the experience Moses had of seeing God's back. God revealed his glory in Jesus Christ.

JESUS: THE GLORY OF GOD
In the Old Testament, God's glory remains obscure, an elusive concept, difficult to comprehend. In the New Testament, God's glory takes on flesh, and his name is Jesus. If we want to know what glory is, we need to look at Jesus. In Jesus we can look directly at the eclipse without burning our eyes. "The Word became flesh and made his dwelling among us. We have

seen his glory, the glory of the One and Only, who came from the Father, full of grace and truth" (John 1:14).

And what do we see when we turn to Jesus? At first glance, we see a humble carpenter's son, one who "had no beauty or majesty to attract us to him, nothing in his appearance that we should desire him" (Isa. 53:2). We see one who served others and submitted himself to the suffering of the world. In the apostle Paul's words, Jesus was the one who

> being in very nature God,
> did not consider equality with God something to be grasped,
> but made himself nothing,
> taking the very nature of a servant,
> being made in human likeness.
> And being found in appearance as a man,
> he humbled himself
> and became obedient to death—
> even death on a cross!
> Therefore God exalted him to the highest place
> and gave him the name that is above every name,
> that at the name of Jesus every knee should bow,
> in heaven and on earth and under the earth,
> and every tongue confess that Jesus Christ is Lord,
> to the glory of God the Father. PHILIPPIANS 2:6-11

Jesus is God; he is God's glory. When he is present, it means that God is present. He has the power, the authority, the distinction, and the importance of God. As we come to know Jesus, we come to know God himself. As the glory of God, Jesus deserves our respect, honor, esteem, and worship. Revelation 5:12 gives us a window into the heavenly worship of Jesus Christ, the type of worship that he so richly deserves here on earth: "Worthy is the Lamb, who was slain, to receive power and wealth and wisdom and strength and honor and glory and praise!"

That the glory of God is enfleshed in Jesus means that

for us to enhance the glory of our spouses, we must do two things: we must help our spouses become more Christlike, and we must allow our spouses to draw Christlikeness out of us.

What does it mean to be Christlike? Christlikeness expresses itself in a tenderness and mercy that forgive sin and in a strength and boldness that pursue the offender regardless of the cost or the risk. It means being willing to submit ourselves to suffering, even death, for our spouses. It means remaining committed in spite of conflict within the marriage.

Every marriage has moments when it is far easier to lapse into indifference or defensive flight. Few couples have escaped the chasm that sometimes exists in bed after a fight. Although only a few inches separate the two bodies, it feels as if the distance between them is a gap of insurmountable proportion. My (Tremper's) wife, Alice, recently told me after a party that I had talked too much about my children's sports exploits. I am a proud father, but at times I am boastful rather than supportive. I felt wounded. Her words seemed unfair and cruel, and we separated into two different worlds. I was not unkind; I was silent and withdrawn.

It is at that kind of moment that I am aware my controlling passion is not to enhance my wife's glory, but to protect and deepen my own. Not only had I failed at the party, but I had cowered at the prospect that my wife had seen my failure. I communicated to her that relief of shame is more important to me than glory.

I do not live out the glory of God as my heart desires or as my wife hopes, and my wife encourages me time and again to face my arrogance and to flee from self-righteousness. Not that she does so perfectly, but her heart toward me is good, and eventually I find myself thawing and turning back to her to repent and move toward the man I am meant to be. In this way, Alice enhances my Christlikeness; she desires to see me in constant communion with my heavenly Father.

MEN AND WOMEN: REFLECTIVE GLORY OF THE IMAGE OF GOD

God gives his glory to his creatures. An earlier look at Psalm 8 reminded us that God "crowned" people with glory. Psalm 3:3 says, "But you are a shield around me, O Lord; you bestow glory on me and lift up my head."

At first, the idea that human beings have glory seems unbiblical, bizarre, perhaps more like New Age thinking than biblical thinking. The psalmist's confession that he was "a worm" (Ps. 22:6) seems more accurate than saying that humans are glorious creatures. Later we will see how these two true biblical teachings—that humans are glorious and sinful— are totally compatible with one another, but for now we note that the Bible teaches that human beings have glory.

It is important to note that our glory is a derivative glory. It is not a glory that is inherent in human nature; God gives it to us. The image of God crowning humanity with glory is apt. A person is not born with a crown; it is given by another person. The crown is the external sign of an intangible status of royalty. But though it is intangible in one sense, it has a very real impact on the world. People who have royal status can do things that other people cannot.

So the point of the two psalms is that God gives human beings glory. They have significance, importance, esteem, and honor in the world. Men and women are the kings and queens of creation. God has given them the joint royal task of subduing and shaping the cosmos. They are deserving of respect and dignity from their fellow creatures and the rest of creation. They are not the slime of the world but the kings and queens of creation. They are the pinnacle of God's creation, made in order to rule the world at God's command.

John 17 is popularly known as the High Priestly prayer. Jesus serves as our High Priest here when he intercedes for his people and asks that God care for those who follow him. The prayer begins with Jesus' request for himself. He asks that God glorify him, that he reveal Jesus' glory in the presence of the whole world. It is true that Jesus' glory has been visible wherever he has ministered through word and miracle, but now something bigger and better and more exciting is about to happen—his death.

MEN AND WOMEN ARE THE KINGS AND QUEENS OF CREATION.

And this is the paradox of the gospel. Glory comes through suffering and death. Indeed, the Resurrection follows, but first comes the Cross. But Jesus' glory is the glory that he had "before the world began," and this indicates his overwhelming power, beauty, sovereignty, which is rightfully his as a member of the Trinity.

Jesus' prayer continues beyond himself and includes his disciples, not only his immediate disciples, but specifically those who "believe in me through their message"—Christians throughout the ages.

> "My prayer is not for them alone. I pray also for those who will believe in me through their message, that all of them may be one, Father, just as you are in me and I am in you. May they also be in us so that the world may believe that you have sent me. I have given them the glory that you gave me, that they may be one as we are one: I in them and you in me. May they be brought to complete unity to let the world know that you sent me and have loved them even as you have loved me.

"Father, I want those you have given me to be with me where I am, and to see my glory, the glory you have given me because you loved me before the creation of the world.

"Righteous Father, though the world does not know you, I know you, and they know that you have sent me. I have made you known to them, and will continue to make you known in order that the love you have for me may be in them and that I myself may be in them." JOHN 17:20-26

He prays that we all may see his glory, the glory of his victory over death. But he prays that we may also share in his glory, a glory that he has already given us. The main theme of this passage is that all believers are one through a common sharing of this divine glory. Finally, this united glory of the church becomes a preeminent sign that God has sent Jesus. It is through our unity that the world knows that God sent Jesus to die on the cross.

Here we see the relational aspect of glory. Jesus' glory is glory that he shares with the Father. This shared glory demonstrates Jesus' unity with the Father. Jesus gives us glory, once again showing the relational unity that we have with one another and with Jesus himself. While these truths are not tied directly to marriage in the Bible, they have tremendous implications for the marriage unity of a Christian man and woman.

The marriage relationship is the first building block of the church. If marriages are not growing in glory, then the church will be made up of crumbling stones. If the leadership of the church is not struggling, repenting, and growing in a passionate union of intimacy, then the effect will be a "business" model of contractual relationships in the church and not a "family" model of organic relationships that spur one another to growth. What is this glory to look like?

We enter this discussion through the biblical picture of the wedding, the ceremony that initiates the marriage relationship.

WEDDING

Psalm 45 is universally recognized as a wedding song. We do not know the people for whom it was originally written, but that is unimportant. The placement of this wedding song in the Psalms means that it was used for many occasions.

> *You are the most excellent of men*
> *and your lips have been anointed with grace,*
> *since God has blessed you forever.*
> *Gird your sword upon your side, O mighty one;*
> *clothe yourself with splendor and majesty.*
> *In your majesty ride forth victoriously*
> *in behalf of truth, humility and righteousness;*
> *let your right hand display awesome deeds.*
> *Let your sharp arrows pierce the hearts of the king's enemies;*
> *let the nations fall beneath your feet.*
> *Your throne, O God, will last for ever and ever;*
> *a scepter of justice will be the scepter of your kingdom.*
> *All glorious is the princess within her chamber;*
> *her gown is interwoven with gold.*
> *In embroidered garments she is led to the king;*
> *her virgin companions follow her*
> *and are brought to you.*
> *They are led in with joy and gladness;*
> *they enter the palace of the king.* PSALM 45:2-6, 13-15

Because of the psalm's royal language, it is usually assumed that the song was written for a king, and perhaps it was. But once again, it was probably used in common weddings as well as time went on. After all, every married couple is a king and a queen in God's universe.

The psalm describes the splendor of the day as two glorious creatures are brought together to become one. The description of both bride and groom is impressive. The groom is described as competent, majestic, powerful. The bride is beautiful and radiant. The ceremony itself is one of great joy and happiness.

A passage from the Song of Songs alludes to Solomon's wedding day.

Who is this coming up from the desert
like a column of smoke,
perfumed with myrrh and incense
made from all the spices of the merchant?
Look! It is Solomon's carriage,
escorted by sixty warriors,
the noblest of Israel,
all of them wearing the sword,
all experienced in battle,
each with his sword at his side,
prepared for the terrors of the night.
King Solomon made for himself the carriage;
he made it of wood from Lebanon.
Its posts he made of silver,
its base of gold.
Its seat was upholstered with purple,
its interior lovingly inlaid
by the daughters of Jerusalem.
Come out, you daughters of Zion,
and look at King Solomon wearing the crown,
the crown with which his mother crowned him
on the day of his wedding,
the day his heart rejoiced. SONG OF SONGS 3:6-11

The Song is not a drama, but a collection of love poetry. Marriage is rarely explicit but probably assumed in many of the poems. Relevant here is the opulence, grandeur, and sheer joy associated with the day when a marriage begins. Once again, here, as throughout the Song of Songs, the relationship is royal; the groom is spoken of as a king, while the bride is a queen. This is not because the Song of Songs is a historical report of an actual royal wedding; it is rather celebrating the relationship of ordinary human beings, who are divine image bearers.

Marriage today is a beleaguered institution. At best people are ambivalent about it. Statistics vary, but many suggest that approximately half of all marriages end in divorce and that many people who remain together are miserable. As young people contemplate marriage, they need to be reminded of the grandeur and majesty and joy that are possible in a life together. These Old Testament descriptions of marriage certainly send the signal that something special and wonderful is happening.

Marriage unites two image bearers, two reflectors of God's glory. The marriage of two Christians has the potential to be truly wonderful and fulfilling. However, it is not something automatic, especially since we are image bearers who have rebelled against the one we reflect. In other words, marriage also brings together two sinners. The combination of glory can multiply the glory, and the combination of sin can enhance the sin.

In marriage, both happen. Marriage is an institution of joy and grief. And the glory often comes through the struggles in communication, goals, priorities, child rearing, and sex. Anyone who expects glory without a fight is foolish. In a fallen world, problems, both small and great, will arise.

If we recognize that we are both sinners and if we expect that conflict will happen, we can avoid thinking something is uniquely wrong with our marriage. If we recognize that we are both creatures of glory, reflecting the majesty of God as image bearers, we can have hope that we will find joy in the midst of pain.

Those who get stuck in the struggle have marriages that

degrade the partners. Realizing that our spouses are glorious creatures of God helps to push us out of the rut; it restrains us from shaming ourselves by degrading our spouses.

That our spouses are glorious means that they are distinctive. My spouse is like no other. To love my wife truly and rightly, I must have a vision of how she is different from every other woman on the face of the earth. I must study glory. I must be captured by my wife's potential, her giftedness, her burdens, her passion.

But even more than that, I must learn what it means to draw out my wife's uniqueness, to draw her to live out God's glory in a way that no one else can or should do.

I MUST LEARN WHAT IT MEANS
TO DRAW OUT MY WIFE'S UNIQUENESS,
TO DRAW HER TO LIVE OUT GOD'S
GLORY IN A WAY THAT NO ONE ELSE
CAN OR SHOULD DO.

THE CHOICE BEFORE US:
GLORY OR SHAME

In the next part of the book, we will expand our discussion of glory to include how we enhance our spouse's glory. Before that, however, we will dispose of the topic of degradation by exploring various ways by which relational distance is increased. Marriage is the closest of all relationships, but often we fall into a pattern where we push our spouse away from us. We will look briefly at five signatures of degradation, each illustrated with a marriage story from the Bible.

In his letter to the Philippian church, the apostle Paul

challenges the people with a choice. It is a forced choice, with only two options; there is no middle ground. Do we live with our eyes on the earth or with our eyes on Jesus? Do we live for our glory or for God's glory? If we live for ourselves, our glory turns to shame. If we live for God's glory, our bodies will be glorious.

> Join with others in following my example, brothers, and take note of those who live according to the pattern we gave you. For, as I have often told you before and now say again even with tears, many live as enemies of the cross of Christ. Their destiny is destruction, their god is their stomach, and their glory is in their shame. Their mind is on earthly things. But our citizenship is in heaven. And we eagerly await a Savior from there, the Lord Jesus Christ, who, by the power that enables him to bring everything under his control, will transform our lowly bodies so that they will be like his glorious body. PHILIPPIANS 3:17-21

Signatures of Degradation

What does marriage look like when one of the spouses lives for his or her own glory? The Scriptures give us many pictures of degraded marriages.

FALSE GLORIFICATION: JACOB AND RACHEL.   Marriage brings together two human beings, created in the image of God, and makes them one. The husband and the wife both reflect God's glory, and as they treat one another with appropriate honor and respect, they move closer to one another. Their relationship becomes increasingly intimate.

On the other hand, if married partners degrade each other, they introduce relational distance. They grow alienated from one another.

It seems paradoxical, but one way we can mistreat and push

46

our spouses away from us is by "putting them on a pedestal." This cliché reveals what we are really doing; we approach our spouses as if they were idols. We attribute to them a kind of false glory.

Some people might respond to this by saying they would love to be treated like a god or goddess. However, to be treated as gods or goddesses is to be treated as someone we are not; thus the relationship is built on an illusion. Not only that, but to treat spouses as gods or goddesses blocks intimacy. A proper distance must be preserved between worshipers and the object of their worship.

The story of Lynn and Jacob is the account of a husband who pushes his wife away from himself by treating her as something she isn't. He never really connects with the real Lynn. She is repelled by Jacob because she believes that he doesn't really love her; rather, he loves an idea of her.

The story of Jacob and Rachel in the book of Genesis gives us a variation of this theme. "So Jacob worked for Laban seven years so he could marry Rachel. But they seemed like just a few days to him because he loved Rachel very much" (Gen. 29:20, NCV).

The glimpse we get of the relationship of Jacob and Rachel is revealing. We hear that Jacob deeply loved Rachel because of her incredible beauty. We learn that he agreed to work for fourteen years in order to earn the right to marry the woman of his desires. On the other side, we don't hear a word from Rachel concerning her feelings toward Jacob. In her actions, however, we note a hardness, a lack of intimacy. Although Jacob treated Rachel like a goddess, their relationship, at least as it is narrated in the Scriptures, was never close.

We see this clearly in the interchange between them in Genesis 29:31–30:24. Her actions are dictated not by a love for her husband but from a rivalry with her sister. The Lord had blessed her with the love of a husband, but she was not satisfied with that as she observed her sister's growing family.

Jacob reveres Rachel and allows her to manipulate him. She complains to him that she has no children, then she orders him to sleep with her servant. Her constant demands on Jacob make her seem like a goddess ordering around her worshiper. The result is a continuing distance between Jacob and Rachel as well as between Rachel and the other people around her, like Leah and the two servants. Indeed, the family conflicts that are generated by the distance between Rachel and Jacob continues into the next generation as Joseph, Rachel's favored son, comes into conflict with the sons of Leah and the servants.

We are to adore our spouses, but adoration becomes idolatry when we refuse to stand in the way of their sin. In Jacob and Lynn's marriage, Jacob needed to stand up to Lynn, not make excuses for her when she was wrong or simply cold. By glossing over her sin, he encouraged the growth of that sin and created a distance between them. He also felt uncomfortable around her and adopted a pleasant but false persona in her presence. Their marriage was not the union between two people; rather, Jacob worshiped a picture of Lynn, a false representation of who she was. If we see only "good," then it is a sure sign that degradation of idolatry has occurred. Idolatry puts our spouses in the position of never failing and of being responsible to save us from loneliness. To be a god or a goddess is to be given a power that only corrupts the one worshiped and makes the one who worships blind and needy.

BLAMESHIFTING: ADAM AND EVE.   Most of us do everything we can to keep people from knowing of our faults. We become masters at covering up our mistakes. Once it becomes clear that our acts will be revealed for what they are, we do whatever it takes to shift the focus of attention elsewhere. Often we blame others, claiming that we are the victim of another person's mistakes or maliciousness.

A marriage provides a ready object for our blameshifting. Some situations merit blame. For example, a spouse must clearly not only blame but also confront his or her spouse who drives when intoxicated. Or a spouse should blame a partner who pays inappropriate attention to members of the opposite sex. But we also have to watch out for our desire to avoid blame at all costs. Guilt and responsibility for mistakes and sin are like hot potatoes. We can't get rid of them too quickly, and we often push the blame onto the person closest to us, our spouse.

Blame not only pushes away our guilt, but it also pushes away our spouses. It is hard to feel affection toward someone who is pointing a finger at you. Jesus teaches us to forgive each other of sins that are committed toward us, not to blame people for acts that we ourselves have done.

Adam and Eve provide a biblical example of blameshifting. "When the woman saw that the fruit of the tree was good for food and pleasing to the eye, and also desirable for gaining wisdom, she took some and ate it. She also gave some to her husband, who was with her, and he ate it. Then the eyes of both of them were opened, and they realized they were naked; so they sewed fig leaves together and made coverings for themselves" (Gen. 3:6-7).

The question of who is more at fault here is not relevant. The issue is that both Adam and Eve failed God and each other. They each contributed to the other's downfall with its tremendous implications for them, for their children, and even for us.

Blameshifting would place the blame on the serpent. The serpent is the one who challenged God's authority and inter-pretation. But the woman, who knew what God had said about the tree, accepted the serpent's lies and then ate from the forbidden tree. She then gave some to her husband. Starting with Adam himself, men want to point the finger at Eve here. She took the first bite and handed the fruit to her husband. Notice, however, that while the serpent was talking with Eve and while Eve reached for the fruit, Adam "was with her," apparently watching the whole scene. And when Eve turned to him and handed him the fruit, he did not put up an argument. He simply "ate it."

Degradation begins when a man is silent and a woman controls. And it seems that a man's refusal to act on behalf of his wife as she presents him with the difficulties of life only deepens her commitment to take charge. When this pattern is played out repeatedly, the marriage relationship becomes a vehicle for evil. The result for Adam and Eve was marital alienation and expulsion from the Garden. Their troubles were just beginning.

VIOLENCE: SAMSON AND DELILAH. Marriage unites two people in an intimate bond that allows and even requires a great deal of vulnerability. Husbands and wives know each other better and more closely than they know and are known by anyone else. Vulnerability implies the potential of harm. Most people enter the marriage relationship with someone whom they trust, whom they feel cares for them and wants the best for them.

Sadly, many people enter into a relationship with someone who not only refuses to care for them, but actually exploits them and harms them. Physical violence toward a spouse is an obvious form of degradation within a marriage. A husband who hits his wife does not see her as the image of God, a glorious being who reflects her Maker's splendor, but as something less than human, an object of his anger and frustration.

A spouse can be abused with emotional violence as well. A wife does not have to hit her husband to exploit him violently. She can cut him to ribbons with her words. She can make him feel that he is subhuman. Spousal abuse, whether it is physical or emotional, devastates a relationship; it runs counter to reality because marriage unites two beings who are "a little lower than God" (Ps. 8:5, NRSV).

The story of Samson and Delilah presents a picture of the depths to which the moral and spiritual health of Israel had sunk. Oppressed by the Philistines, Israel had become so faithless that the one whom God used to deliver them was a self-seeking, lustful buffoon named Samson. This hulk of humanity couldn't have cared less about God and his people.

The climax of Samson's story comes when he enters into a dangerous relationship with Delilah, a Philistine (Judg. 16). Though lust motivated Samson, the account emphasizes how God overruled Samson's evil inclinations and brought a great Israelite victory. God even used Delilah's exploitation and abuse of Samson to bring him into his final captivity, where he destroyed Dagon's temple and killed many Philistines. The relationship between Samson and Delilah presents a biblical example of relational violence.

The book of Judges presents Samson as a crude and self-centered man. A large part of Samson's moral downfall involved his lust toward women, and for our purposes we will concentrate on the relationship between Samson and Delilah. Delilah was just another woman with whom Samson fell in love, another woman whom he could use to satisfy his sexual desires.

Delilah, on the other side, had a purpose in letting Samson get close to her. She was at the center of the Philistine plot to neutralize this Israelite freak of nature. She tried to discover the secret of his incredible strength. We know that his strength was a gift from God. He was also a Nazirite who was not permitted to cut his hair as a sign of his dedication to God. So his hair was not some kind of magical provider of power but rather a sign of the divine favor that he enjoyed.

This story is one of exploitative love. It is a picture of a tragedy that occurs when a relationship is established on no other basis than lust and utilitarian benefit. Each partner viewed the other with the question, What can you do for me? This leads only to the debauchery of love and the destruction of the self.

A husband who demands sex in order to feel alive bears a tragic resemblance to Samson. A woman who toys with her husband and uses him to achieve a position of power is the sister of Delilah. A wife who uses her husband's money, status, or power to assert her claim of relational dominance is a violent woman, just as a man who lives for little other than his comfort is a violent man.

SHAMING: DAVID AND MICHAL.   When we shame someone, we are giving them an emotional shove away. We don't want them near us, so we say or do something that makes them want to run away. Of course, it is necessary for spouses to be honest and to point out faults to one another. But how we expose sin in our spouses makes all the difference in the world.

The other day my wife, Alice, noticed I was avoiding a conflict with one of my sons. I was tired and distracted by various other responsibilities. I did not want to tackle the problem. Alice could have ignored my cowardice. She could have intruded into the matter with our son and solved the problem with him. Both options would have been wrong at that moment.

Alice spoke to me in a way that helped and did not push me away. She looked at me kindly and said: "I know you are tired, but I suspect you simply don't want to get into a real battle with Timmy. I trust your heart, but I think in this case you are choosing the easy way out. Let me know if there is anything you want me to do."

I was stunned. She succinctly cut to the heart of my refusal to become engaged. But she did so without an air of superiority or arrogance. She did not leave me room to attack her confrontation; I was left looking at myself in a moral mirror, and I did not like what I saw.

If she had attacked, smirked, or stood apart from my sin with a judgmental heart, then she would have shamed me. The result would have been a loss of intimacy and a withdrawal from relationship. This is what happened in the relationship between Michal and David. "When David returned home to bless his household, Michal daughter of Saul came out to meet him and said, 'How the king of Israel has distinguished himself today, disrobing in the sight of the slave girls of his servants as any vulgar fellow would!'" (2 Sam. 6:20).

Michal was angry. She had looked out her window and had seen her husband dancing wildly in front of the ark of the Lord. However, she had her eyes focused on the young women who were watching her handsome royal husband dance. In his joy David danced with few clothes on, and she was angry that the young women who were watching were lusting after him.

David danced as if no one were present. He had made himself vulnerable as he danced with abandon in celebration of the arrival of the ark, which symbolized God's presence, into Jerusalem. God, too, was pleased with David. But Michal could not share her husband's joy. Instead she stripped him by shaming him for his behavior. God was not pleased with Michal's response (2 Sam. 6:23). From everything we know about the relationship between David and Michal, it was shattered from this point on.

USING: AHASUERUS AND VASHTI. A husband and wife enter into the most intimate relationship possible among human beings. A spouse is a complex being who thinks and feels, not an object to be manipulated or paraded about. Even if a spouse is treated like a beautiful or wonderful object, the dehumanization leads to incredible relational distance and marital harm. The story of the Persian king Ahasuerus and his queen,

Vashti, illustrates this. "On the seventh day, when King [Ahasuerus] was in high spirits from wine, he commanded the seven eunuchs who served him . . . to bring before him Queen Vashti, wearing her royal crown, in order to display her beauty to the people and nobles, for she was lovely to look at. But when the attendants delivered the king's command, Queen Vashti refused to come. Then the king became furious and burned with anger" (Esther 1:10-12).

It is true that Ahasuerus and Vashti were a pagan couple, but nonetheless they were made in the image of God. Their relationship would thrive only as they related to one another as human beings with respect, honor, and love.

But Ahasuerus used Vashti like a beautiful object to be displayed before his drunken friends. She reacted valiantly by refusing to come to be ogled by them with the result that she was ordered out of the court for the rest of her life. While we learn of this story because God used it to bring Esther into a position of influence in the Persian court, we nonetheless learn something about the dynamics of marriage from this brief interchange.

Love Wins Out: Ruth and Boaz

The Bible also gives us illustrations of marriages that are based on love, honor, and respect. Ruth and Boaz are not ideal creatures; they live in the real world of struggle. But as they relate to one another, they grow increasingly intimate and encourage us in our own marriages. "So Boaz took Ruth and she became his wife. Then he went to her, and the Lord enabled her to conceive, and she gave birth to a son" (Ruth 4:13).

God chose to work through the relationship of a man named Boaz and a woman named Ruth. In their courtship and eventual marriage we get a glimpse of two image bearers coming together. They are not perfect, as we will see, but this is a love story that encourages us centuries later.

When Ruth and her mother-in-law, Naomi, arrive in Bethlehem from Moab, they are in sad shape. They are poor, and they have lost the rest of their family. Most frightening of all, there are no men in their life to establish their status in the society of their day. Naomi is sour on life, but Ruth supports her and gets on with the needs of the day.

Ruth goes in search of food. According to Hebrew law, the poor of the land were permitted to glean the leftovers of a harvested field. So Ruth goes to the field of Boaz, who is a relative of some sort to Naomi and also a wealthy man. She goes with no designs on him, but soon he notices her and gives her preferential treatment.

Soon Boaz is speaking to her protectively and lovingly: "My daughter, listen to me. Don't go and glean in another field and don't go away from here. Stay here with my servant girls. Watch the field where the men are harvesting, and follow along after the girls. I have told the men not to touch you. And whenever you are thirsty, go and get a drink from the water jars the men have filled" (Ruth 2:8-9).

Ruth goes home and excitedly tells her mother-in-law these wonderful developments. In her words, she is deeply appreciative and respects this man. Soon Naomi urges Ruth to pursue this relationship.

The scene that follows may offend some and turn Ruth into a villain rather than a heroine. That would be unfortunate. She intends by her act to initiate a lifelong relationship with Boaz, not have a one-night stand. Ruth steals into the threshing floor at night after Boaz has gone to sleep. The language that describes this move is clearly provocative in its Old Testament setting: "When Boaz had finished eating and drinking and was in good spirits, he went over to lie down at the far end of the grain pile. Ruth approached quietly, uncovered his feet and lay down" (Ruth 3:7).

In a word, she made herself completely vulnerable to him.

She opened herself up to him because she trusted him. She offered herself to him because she held him in the deepest respect. He in turn did not degrade her, but he showed her respect: "The Lord bless you, my daughter. . . . This kindness is greater than that which you showed earlier: You have not run after the younger men, whether rich or poor. And now, my daughter, don't be afraid. I will do for you all you ask. All my fellow townsmen know that you are a woman of noble character" (Ruth 3:10-11).

Boaz treated Ruth as a woman of dignity, a woman who is a reflection of God's glory, not taking advantage of her when she was in a difficult situation. Ruth showed great respect for Boaz. And together they enhanced the glory of the other as they came together, united in marriage.

Our options in our marriages are simple: We can enhance the glory of our spouses, or we can degrade them. If we see our options as that simple, then we will have a measuring stick to consider each moment in the light of what our heart most deeply desires. And if our heart desires the glory of God, then we will begin to ask the difficult question: What does it look like to enhance the glory of our beloved?

QUESTIONS FOR REFLECTION AND CONVERSATION

1. In what ways has your relationship with your spouse changed you? At this point concentrate on how you have changed for the better. How has your spouse influenced you to reflect God's glory more clearly?
2. In what way is your spouse special? How is he or she like no other person in your life?
3. Spend fifteen minutes quietly thinking about your spouse. Ask yourself, "What do I know and what don't I know about my spouse? What intrigues me about my spouse?"
4. What are your spouse's potential, giftedness, burdens, and passions? Make a list for each of the four areas.

5. What is most beautiful and wonderful about your spouse?
6. What about your spouse makes you thankful?
7. Does thinking about your spouse lead you to worship God? Explain your response.
8. How is your spouse like Christ?
9. Once again reflect on your spouse. Ask yourself, "Does my picture of my spouse correspond to reality or fantasy?"
10. Think about the following categories and ask in what way they describe your marriage: false glorification, blameshifting, violence, shaming, and using.

4

Jacob and Lynn Become Intimate Allies in Discovering Who They Are

Three months later . . . Jacob was lost. He turned down a street that he thought would take him to the restaurant, but it quickly became clear he had turned down a dead-end street. Lynn sat quietly. In the past, Jacob would laugh, make a joke, and apologize for his error. This time he bellowed. He actually swore.

Jacob turned and looked at Lynn: "Why didn't you ask how to get to this place? You should have known I had no idea how to get there." In the past three months, partially due to counseling but more simply because Jacob was honestly looking at life, he had become more aware of an ache, an inner emptiness that he had never acknowledged in his life. He had begun to admit he was not as happy with Lynn as he claimed. In fact, he was far from happy in any area of his life. In many ways, he had become an unpleasant, troubled man.

Lynn looked out the window. She had learned not to offer quick comfort, cheap advice, or tell him what he craved to hear. Each response seemed only to set him off more deeply. She was not afraid of him or fearful he would do something to himself, but she felt it was better to let him struggle on his own. Jacob had wanted her to do more, but he also had come to a point of respecting her reticence. She seemed to trust that he would face his sin, struggle, be broken, and move toward her or the others he had failed. Jacob has a good heart, and though he fails more often and more dramatically than ever before in their marriage, Lynn feels more joy, passion, and freedom in their love than ever before.

Lynn and Jacob wrote letters to one another during the hard weeks of looking at their lives. They put words to their confusion, heartache, and growing hope. I was given permission to print two letters that give some scope of what has happened in their marriage.

Dear Lynn-Girl,

Do you remember when I first called you girl? I do. It was on the steps of Gray Chapel. We had just walked down the stairs from the old library above Stephens Hall. The one with the old, brittle planks for a floor that creaked every time you took a step so no one who wanted to study went there. I loved to go there with you. I knew the one study desk that was farthest from the door and tucked into the corner by the old volumes of Euripides' War Journals.

We had studied until 8:30. We could hear the party animals carousing next door at the chapel prior to a rock concert. If I recall it was Frank Zappa and the Mothers of

Invention, and I think he had two original members of the Turtles singing with him on that tour. I had asked if you wanted to go, and you turned up your nose and laughed. I called you a girl. You looked so much like a little schoolgirl who had been invited to drink sour milk. I couldn't stop laughing and laughing. I know a few of the stone-heads hanging out near the pillars thought we were tripping on some mushroom, but we knew we were laughing with fresh and free innocence.

What I never admitted to you is that I loved Frank Zappa. He was performing his *Billy the Mountain* album, and I loved the way he not only tweaked the noses of the Nixon majority but also mocked the foolishness of the mindless war protesters. He was good. But you looked so girlish and pure that any mention of my intrigue in Franky-boy would have ended our nascent dating relationship.

How I worked to win you! It is so sad to me that I could cry. I never, never believed you might actually love me or want me. I figured I had no chance of winning you unless I was funnier, smarter, more pious, more consistent, more devoted than any other man in your life or your dreams. And I worked hard enough that I had no equal in your life.

But the more I worked to win you, the more I had to make you a prize more valuable than life itself. If I was going to give my life to gain you, then you had to be a pearl of such price that it made the sacrifice, the pain, the fear worth it.

I set you up. In fact, I ruined the real possibility of delight in our marriage. I know I smothered you with my adoration. I know that I also put you in a straitjacket of compliance. If I was going to be the faithful Sir Gawain, the shining knight who loved you with utter simplicity and sincerity, then you had to be Lady———, the woman of chaste, pure, and delicate features that would wait until I slayed the Green Knight that opposed your reign. Sick. Sick. Sick. And worse, it is sinfully tragic.

I have deprived you of what I do feel and do desire. I love

you. I am now somewhat hesitant to use that phrase, knowing how hackneyed it has become and how demanding it has been in the past. But I do love you, and as I have faced the reality that you are not a refined, pure, sinless Lady, I have come to see I really have more than a role in your life;

I actually have a calling in your life.

And that calling, my girl, is what I want to describe. I am committed to seeing your beauty grow. You are beautiful, and your memory will exceed and outlive all others. I believe that deeply. Yet, you are at times distant, impatient, critical. You often offer yourself only at the level that is expected, and you avoid conflict with tragic brilliance. I suppose that is why we were able to survive for so long in a sinful marriage when I broke your heart a thousand times.

After all these years of marriage, I hardly know but a few stories as to what has provoked your pain, shaped your perspective, and intensified your commitment to make sure you would not be devastated again. I hardly know you. I have hardly ever dealt with your heart. I have seldom offered you all my heart—both bad and good. To whatever degree I can enhance your beauty and undermine your depravity, then I will because I want you to look more and more like the Lord. I want the same for me. And I hope your life is as equally directed to helping me gain the splendor and honor that is befitting a warrior-king. I want to be like Jesus. I know you do as well. And I am glad.

Love,
Jacob

Dear Jacob,

You like Frank Zappa? Are you a Christian? Certainly, I would never tell that to the elder board or to our kids. I would not want them to think their father was a hippie. I know you weren't, but honestly I always thought you would look good with long hair. Sad, it is too late for that. Sorry.

Darling, that is a good indication of the new freedom I

feel. I know you hate your balding head. I am frankly not fond of it either. But now I know you will not sulk, start on a program of Rogaine, or get a toupee. I feel as if you will look realistically at me for the first time. I know I am vain. I know I am more concerned with the superficial than I am with the deeper matters of God. For the first time, I feel as if you are actually calling me to see what I am and what I could be.

And it is terrifying. I mean really, really frightening. I thought I wanted you to adore me with deep and honest eyes, but now that you are, I find I wish you were as blind and devoted as you were before. You are actually calling me to be like the Lord. I am excited too, but I sometimes wish we were back in our old comfortable patterns. Don't quit. I really want to be even more lovely. And I want to be part of seeing you live out your splendor and honor.

But I don't know how to do that. It is a right desire, but I am more than ever confused as to what it would mean for us to invite the other to live out more deeply the glory of God. I hope the days ahead will lead us to that place.

Yours forever,
Lynn

Part Two

WHAT ARE OUR ROLES AS HUSBANDS AND WIVES?

5

JACK AND MARTHA:

THE COUPLE WHO DIDN'T

KNOW WHAT TO DO

Jack got in line under the sign: First Class and Premier Members. The thought passed quickly through his mind: *I hate my life and my travel, but at least I get the benefits of going first class.* The line in the economy section was long, and the people looked tired and defeated by the wait. With only one person in line ahead of him and with three airline personnel checking in the first-class passengers, Jack felt assured of a quick turnaround for his flight home.

One ticket agent ended with a customer and departed. Another agent was busy with a person who looked as if he was buying tickets to go on a long trip. When the person in front of Jack finished checking in, Jack eagerly moved forward. But the agent said, "I'm sorry, but I must take the people in this other line first." He had not noticed that she was an agent for the passengers flying economy class, not one designated for first-class passengers.

Jack's blood began to boil. He was tired. He had had a good but long day, and he wanted to get home as quickly as possible. He quickly responded, "Look, I need to see if I can get on an earlier flight, and I know one leaves in only twenty-five minutes. I need to check in *now.*"

The agent looked at him and said: "You'll need to wait for the other first-class agent." He fumed and waited nervously, moving from foot to foot. He could feel his eyes bulge with pulsating anger.

The ticket was soon changed to the earlier flight, and he felt better. In the few minutes left before he needed to board the plane, he called his wife. In a matter of moments, she informed him their son's basketball was lost at school; new shoes that fit his ten-year-old daughter's feet about six weeks ago were now hurting her feet; and their oldest daughter had pitched a world-class fit in front of friends who attended the same church. In a moment, his frustrations with life escalated to a fever pitch, and he curtly ended the phone call and slammed the phone down on the receiver. All in a day's work.

Life was good, decent, and sad for Jack and Martha. He was a vice president for a growing software firm. He had a stock portfolio that might in a few years provide the foundation for a leisurely and humane life. But now the press of success, the demands of daily feeding the beast of a boss who required more of others than he did of himself, took its toll. Most nights Jack went to sleep with both exhaustion and a low level of dread at what would surface tomorrow.

AT HOME.   Martha was a gracious but empty woman. Her emptiness was a quiet ache, a wistful dissatisfaction that felt like the beginning of a slow slide to despair.

Their three children were all in school. The youngest had

just started school, provoking a level of life reevaluation that she had not entertained since college. She thought about going back to teach. She had wanted to study toward a master's degree in anthropology, but there were very few archaeological digs in their suburban community—it just wasn't practical. Practical. She had come to hate the word. It was Jack's favorite word whenever they discussed the future. It was like the cork that kept in check the tensions in their marriage and the frustrations with their busy lives. *If we stopped being practical,* Martha thought to herself, *we would open Pandora's box— releasing demons and dreams that have been shut up rather than faced in our marriage.*

Whatever happened to our dreams? The thought cut through Martha as if she had stepped on a piece of glass. The shard cut deep, and she could not extract it all day. Fortunately, she had both a tennis drill and then a doubles match in the afternoon. The physical exercise and competition would force her to concentrate.

Unfortunately, the lesson was canceled, and she played a weak match. She had just enough time to pick up the laundry before dropping their younger daughter off at the orthodontist and taking their other daughter to her piano lesson. She couldn't remember if she had promised the neighbor she would pick up their sons from soccer practice.

She could feel the wound from the bleeding question grow dull from the mind-numbing monotony of her daily tasks. In some sense, it was relieving to not feel the pain each time she took a step; on the other hand, the pain from the question was the most real and personal passion she had felt in months. She let the question drift as she recalled the one shot she had missed when she had taken a big risk and had hit the ball hard down the alley. It had been close and felt so good to try, but it was not a high-percentage shot. And she had to learn to be more practical.

AT THE OFFICE.   Jack swore quietly. He had been trying to get Martha on the car phone for over an hour. He knew that her tennis time was over and that she should be in the car. It had been a big expense to get a car phone for her, but he felt it was an important safety device. Plus it would enable them to avoid unnecessary tensions at points when plans needed to be changed—and this was one of those points.

He had to pick up tickets for his flight to Boston, and Martha would be driving by one of the suburban ticket agencies. And it would take her only a second to stop in and save him a trip through that part of town. He wanted to save an hour to grab a cup of coffee with two of his cronies to celebrate his most recent victory.

He was tired, as usual, and harried by the day's demands. But he had just finished a major presentation that could take the company in a new direction—a risky but potentially very profitable path of acquiring another firm that would expand their client base and their reputation, and put them in line in a matter of years to be acquired by one of the giants in the field. Jack reasoned his stocks might be worth fifteen to twenty times what they were worth today.

He felt good. He had pulled off a coup. Even his skeptical and critical boss had been impressed by the presentation. He chuckled as he thought about the old man laughing and patting him on the back.

Just then the redial caught up with Martha. His voice changed. The gleam in his eye became dull, and the bounce in his voice slowed to a tired monotone: "Hey, Mart. Where are you? I have been trying to find you for an age. How was your game? Sorry. Hey, any chance of running by United to pick up tickets for me? I have to fly up to Boston on Friday, and I'm supposed to meet with Martin and John to go over the presentation I made this afternoon."

It was the first moment he realized he was not telling the

whole truth. It was not as if he was going to have coffee with another woman—he was an exceptionally moral man. But he noticed he did not want to tell his wife about his presentation, the celebration with friends, or the potential stock deal. He knew she would be both irritated and matter-of-fact, even cold. He just did not want her to rain on his party.

Somewhere deep in his heart he knew that she hated his work. He felt passionate about his work. It was the one area that allowed him to feel alive and purposeful. He could sit for hours and work on spreadsheets and draw out scenarios for managing different crises. He was creative, risky, and visionary. He sincerely loved his wife. But he dreamed about his work.

"Sure, Jack. By the way, I don't mean to upset you, but I'm going to see the doctor to see if I can get on some kind of antidepressant. I just don't think I can continue with this pace feeling like this. Do I need to pay for the tickets or are they prepaid?"

She was not aware of the non sequiturs, the abrupt shift in topic. It was a normal conversation—task oriented, lightly personal, and devoid of connection in relationship and context. At one point, she noticed her voice sounded hollow and robotlike, but it seemed like more effort than it was worth to ask about his day. If she asked, she knew the four responses that were the possible answers, and she did not care to hear any of them today.

She felt a tinge of anger in her heart, but how could she erupt over something as small as adding one more errand to her day? And to be aware of any other reason for her anger, again, felt like more effort than it was worth.

If someone had asked her what she was trying to tell Jack about the antidepressants, she would have been confused and defensive. She was just telling him a thought. She did not have a whole lot of time with him anyway, so she just said what was on her mind.

Jack and Martha seldom, if ever, had verbal intercourse. Words passed between them with no greater purpose than passing on information and dividing tasks. Jack was not much for long conversations. Martha was not much for conflict. So they each retreated to the world that required their unique skills and energy. He was a successful businessman and a caring family man. She was a good mother and was devoted to her family.

Jack and Martha did their work well. They knew the dues that were required to make their world work, and they paid their debt with dutiful civility.

Martha ended the call. She had to run into the pharmacy for something that she could not even recall. She pulled the car into a space and turned off the engine. She stared out the window for what seemed like a moment, but, in fact, she sat motionless for nearly a quarter of an hour.

Her mind focused on the last volley of the match. She had hit a good serve—deep and in the corner. She hesitated and did not immediately come to the net. But her opponent hit a weak shot off the racket, and it landed short and on her side of the court. She had practiced short shots for weeks, and she felt a rush of adrenaline. Martha slowed her breath; she moved forward. Out of the corner of her eye she saw the woman playing the net edge toward the middle. Martha took a short backswing and hit the ball down the line. Her topspin carried the ball easily over the net; it was hit hard but not too hard. The ball rose and dipped down toward the line. She had looked up a second too soon and had not followed through. The ball was out by an inch. She lost the game. She lost. It mattered—and little else mattered.

6

Re-entering Eden:

Learning to Create,

Offer, and Shape Life

Marriages can become plodding, cyclical routines filled with boredom and obligation. No one expects that a marriage will retain the giddy glow of excitement that comes with the novelty of new love. But it is equally wrong to assume that passion must wane simply because of familiarity. True passion comes from the nature of the purpose of a marriage.

The purpose of every marriage is to shape the raw material of life to reveal more fully the glory of God. Either we labor to enhance glory, or we exploit the beauty of creation for our pride and pleasure. Every marriage moves toward either creativity or exploitation.

Tragically, Jack and Martha exploited one another to serve the purpose of finding passion in arenas other than their marriage. They had lost passion for each other because they did not have a joint, core purpose that united their hearts. Jack's purpose, his core passion was to succeed in business. His greatest joy was not in becoming like Christ. Therefore, his marriage was a convenience that enabled him to pursue what mattered most to his heart.

Martha had grown numb and bored. She lost hope in intimacy; she lost desire for Jack. The doldrums of life drifted these two castaways further and further from each other until Martha's deepest passion was the adrenaline that came from competitive sports.

A marriage is no better than its purpose. And if the purpose is to live out the purposes of God, there will be a growing passion not only for God but also for one another. What is the core purpose of marriage? What purpose will ensure the growth of real passion?

Again we'll look to the first three chapters of Genesis to provide us with insight.

WHAT ARE WE TO DO AS HUSBANDS AND WIVES?

Immediately after God creates the man and the woman, he gives them their job descriptions. "God blessed them and said to them, 'Be fruitful and increase in number; fill the earth and subdue it. Rule over the fish of the sea and the birds of the air and over every living creature that moves on the ground'" (Gen. 1:28).

Our attention is drawn to the fact that God speaks to both the man and the woman, assigning them a joint task in the world. Together they are to fill the earth, subdue it, and rule over all the creatures. In a poetic form called a chiasm, we are told what to do. A chiasm is a poetic stanza that links words in this form:

DIAGRAM OF CHIASM

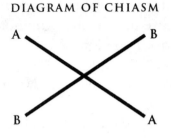

The B elements are synonyms, and the A and C elements add a new dimension to the meaning of the stanza. Notice this pattern in the verse:

(A) Be Fruitful—(B) Increase
(B) Fill————(C) Subdue

We are to be fruitful and increase. As we increase and fill, we are to also subdue. And our fruitfulness and our subduing should lead to ruling. Or, put in a formula: Fruitful + Subdue = Rule.

We are to make, to shape, and to own the world around us. In our culture we have learned to see contradictions between being, doing, and having. Too often we become what we do; or we define ourselves by what we own; or we make in order to possess. Today we feel tensions between the three most important verbs of life: *be, do, have.*

WE ARE TO MAKE, TO SHAPE, AND TO OWN THE WORLD AROUND US.

Before the fall of humankind into sin, no contradictions existed between these actions. Adam and Eve's existence as image-bearing persons enabled them to live righteously and rule as God's representatives on earth. Even though sin has severed the natural link between being, doing, and having, we are still called to live out the job description given to us by God. What does that mean for us?

Be Fruitful and Increase in Number: Bold Creativity

We are made to make. We are deeply wired by God to create. In the deepest sense of the word, we are creative, imaginative beings who long to take what God has already created and bring it into a new existence.

The Genesis passage is primarily referring to the human calling to create children in families. We are to procreate and to increase in number. But it would be an error to think that the mandate to create is limited to nothing more than bearing children. We are to be fruitful. Part of Adam's calling was not only to plant seeds in Eve but also to seed the creation with new plants. He was a farmer, artist, and scientist; Eve was called to be the same.

WE ARE DEEPLY WIRED BY GOD TO CREATE.

One of the most profound pictures of that creative work is Adam's naming of the animals. In the ancient Near Eastern culture, to name was to create, to set the course of the thing being named. In many ways, it was similar to God's calling all existence into being through his own divine "naming" or speaking. Adam was to draw forth from his own being a name for all of God's creation—God shares the glory of making.

Obviously, Adam and Eve had different capacities, but neither could fulfill the entirety of the task without the other. God created interdependence to reflect his Trinitarian being.

HUMAN CREATION.   What does it mean to create? To create is to take something that already is and draw it forth into a new form. We create a vase by transforming a lump of clay into a new form. Or we create a vacation by transforming an idea or a wish.

TO CREATE IS TO TAKE SOMETHING THAT ALREADY IS AND DRAW IT FORTH INTO A NEW FORM.

Think about vacation plans. Creation begins with desire. A father wants to relax and enjoy the company of his family without the normal toils of life. It spurs him to begin to talk about next summer's vacation. He talks over his ideas and desires with his wife. Last summer they visited their extended family. This year they want to take their kids out West. But where will they go? And what will they do? Recently they both watched the movie *A River Runs through It,* and they began to joke about how much fun it might be to fish as a whole family. They love fishing, but no one has dared to pick up a fly rod. One of them noticed an ad in a brochure for a two-weekend fly-fishing course at a local junior college. They decide to attend the class, book lodging at a ranch in Montana, and buy the airplane tickets—all on the basis of imagining the possibility. Creation has occurred. Desire leads to dreaming; imagining moves the heart to action; and choice leads to creation.

Men and women are called to be imaginative, to dream. We are called to envision and then to act to see our creation come into existence. It is impossible not to create. We create when we prepare a meal, make plans for the day, or put on clothes in the morning. But often we create by rote. We paint by number and lose or stifle the passion of dreaming. And when we do dream, we often limit our dreams to the mundane rather than to what we can desire, dream, and create for God.

Jack was a dreamer-creator. He loved his work, and his imagination soared as he envisioned new levels of expansion, acquisition, and growth. He was an artist who painted on the canvas of reality the colors of his imagination. Imagination is our capacity to envision what could be. And Jack lived for his art.

MEN AND WOMEN ARE CALLED TO BE IMAGINATIVE, TO DREAM.

But he did not bring his imagination to bear on the clay of his own life. He refused an honest look at his character, heart, and existence. He ignored the raw chaos of his life. Consequently, he did not face what could be. He refused to imagine what he could be if God were to rule his heart more deeply. Jack's refusal to see his own soul as the prime ground for creation left him dream-less as he thought about his wife and children. He had no more vision of who they were and who they were meant to be than he had for himself. In harsh terms, Jack loved them, but he never dreamed about their existence. He was a creator in his job but not in his family. Therefore, his family was left in middle-class chaos—moving aimlessly, circling in the tiresome, dark loneliness of the status quo.

OUR GREAT WORK OF CREATION.   We are creators, with God, of life. Obviously, through physical birth we have the capacity to be part of the birthing of a new human being. Even here our creation is derivative; anything we make comes out of what God has already made. In that sense we are always co-creators with God.

But we are not limited to a creative participation only in the physical sphere. We are also invited to participate in the spiritual realm of creation—called the second birth.

Without question, the new birth of Christ in a human heart is entirely the work of God. The apostle John says, "Yet to all who received him, to those who believed in his name, he gave the right to become children of God—children born not of natural descent, nor of human decision or a husband's will, but born of God" (John 1:12-13). Yet, the apostle Paul claims that his involvement with people who come to know Jesus is similar to being their birth parent.

New birth is the domain of God. A husband and wife provide the sperm and egg, but God is the one who creates the child in the womb. In the same way, we provide the Word and the relationship for conversion, but it is God who forms Christ in a human soul. In both cases, we are the most honored of creation in that we are co-creators with God. The work of creation must be done not only together with God but also in intimate involvement with one another.

When we see the mandate to be fruitful in terms of giving birth to children, it is obvious that it would be impossible for either sex to fill the earth alone! Only together—and, as we will soon learn, only in the context of marriage—can men and women fill the creation with glory.

At the core of filling the earth is reflecting God's character as a maker of life and becoming co-heirs in creation. To do so with regard to children and in all other creative endeavors, we must live in a core commitment to mirror the character of God in our home and in our church. We must provide a solid foundation of honor and love to sustain and nurture growing relationships.

Marriage must be a picture of or testimony to new birth. Marriage must reflect the fruits of new birth and the creative, Trinitarian God who is the author of life. In that sense, a marriage is the foundation of evangelism and the declaration of the possibility of being a son and a daughter—being a member of the family of God. The central task of a marriage is first to create and offer life and then to take new life and shape it in the direction of maturity.

THE CENTRAL TASK OF A MARRIAGE
IS FIRST TO CREATE AND OFFER LIFE
AND THEN TO TAKE NEW LIFE
AND SHAPE IT IN THE DIRECTION
OF MATURITY.

Fill the Earth and Subdue It: Tender Cultivation

We are to subdue the earth. This biblical teaching has been much abused in the exploitation of the creation for selfish ends; thus we tend to ignore it or explain it away. But there is a proper, productive sense in which God's human creatures are not only to create but also to mold creation as God does.

Creativity is visionary movement that brings something into existence. Subduing is shaping the creation into a higher order of beauty and usefulness. It is cultivating the young plant into mature fruit.

God created something out of nothing, and then he began to shape it from raw chaos into a form that reveals his glory. God is a potter. He takes the clay of creation, shapes it, and then breathes his presence into its soul. He shapes chaos into beauty, and then he stamps it with his name. We are to do the same.

We do not create ex nihilo, out of nothing, but we are to shape his creation into even higher forms of useful splendor. To subdue means to tread down or to cut a path in a virgin forest and then cultivate the land. Adam and Eve were to be explorers and scientists who took the original creation, envisioned something new, and then cut a new path in the world.

SUBDUING IS SHAPING THE CREATION INTO A HIGHER ORDER OF BEAUTY AND USEFULNESS.

The by-product would then reflect the beauty of the Creator and serve the purposes of knowing more about God, one another, and creation itself. All our subduing ought to reflect glory—increasing a sense of awe—and ought to deepen our knowledge of God's goodness—increasing our sense of gratitude. Subduing is not ruining; it is living out glory to increase beauty. Subduing therefore increases our worship of God.

We live out glory each time we compose a symphony or cut the lawn. We are to take a grass-covered field and turn it into a harvest of flowers or plant rows of grapes. We are to shape the fields of life to satisfy our hunger and quench our thirst; we live to feed our craving to know more and more of God's infinite goodness.

In the story about Jack and Martha we see two people whose creative energies are not claimed by a passion to see new birth, to see God. Instead, Jack and Martha give themselves over to work and play. They cultivate dreams that have little to do with the glory of God.

CULTIVATING GLORY. To subdue the earth means to work the creation to a higher and higher reflection of God's glory. To Adam and Eve the mandate to subdue the earth meant especially that they should cultivate the land so that it would

81

produce food for them to eat and enjoy. To us in our highly developed technological society, the mandate to subdue the earth has taken on a much broader meaning. Very few of us are involved in farming, but all of us can live with the heart of a co-creator, an artist, so that the earth can be used and enjoyed in God-honoring ways.

An architect, for example, uses his or her intelligence, training, and experience to design a house; thus, the architect uses the resources of the earth to provide shelter and to create a beauty that makes us long to be home. A garbage collector subdues the earth by ordering and disposing of waste so that our homes and streets are not littered and spoiled. A homemaker subdues the creation while he or she manages the household finances, mops the floor, works with the children's schedule. The possibilities are as numerous as there are people.

OUR GREATEST PRIVILEGE IS SHAPING THE CHARACTER OF THE SOUL TO REFLECT THE IMAGE OF CHRIST.

Our greatest privilege is not in shaping a symphony, learning to fly-fish, directing a ministry, or even providing food and clothing for our children. Our greatest privilege is shaping the character of the soul to reflect the image of Christ.

We are to invite one another to become more like our God. When we reflect his character, we most effectively live out his glory. We are called to disciple one another; that is, we are called to participate with God in shaping one another to reflect more gloriously the beauty of God. Paul compares his experience of discipling to childbirth. He says, "We proclaim him, admonishing and teaching everyone with all wisdom, so that we may present everyone perfect in Christ. To this end I labor, struggling with all his energy, which so powerfully works in me" (Col. 1:28-29). He labors to present each person full, complete, mature in Christ.

To subdue and/or cultivate is to put our hands in the clay—to get dirty, to throw the clay, beat it, and then spin it—molding it to the purpose that best fits the Master's desire. It requires the labor, the sacrifice, the sorrow of a woman who in childbirth is willing to spend her life to give birth to a child.

GOD'S INTENTION FOR MARRIAGE
IS TO GROW OR SUBDUE EACH PARTNER
IN RELATION TO THE OTHER
IN ORDER TO DRAW EACH
AND EVENTUALLY THE MARRIAGE
ITSELF TO REFLECT THE
CHARACTER OF HIS SON.

I (Dan) recall in a college art course the enormous labor involved in shaping a lump of clay into a usable, lovely vase. The patient labor of pounding out the clay to dissolve the air bubbles was tedious. I soon tired of the work, and I wanted to move quickly to molding the clay. The work soon became more than tedious; it was painful. My hands were filthy, my fingers ached with pain, and my arms were exhausted. But over time perseverance was rewarded with the pleasure of forming a vase that was both useful and lovely. The same is true for people who disciple others. They must be patient, endure great pain, and persevere to see the vessel completed and ready for use. It requires the vision of an artist and the suffering of a mother both to bring into existence and to shape beauty.

The purposes of our marriages are to create life and to shape life to maturity. A marriage is no better than the vision we have for one another and the willingness we have to sacrifice for each other, to suffer to see growth occur. Many marriages survive by merely providing a partner for activities—a resource to counter occasional biological and personal needs. But God's intention for marriage is to grow or subdue each partner in relation to the other in order to draw each—and eventually the marriage itself—to reflect the character of his Son. The high calling of God is to create life and then to shape it in his image. Our marriages are not only the context for evangelism but also the soil for discipleship. And to what end? Ultimately, our marriages are the foundation for the kingdom of God to grow on earth in anticipation of its full realization in the new heavens and earth.

TO RULE AND TO SERVE.   God wants us to rule over the creation. Here we see another connection with our creation in the image of God. God is the King of the universe. He created it, so he rules over it. But the amazing teaching of the Genesis passage is that God reflects his rule over the rest of his creation through us! Men and women are the rulers over God's vast creation.

MEN AND WOMEN ARE THE RULERS OVER GOD'S VAST CREATION.

Astounding as this teaching is to us on its own, it is even more astounding in the light of common thought in the ancient Near Eastern cultures that surrounded Israel when Genesis was first written. The creation accounts we have from Mesopotamia, for instance, inform men and women that they are the "fodder of the gods." The gods were tired of working, so they created humanity, a race of slaves that would do their bidding. The Bible teaches just the opposite: Men and women are the kings and queens of creation. We are God's representatives who are equipped and called to create and shape creation. But for what end? And in what manner?

Men and women are to rule in order to serve, and we serve through sacrifice. Jesus taught that we are not to rule like the Gentile leaders, but we are to serve with and through the humility of God. He said, "You know that those who are regarded as rulers of the Gentiles lord it over them, and their high officials exercise authority over them. Not so with you. Instead, whoever wants to become great among you must be your servant, and whoever wants to be first must be slave of all. For even the Son of Man did not come to be served, but to serve, and to give his life as a ransom for many" (Mark 10:42-45). To rule is to serve. We are servants of creation. In some sense, we are servants of our own creation. When a book is published, it takes a life of its own. When it goes out into the world, I must assume responsibility for its errors, and I must also further its good. In conversations with others who have been helped, I must take what was planted and develop it to the end of seeing growth that spurs the soul to desire to live out the life of Christ. In other words, I must serve others through whatever creative endeavor I have been privileged to pursue.

MEN AND WOMEN ARE TO RULE IN ORDER TO SERVE, AND WE SERVE THROUGH SACRIFICE.

We are called to cultivate Christ in others by sowing words of life on ground we have worked—guided by a vision of what is and what could be. In my marriage, I must see my spouse as the first and primary person that I am to labor to create and shape. As well, I must open my heart to be the palette of my spouse. She is to envision and paint on my soul the being that I am to become.

Not to see one's spouse as a work of art and not to give one's soul to the other to create and shape is to fail at the most primary task of life. We are to serve one another so that we become like Christ and so that the other equally is molded in his image. In so doing, our marriages become the fertile ground to offer new birth and the growing of life to others.

To rule is to be the first to serve and the first to sacrifice in order to bring the benefits of creation to those we love. As royalty, we are to serve our great King as servants who rule in his place, ordering creation to bring joy and wonder to others. Built deep within every human heart is the passion to serve, to rule by honoring others.

TO RULE IS TO BE THE FIRST TO SERVE
AND THE FIRST TO SACRIFICE
IN ORDER TO BRING THE BENEFITS
OF CREATION TO THOSE WE LOVE.

In marriage, we are both kings and queens who rule by ordering creation to enhance the glory and pleasure of each other. We are to rule through sacrificing on behalf of one another.

Further, we must recognize that the job description is given equally to men and women. At this point, God makes no distinction about who is to do what. Women are not the slaves or servants of men; men are not the slaves or servants of women. Men and women together fill, subdue, and rule over all of creation.

Summary for Marriage: Our spouses are joint heirs and rulers over creation. We are called to create order and beauty out of chaos and to form in one another an even clearer picture of God, the divine ruler. Our only option in responding to our roles as spouses is either to create or to use creation for our own selfish purposes.

QUESTIONS FOR REFLECTION AND CONVERSATION

1. We are called to create. To create requires artistry and imagination in order to shape the raw material of life. In what areas of life are you most imaginative? Where do you find it hard to dream in your marriage?
2. What specific vision do you have for your spouse? Compare what your spouse is now to what you might imagine him or her to be if God truly were to rule in your spouse's life.
3. In what ways do you refuse to suffer—that is, to be patient, to bear pain, and to persevere with your spouse? What would need to occur in your life for each of you to develop a vision and to be willing to bear the pains of childbirth on behalf of your spouse?
4. At times every marriage gets bogged down in the mundane and survives on busyness rather than creativity. Consider the time(s) that you and your spouse have worked together to create an unusual outcome to a significant problem. What was it like? How did it occur? What were the results?
5. Where do you wish you and your spouse colabored in a way that would reflect greater creativity?

7

Shaping Beauty and
Order out of Chaos

We are called to cultivate Christ in our spouses by the power of the spoken word. To do so effectively, we must be guided by a vision of who they are, a picture of who they were meant to be (like Christ), and a grasp of our role in helping them become like Christ.

As Christians, my wife and I are called to glorify one another. To put it another way, we are called to shape Christ in one another; that is, we must encourage each other to know the heart of the Father through the passion of Christ.

I need to draw Christ out of my wife, and she needs to draw him out of me so that we can in turn subdue or better shape the world. This is the message of Genesis 1:28 for the Christian who reads it in light of the New Testament, and this is what we are exploring in this section.

What does it mean to shape the world? Why does the world need shaping?

I NEED TO DRAW CHRIST OUT OF MY WIFE, AND SHE NEEDS TO DRAW HIM OUT OF ME SO THAT WE CAN IN TURN SUBDUE OR BETTER SHAPE THE WORLD.

When Adam and Eve were in the Garden, they were called to subdue the earth. This included taking care of the Garden (Gen. 2:15). Apparently, there was work to do in the Garden of Eden! God gave them the task of gardening in the Garden. And in this task, somehow God would reveal more and more of himself.

The work of caring for the Garden was tantamount to going to school. It was the place of investigation and the expansion of their grasp not only of the world but also of the God who made it. In other words, we are to shape in order to be shaped. We engage in change to be changed. We are to be known in knowing and in knowing know about God something that could not be experienced without shaping the world and others.

This shaping would be similar to the type of shaping that God himself did during creation. Genesis 1:1-2 informs us that God created the heavens and earth, but when he first brought them into being, they were "formless and empty." It was the divine task of the next six days to take this shapeless matter and bring it to the beauty of the created universe.

Indeed, it was so beautiful that God kept repeating "It is good" after each step.

But the shaping takes a more dangerous and burdensome direction after Adam and Eve sin. First of all, the earth itself is no longer a friendly place. No longer do men and women live in the Garden. They confront a hostile environment that sometimes has too much or too little rain, too much sun, or too much wind.

But it is more than the earth itself that confronts human beings. We become our own worst enemies. Instead of seeking the common good as we confront the forces of nature, we turn on each other, seeking to gain an advantage.

This selfish impulse not only leads to societal problems but also affects our relationship with nature. "Subduing" creation becomes raping it. We exploit the earth for our own profit and gain. In their efforts to subdue the earth, some people have used Genesis 1:28 as a license to rip great ugly holes in the earth, pour poison into the waters, and belch toxic gases into the air.

It is not to be doubted that greedy men and women have used Genesis 1:28 as their excuse, but their greed is fueled by an obvious misuse of the text. As author Wendell Berry has insightfully pointed out, those who believe that Genesis 1:28 justifies a misuse of the earth's resources "are guilty of an extremely unintelligent misreading of Genesis 1:28 itself. How, for example, would one arrange to 'replenish the earth' if 'subdue' means, as alleged, 'conquer' or 'defeat' or 'destroy'?"[1]

SHAPING THE CHAOS

The point, however, is that after the Fall, we are called to shape not just a formless world but a hostile world. We will use the term *chaos* to describe the world that has fallen into sin. Nature, society, and our own inner world present a level of chaos that is both evil and dangerous.

As marriage partners, a husband and a wife have a clear

alternative as they relate to one another and then as they relate to the world, both social and natural: Marriage partners either call order and beauty out of chaos or intensify the chaos. We may either shape beauty and relational unity or enhance what is ugly and chaotic.

CHAOS IS A WORLD
THAT HAS FALLEN INTO SIN.

In the first place, a married couple has to recognize what is chaotic and unformed within themselves, both as individuals and as a couple. After we become Christians, sin still remains within us (Rom. 7:7-25). The result is that even Christian marriage partners act harmfully toward one another and cause conflicts.

That was the case for Jack and Martha. They were slowly and with hostility drifting from one another. They weren't helping one another grow toward Christ; they weren't sharing the same dream. They were living for their own vision and resenting the presence of the other. They were enhancing the chaos in their spouse's life, not shaping one another toward beauty.

MARRIAGE PARTNERS EITHER CALL
ORDER AND BEAUTY OUT OF CHAOS
OR INTENSIFY THE CHAOS.

We are made to shape and form the world around us. When we refuse to be shaped or to shape others into the image of Christ, then we serve lesser gods, like our work or hobbies. The emptiness of living for so small a purpose ends up creating a desperate drive to find satisfaction in someting that cannot provide life. Jack and Martha are tragic pictures of upper-middle-class lives that revolve around shaping one's own glory rather than God's glory. Self-glory always leads to greater chaos.

A married couple faces chaos not only within themselves and in their marriage relationship but also in their other relationships. For example, young married couples often find relationships with in-laws to be one of their most difficult struggles. Well-meaning or malicious parents often try to barge into a new, tender relationship. Perhaps they just want to "help out," but if the help comes with strings attached, then it is just so much pretense.

The couple faces further chaos in the natural world: cutting the grass, fixing the roof, paying the bills, getting gas in the car, finding a job, keeping a job, getting a job that pays enough. The list is endless, and life often seems like an uphill battle.

And, indeed, life is a battle. Life is a battle to stay alive, a battle to cope with everyday aggravations, a battle to control ourselves and get along with our spouses, a battle to pay the bills, a battle to get all the house chores done. In a word, life is a battle against chaos.

LIFE IS A BATTLE AGAINST CHAOS.

How does the battle affect my marriage? How can we fight the battle?

Let's look at various biblical passages that help us define the battle as well as how to engage in it. We will find that the Bible does not see the battle as a life of drudgery and fear. Far from it. The Bible describes life as a colaboring with God in the exciting task of shaping a world plunged into chaos.

CREATION: GOD, THE SHAPER

Genesis 1 recounts how God first created matter and then shaped it into existence. The creation account in Genesis 1 contrasts sharply with the creation accounts of the surrounding nations of Egypt and Mesopotamia. In all other ancient Near Eastern creation accounts matter was already present. It was there at the same time as the beginning of the gods.

Israel's God, in contrast, has always been there, and at a certain point, he called creation into being. The moment he created matter, history began. Space came into being, and time began. At the beginning, the earth was "formless and empty" (Gen. 1:2). God then launched into his six-day plan for shaping the cosmos.

In order to see how our God shapes order and beauty out of disorder, we focus briefly on the fourth day. In its similarities to the other creation days, it illustrates important points concerning God as Shaper of disorder.

> And God said, "Let there be lights in the expanse of the sky to separate the day from the night, and let them serve as signs to mark seasons and days and years, and let them be lights in the expanse of the sky to give light on the earth." And it was so. God made two great lights—the greater light to govern the day and the lesser light to govern the night. He also made the stars. God set them in the expanse of the sky to give light on the earth, to govern the day and the night, and to separate light from darkness. And God saw that it was good. And there was evening, and there was morning—the fourth day. GENESIS 1:14-19

Something that casual readers of the Bible often miss is the relationship between the six days of creation. It is significant to show the pattern of the creation days so we can see day four as the cusp from God's creation of realms to the creation of inhabitants of those realms.

The first three days result in the creation of three spheres of existence. The first day God creates light and darkness. The second day he creates water and sky. And the third day he creates earth.

The next three days fill those spheres in the exact order in which they were created. The fourth day, the day that we are focusing on for illustrative purposes, fills the realm of light and darkness with sun, moon, and stars. The fifth day fills the sphere of the water and sky with fish and birds. The sixth, the climactic day, populates the dry ground with creatures, most notably human beings.

Perhaps the most startling aspect of the creation process is the means God uses to bring reality into existence: He speaks, and it is done. His word brings things into existence. In the fourth day, he commands lights to appear in the sky, and the result is the moon, the sun, and the stars.

These mighty heavenly bodies, so huge and so incredibly distant from each other, are brought into existence by the divine fiat. The sizes, the distances, the temperatures, the variations, the mind-boggling ages represented in our cosmos are nothing to the God who created them in a word.

And God brought these mighty heavenly bodies into existence by the power of his word alone. He is like and unlike a potter. He is unlike the potter in that he creates the clay out of thin air, but he is like the potter because his word takes the blob of clay and shapes it into a beautiful vase.

Genesis 1 describes God, the Shaper, the one who creates beauty and form out of disorder and formlessness. However, after the Fall, God's shaping and ordering takes on a new, sharper edge. Psalm 74 gives us a glimpse into God's role of conquering chaos after the Fall.

CHAOS: GOD, THE CONQUEROR

How long will the enemy mock you, O God?
Will the foe revile your name forever?
Why do you hold back your hand, your right hand?
Take it from the folds of your garment and destroy them!

But you, O God, are my king from of old;
you bring salvation upon the earth.
It was you who split open the sea by your power;
you broke the heads of the monster in the waters.
It was you who crushed the heads of Leviathan
and gave him as food to the creatures of the desert.
It was you who opened up springs and streams;
you dried up the ever flowing rivers.
The day is yours, and yours also the night;
you established the sun and moon.
It was you who set all the boundaries of the earth;
you made both summer and winter.
Remember how the enemy has mocked you, O Lord,
how foolish people have reviled your name.
Do not hand over the life of your dove to wild beasts;
do not forget the lives of your afflicted people forever.
Have regard for your covenant,
because haunts of violence fill the dark places of the land.
Do not let the oppressed retreat in disgrace;
may the poor and needy praise your name.
Rise up, O God, and defend your cause;
remember how fools mock you all day long.
Do not ignore the clamor of your adversaries,
the uproar of your enemies, which rises continually. PSALM 74:10-23

Psalm 74 is a cry of the soul by an individual on behalf of the whole community. The people of Israel have just suffered a humiliating defeat at the hands of their enemy. The psalmist is upset that God seems absent—or worse, that he is on the enemy's side. The people hear the mockery of evil people denouncing their God, and God seems to do nothing to defend his name or his people.

In the midst of his confused prayer to God to pay attention to them once again, the psalmist describes the Lord as one who brings order to chaos—in this case, not the formless matter of creation but the hostile and dangerous chaos of a world after the Fall.

The psalmist reminds God of his victory against Leviathan. As we read, we must keep in mind that we are reading poetry. The poet has more freedom than the writer of historical narrative to speak in figurative language. Leviathan is the great monster of the sea. The sea itself represents the forces of chaos, disorder, evil, and the demonic. Sea monsters are a horrific and powerful personification of evil in the world. Leviathan is the multiheaded demon who ranges himself against God.

The point of the psalm is that this potent image of chaotic evil stood no chance against the Lord. God conquered Leviathan and used its body as food for his creatures.

But the psalmist is not interested in the past for the sake of the past. Chaos reigns in the present. This chaos is not the cosmological chaos represented by Leviathan but rather the sociological chaos of evil people who have just destroyed the temple, adding to the confusion of whether God was going to keep his promises to his people. The psalmist calls the Lord to the battle of the present, a battle against the uproar of the enemy. The psalmist cries out for a word from God to be spoken against the contemptuous words of his enemies. With just a word, God could heal or destroy.

WORDS: THE POWER OF LIFE AND DEATH

Words have great power. With a word God called into being the beauty of the cosmos. With a word he can silence the most threatening forces of evil. His word brings life. As he speaks and acts in the world of sin, he pushes back the chaos by his powerful word.

God also calls husbands and wives to use our words to push back the chaos and shape our lives into order and beauty. He calls us to use our words to bring life to those who hear them.

Jack and Martha had a problem with words. They talked to each other, but they didn't communicate well. They spoke *by* each other, both consciously and unconsciously. They each had their separate visions and aspirations, and they didn't want to share them with one another. Somehow they avoided the truth that the spoken and written word expose the heart. When we talk about our passions, hurts, desires, and troubles, we expose our hearts. Jack and Martha didn't want their separate, parallel lives exposed, so they spoke *by* each other rather than *with* each other.

GOD ALSO CALLS HUSBANDS AND WIVES TO USE OUR WORDS TO PUSH BACK THE CHAOS AND SHAPE OUR LIVES INTO ORDER AND BEAUTY.

Neither Jack nor Martha had a good sense of how words had an impact on the other. As a result, their communication was both a symptom and a cause of their growing alienation. When spouses engage in honest and lengthy conversation, they expose the core battle with self-glory and the many forms of degradation in a marriage. But it is this embattled conversation that is necessary to enhance the glory of the other.

By the time most couples get married, most of them have already discovered that their spouses are not perfect. Those who are honest with themselves also realize more deeply than ever before that they are far from ideal themselves. Marriage does not magically dispel the problems that existed before the wedding. If anything, marriage enlarges the problems. Living in close proximity, minor faults and idiosyncrasies balloon to gargantuan proportions, and major problems loom large.

It is not unusual for the thrills of a new marriage to obscure these difficulties, but "the honeymoon doesn't last forever." Every married couple confronts troubles and crises. The question is not whether a marriage will be tested, but how the test is met.

Marriages are challenged in many ways. How we talk to each other reflects the quality of our relationship as well as the depth of our character. Good speech quells chaos and promotes joy and life; bad speech produces chaos and leads to despair and death. The book of Proverbs teaches this well. "The tongue has the power of life and death, and those who love it will eat its fruit" (Prov. 18:21).

HOW WE TALK TO EACH OTHER REFLECTS THE QUALITY OF OUR RELATIONSHIP AS WELL AS THE DEPTH OF OUR CHARACTER.

Proverbs is full of poetical lines that contain a sharp contrast. Most of the proverbs included in this chapter speak of both life-words and death-words. The impact of such constant contrast is to persuade us that there are no alternatives in our communication: We either promote well-being or enhance trouble with our speech. While the following proverbs generally address all speech, we will apply the principles to marriage. Words spoken between spouses either build up or break down a marriage.

Proverbs: Words That Make Marriages Whole

The book of Proverbs is a rich source of diagnosis and treatment for the ills of everyday life. Although at times it seems like no more than a collection of pithy mottoes, Proverbs has an impressive unity that places ordinary life in an intensely religious context.

While our purpose is to draw out the book's teaching about communication and apply it to our marriage relationships, we need to set the book in its broader context. From the very start Proverbs creates an opposition between wisdom and foolishness. The book uses personification to help readers identify with a young man who faces choices to follow one of two women, Lady Wisdom or Lady Folly (see especially Prov. 9). As we probe into the nature of these two women, we observe signals that indicate that Wisdom is in actuality Yahweh, the true God of the Bible, and Folly represents all the false gods and idols that tempt Israelites to leave the worship of the true God. Proverbs 9:18 reveals the ultimate fate of those who choose to follow Lady Folly when it comments, "her guests are in the depths of the grave." After the introductory chapters, the rest of the book includes the practical one-liners that we usually associate with the book.

WORDS ARE THE TOOLS THAT SHAPE THE HEART.

Words are the tools that shape the heart. When we speak in accordance with the heart of God, we shape order, purpose, and beauty out of chaos. When we speak in accord with the Author of Death, our words will kill; they will incite chaos, ferment pointlessness, and draw forth ugliness. We either create and shape life through words or destroy it.

The following proverbs give wisdom about communication. Let's look at these proverbs through the filter of our marriages.

The mouth of the righteous is a fountain of life,
but violence overwhelms the mouth of the wicked.
PROVERBS 10:11

Reckless words pierce like a sword,
but the tongue of the wise brings healing. PROVERBS 12:18

A gentle answer turns away wrath,
but a harsh word stirs up anger. PROVERBS 15:1

The tongue that brings healing is a tree of life,
but a deceitful tongue crushes the spirit. PROVERBS 15:4

A wise man's heart guides his mouth,
and his lips promote instruction. PROVERBS 16:23

Pleasant words are a honeycomb,
sweet to the soul and healing to the bones. PROVERBS 16:24

A word aptly spoken
is like apples of gold in settings of silver. PROVERBS 25:11

A quick reading of these proverbs leads us to see that our words are powerful—either to create or to destroy. We are most like God in that our speech brings about profound change. God speaks—to create or to destroy. He creates beauty; he destroys sin. Too often we create chaos and destroy beauty with our words.

If I am to grasp the power and importance of my words, then I must see each word spoken in light of calling beauty into existence or destroying beauty by the force of my cruel, unkind, heartless words. I am not to flee from the power of words by remaining silent, and I am not to speak with a cavalier disregard of my power to create or destroy. I am to sow words like seeds to bring a harvest of fruit that blesses God.

In contrast are the quarrelsome words spoken to destroy or use someone for our own glory. The proverbs below address this issue in light of the "quarrelsome wife." Perhaps no other issue is spoken of so often in the book. But before husbands use these verses to club their wives over the head, they need to remember that the book was originally written to men, not women. But as we apply the book to the church at large, we are required by its status as part of the canon to broaden its application to women and men. The point is these same things may be said about a quarrelsome husband.

A foolish son is his father's ruin,
and a quarrelsome wife is like a constant dripping.
PROVERBS 19:13

Better to live on a corner of the roof
than share a house with a quarrelsome wife. PROVERBS 21:9

Better to live in a desert
than with a quarrelsome and ill-tempered wife.
PROVERBS 21:19

As charcoal to embers and as wood to fire,
so is a quarrelsome man for kindling strife. PROVERBS 26:21

A quarrelsome wife is like
a constant dripping on a rainy day;
restraining her is like restraining the wind
or grasping oil with the hand. PROVERBS 27:15-16

A fool gives full vent to his anger,
but a wise man keeps himself under control. PROVERBS 29:11

Do you see a man who speaks in haste?
There is more hope for a fool than for him. PROVERBS 29:20

Living with an argumentative spouse is like living with water torture. One method of psychological warfare used to break POWs was to place them under a constant dripping of water. After a while the monotony, the minor irritation became unbearable, and the prisoners would offer any information to their captors to avoid the suffering.

To live with a spouse who is constantly nagging, complaining, seeing the down side of life is like living under psychological warfare. It wears a person down. It makes life unbearable, and anything—even living in a dark, lonely corner of the house or even the desert—is better than that.

It may be, though, that a husband wants to drive his wife away by his words. He wants a wife to cook for him, care for him, take care of his kids for him, but he doesn't want a wife to cramp his lifestyle. He doesn't want a wife who will tell him when to be home or when he needs to spend more time with his family. He doesn't want a wife to tell him that he is spending too much time or too little time doing his work. He wants to set his own agenda, be his own person, and not answer to anyone else.

Such a strategy may not even be a conscious one in the mind of the quarrelsome person. A wife may just feel annoyed with her husband, and his moving away from her may just intensify her anger. But the real object of her quarrelsomeness may be to avoid sexual intimacy because she is bored with him or too busy with other matters.

Proverbs identifies such people as fools. "Folly" in the Wisdom Literature of the Bible does not simply mean befuddlement or stupidity. Folly is intimately tied with evil, with wickedness. Or to use the language of this book, folly promotes chaos rather than seeking God's order.

The lips of the righteous nourish many,
but fools die for lack of judgment. PROVERBS 10:21

The lips of the righteous know what is fitting,
but the mouth of the wicked only what is perverse.
PROVERBS 10:32

The tongue of the wise commends knowledge,
but the mouth of the fool gushes folly. PROVERBS 15:2

The lips of the wise spread knowledge;
not so the hearts of fools. PROVERBS 15:7

He who answers before listening—
that is his folly and his shame. PROVERBS 18:13

And nothing is more powerful for promoting chaos than the tongue. A single word can result in all hell breaking loose in a household.

Proverbs reminds us that words can bring life and they can bring death. They can lift a marriage to the heights of ecstasy or even rekindle a dying love. But they can also devastate a marriage.

Proverbs warns us of the kinds of speech that need to be avoided—gossip and quarrels, perverse, violent, harsh, deceitful, or hasty words—and it directs us toward speech that promotes life—fitting for the situation, gentle, knowledgeable, pleasant.

A scoundrel plots evil,
and his speech is like a scorching fire. PROVERBS 16:27

A perverse man stirs up dissension,
and a gossip separates close friends. PROVERBS 16:28

Starting a quarrel is like breaching a dam;
so drop the matter before a dispute breaks out. PROVERBS 17:14

He who loves a quarrel loves sin;
he who builds a high gate invites destruction. PROVERBS 17:19

We must choose our words as if we were choosing an instrument of life or death. If we know the power of words, then we will neither refuse to speak because of fear nor speak often and sow seeds of destruction. We are to speak words of encouragement to draw forth the heart of God in those we love; we are to speak words of rebuke to disrupt the natural bent of our hearts to pride and self-righteousness. We are to know our spouses, know ourselves, and use a common sense that is based on an ever-deepening understanding of Scripture.

However, even when we know that our words can promote love-order or hate-chaos in our relationships, we don't always have the ability to control our speech. A spouse may know the right thing to say and even desire to say it on one level, but deep down something seems to prevent him or her from saying the right thing the right way. Verses from the book of James provide information about this problem.

> When we put bits into the mouths of horses to make them obey us, we can turn the whole animal. Or take ships as an example. Although they are so large and are driven by strong winds, they are steered by a very small rudder wherever the pilot wants to go. Likewise the tongue is a small part of the body, but it makes great boasts. Consider what a great forest is set on fire by a small spark. The tongue also is a fire, a world of evil among the parts of the body. It corrupts the whole person, sets the whole course of his life on fire, and is itself set on fire by hell. JAMES 3:3-6

James reiterates much that we have already seen in the book of Proverbs. The tongue is the most powerful part of the body. Although small, it can make a big impact. It can create a tremendous amount of relational damage. He also tells us that an unrestrained tongue will ultimately destroy itself and the person who uses it.

The metaphors James uses give simple, yet horribly difficult advice. In a word, he says "Stop it." We need to treat our tongue as a runaway horse or a rudderless ship: We need to rein in the horse or put a rudder in the ship.

James does not give us any techniques by which to stop our tongues. Instead, he asks us to develop a sense of horror over the damage that we do. He asks us to sit in a burned-out forest, seeing the death and destruction that one small match can bring and see that same destructive power in the words we use. Coming face-to-face with that destruction leaves us in a position either to struggle to heal or to join the Author of Chaos.

A LIFE OF WARFARE

Life is full of conflict and chaos. The Bible understands this and describes our time on earth as warfare.

> Finally, be strong in the Lord and in his mighty power. Put on the full armor of God so that you can take your stand against the devil's schemes. For our struggle is not against flesh and blood, but against the rulers, against the authorities, against the powers of this dark world and against the spiritual forces of evil in the heavenly realms. Therefore put on the full armor of God, so that when the day of evil comes, you may be able to stand your ground, and after you have done everything, to stand. Stand firm then, with the belt of truth buckled around your waist, with the breastplate of righteousness in place, and with your feet fitted with the readiness that comes from the gospel of peace. In addition to all this, take up the shield of faith, with which you can extinguish all the flaming arrows of the evil one. Take the helmet of salvation and the sword of the Spirit, which is the word of God. And pray in the

Spirit on all occasions with all kinds of prayers and requests. With this in mind, be alert and always keep on praying for all the saints. EPHESIANS 6:10-18

The world is a dangerous place to live. God battles Leviathan, and we battle a hostile environment. Paul makes it clear in this passage that life is a battleground.

We lead such an hour-by-hour existence that we miss the great truth that we are caught up in a cosmic struggle, a struggle between good and evil. It is not always clear who or what is on which side. People do not wear black and white hats. But the Bible describes the Christian life as a struggle against the "powers and principalities" (KJV); sometimes those powers take form in other people.

LIFE IS A BATTLEGROUND.

Marriage is part of the battle. It is a battle that calls us to engage the enemy and push back the forces of chaos. The beauty of marriage is that it is God's gift of an intimate ally in the struggle. Although at times it appears that husband and wife increase rather than diminish the chaos of life, marriage intends to unite two people into a joint ministry of subduing, shaping, conquering, in order to produce beauty.

At the end of his letter to the Ephesians, Paul encourages the believers in their struggles by placing their conflicts in the broader context of God's war against evil. Paul knows that life is a battle, and the opposition is not just what our eyes can see. The ultimate opponent is the Master of Chaos himself, Satan, and his minions.

A married couple will find out only too soon that romance does not protect them from the forces of the warfare. If warm, fuzzy feelings are all they have between them, then the conflict will soon cause those to disappear.

As married couples, we are jointly called to shape a world that resists shaping. We are called to join the army of God in order to conquer chaos. In our marriage we are called to help one another "stand firm." This is a military term that means to be prepared for the assault. We are to be "ready"; we are not only to be prepared with our armor on and our sword sharpened but actually to be "looking" for the signs of attack. I am to help my spouse see the war with our children, family, friends, and neighbors. Even more, I am to help my spouse prepare for war, train for war, and use God's weapons to fight the war that rages around us each day.

THE BEAUTY OF MARRIAGE IS THAT IT IS GOD'S GIFT OF AN INTIMATE ALLY IN THE STRUGGLE.

Marriage as war sounds just horrible, even if the conflict is an external one only. The bad news is that the conflict will also surface in the marriage. After all, Christians are not perfect. Paul describes the conflict that still remains in the heart of believers. Christians are "new creatures," true, but the "old person" still remains. The conquering of chaos takes place in ourselves as individuals, in our lives as couples, and with outside forces. That is the bad news behind Ephesians 6.

But the passage contains the most wonderful news of all. We have available to us the armor and weaponry of God. We are not left to our own resources to wage the war. We are fighting God's war using the weapons that he gives us. And the weapons he gives us for the struggle are powerful.

They may not seem so at first. After all, they are only spiritual weapons. Our human natures fear guns and bombs; we think that is where true power is. But we are wrong. Spiritual does not mean intangible. The weapons described in Ephesians 6 are the most powerful weapons of all: truth, righteousness, peace, faith, salvation, prayer, and the Word of God.

God's weapons require us to fight with eyes that see the unseen and with hearts that know that our own power is useless against the forces we fight. Obviously, it implies that a marriage will be no better than both spouses' willingness not only to fight but also to fight with humbling weapons that appear powerless and pointless.

But these are the only weapons that will protect us from the ultimate damage that the hostile chaos of this world can throw at us. In fact, these weapons will not only protect us but also beat back the enemies of chaos as God establishes his kingdom on earth.

CHAOS WITHIN AND WITHOUT

In order to wage war with power, we must understand not only the dark side of our hearts but also the dark side of the world in which we live.

> What causes fights and quarrels among you? Don't they come from your desires that battle within you? You want something but don't get it. You kill and covet, but you cannot have what you want. You quarrel and fight. You do not have, because you do not ask God. When you ask, you do not receive, because you ask with wrong motives, that you may spend what you get on your pleasures. JAMES 4:1-3

This passage explains that we want to kill with our words because we are empty and demanding. We want good things for ourselves and often care little about others, except as they can help us achieve our goals.

But the paradoxical teaching of the Bible is that the more we seek for ourselves, the less we will get. If through our selfishness we speak death-words, *we* are the ones who will die. The more we seek for others, the more we receive for ourselves. Often our death-words are meant to protect in us something that feels fragile and needy; in fact, our death-words lead to greater weakness and emptiness. Only when our words are oriented to bless will we know the sweet call of life from our Father.

The Bible is a realistic book and describes the world as it is. We don't want to become paranoid, but it is naïve to think that people are always out for our best interests. We are self-centered, sinful human beings who are concerned to satisfy our own needs and desires.

Psalm 55 presents an even more unsettling picture: a close friend who betrays the psalmist. Almost everyone at some point in life can identify with the psalmist when a close friend or relative stabs us in the back.

> *If an enemy were insulting me,*
> *I could endure it;*
> *if a foe were raising himself against me,*
> *I could hide from him.*
> *But it is you, a man like myself,*
> *my companion, my close friend,*
> *with whom I once enjoyed sweet fellowship*
> *as we walked with the throng at the house of God.* PSALM 55:12-14

The book of Romans reiterates this understanding of a world gone amok. People know that God exists, according to Paul in Romans 1, but since they couldn't care less about him, God turns them over to their natural propensities, and the problems of the world are compounded. Then in Romans 8 we learn that it is not just the world of human society that is affected by sin. The natural world as well is dysfunctional.

But perhaps more than anything else, it is death that looms over us all as the greatest external enemy. No matter how well a person's life goes, death will inevitably bring it to an end. Death is the most insidious of all the tools of the Master of Chaos.

WHO WE ARE MEANT TO BE

The Bible has revealed us for what we are, and it is not pretty. But it also shows us what we can be in the power of the Spirit.

> But the fruit of the Spirit is love, joy, peace, patience, kindness, goodness, faithfulness, gentleness and self-control. Against such things there is no law. Those who belong to Christ Jesus have crucified the sinful nature with its passions and desires. Since we live by the Spirit, let us keep in step with the Spirit. Let us not become conceited, provoking and envying each other. GALATIANS 5:22-26

Galatians 5 describes what we are meant to be. It describes the character of people who have the Spirit of God dwelling deeply within them. Since Jesus and the Spirit are ultimately one, the fruit of the Spirit describe someone who is becoming more and more like Christ. As we read about the fruit of the Spirit, then, we see the goal of enhancing beauty in our spouses. This is our goal as we interact with them. We want them to show love, patience, kindness, goodness, faithfulness, gentleness, and self-control. We want them to experience joy and peace.

What does it mean to shape Christ in another? It is to see our hearts become like the radical character of Jesus—who was bold and kind, passionate and patiently tender, fearless and compassionate, holy and human.

Of course, these virtues are contrasted with the list of "acts of the sinful nature": "sexual immorality, impurity and debauchery; idolatry and witchcraft; hatred, discord, jealousy, fits of rage, selfish ambition, dissensions, factions and envy; drunkenness, orgies, and the like" (Gal. 5:19-21).

The basic contrast is between working to meet one's own needs in any way possible, even at the expense of others, versus seeking the good of others, crucifying one's own desires for the sake of relationship. The paradox is that seeking for self leads to chaos and personal destruction, while seeking the good of the other leads to enhancement, not only for the other but also for ourselves. The latter "inherit the kingdom of God," while the former do not (Gal. 5:21).

With that in mind, however, we should not romanticize the fruit of the Spirit. We are held in check by Jesus Christ, because it is Jesus who is the embodiment of the fruit of the Spirit. The gentleness and kindness of the Spirit are such that they did not stop Jesus from chasing the money changers out of the temple area with whips (John 2:13-17). Jesus' perfect self-control did not hold him back from weeping in the Garden of Gethsemane (Matt. 26:36-46).

It is also noteworthy that Paul describes the fruit of the Spirit as a desire of the heart rather than a series of actions. In the words of R. N. Longenecker, "Paul is not so concerned with precisely how each of these matters works out in practice, but with the underlying orientation of selfless and outgoing concern for others."[2] This state of mind, of course, leads to actions, but Paul does not specify them because they will take different shape in different situations.

The fruit of the Spirit become a goal for a husband and

wife as they seek to shape the inner chaos of the heart's immaturity toward the beauty of Christ within.

So much of what we have already said applies here. Life is war, and marriage provides us with a close and intimate ally with whom we may wage this war. The battle requires bold love, forgiveness, confrontation, repentance. It will involve suffering and humiliation.

LIFE IS WAR, AND MARRIAGE PROVIDES US WITH A CLOSE AND INTIMATE ALLY WITH WHOM WE MAY WAGE THIS WAR.

The main thrust of our most effective shaping takes place as we put the great commission, the gospel mandate of Matthew 28, into operation. But it involves more than ministry narrowly defined. As Christians take up their various professions and careers, they do so as members of God's army. As doctors they heal the sick. As homemakers they bring order out of disorder in the home and bring up the next generation. As lawyers they serve the civil peace. As teachers they educate. As landscapers they beautify our local environment. As Christians we are called to excel in those areas where God has called us to labor.

As married couples we are called to join together in our work. A husband and wife rarely have the same job; there is usually a division of labor. The husband may be a nurse, the wife an architect, but they still can and must labor together.

We as husbands and wives must stir each other to love and good deeds. Each must ask of the other: "How does your labor and your heart serve the greater kingdom?" "In what ways are you refusing to fight for God's glory?" "What is your most life-controlling passion: your own glory or God's kingdom?" Words expose. They also shape. We need to encourage one another's labor. Words increase energy to remain faithful, strong, engaged in the battle.

Husbands and wives need to share their successes, weep together over setbacks, encourage each other in their labor, dream together over how their calling can have an impact for the gospel. Every couple ought to be asking, "How is our marriage being used to enhance beauty, seek justice, and destroy evil?" For many, the daily grind of life makes this kind of question seem unrealistic and abstract.

HOW IS OUR MARRIAGE BEING USED TO ENHANCE BEAUTY, SEEK JUSTICE, AND DESTROY EVIL?

The chaos of the world intrudes on this kind of discussion. A man returns after a long, tiring day of meetings, feeling that the last thing he wants to do is talk about it. Or a woman secretly resents her husband being out in the world while she is stuck at home with the kids and the laundry. She doesn't want to hear about it. Such lack of communication squashes dreams and visions and breeds a let's-just-make-it-through-the-day mentality. Chaos enters the relationship and begins to unravel the passion and purpose of the marriage.

The alternative is a husband and wife who respect each other and value each other's view of the world. They share together, plot their lives together, support each other in their common vision. Such a life strategy not only doubles but also multiplies the couple's effectiveness. Chaos is pushed out of the relationship; the kingdom of darkness is thrown back on the defensive. The husband and wife are not just drones or drudges of creation but the conquering servant-rulers of creation.

THEY SHARE TOGETHER, PLOT THEIR LIVES TOGETHER, SUPPORT EACH OTHER IN THEIR COMMON VISION.

God calls us to rule in his creation. We are the kings and queens of the cosmos. We share in Christ's glory. As we read these words with human eyes, we anticipate worldly power, prestige, wealth. For such expectation Jesus has shattering words.

> Jesus called them together and said, "You know that those who are regarded as rulers of the Gentiles lord it over them, and their high officials exercise authority over them. Not so with you. Instead, whoever wants to become great among you must be your servant, and whoever wants to be first must be slave of all. For even the Son of Man did not come to be served, but to serve, and to give his life as a ransom for many." MARK 10:42-45

We find ourselves asking with James and John, "Let one of us sit at your right and the other at your left in your glory" (Mark 10:37). In his response, Jesus defines the nature of our royalty to us. He presents us with a paradox. The ruler is the one who serves. He turns human expectations on their heads. The king and queen are not those who command others; they are the ones who sacrifice their lives for others.

Thus, royalty implies sacrifice. Jesus is our model. Jesus, the great King of the universe, is the one who served others by giving his life as a ransom for many. How does Jesus rule? He rules by going to the Cross.

In marriage, then, we must think of our lives as lives of sacrifice—but not a life of drudgery or merely enduring one another. We live for each other, and because of that we will find that we need to develop a lifestyle of repentance. As sinners who are inherently self-serving, we will find ourselves repeatedly asserting our own desires, our own agendas. As we realize this, we must immediately seek God's forgiveness and our spouses' forgiveness. The most successful marriage is a marriage where forgiveness is often sought and richly given.

IN MARRIAGE, THEN, WE MUST THINK OF OUR LIFE AS A LIFE OF SACRIFICE.

OUR ROLE IN CULTIVATING

Marriage is an arena for growth. We must help each other progress toward Christlikeness.

> Submit to one another out of reverence for Christ. Wives, submit to your husbands as to the Lord. For the husband is the head of the wife as Christ is the head of the church, his body, of which he is the Savior. Now as the church submits to Christ, so also wives should submit to their husbands in everything.
>
> Husbands, love your wives, just as Christ loved the church and gave himself up for her to make her holy, cleansing her by the washing with water through the word, and to present her to himself as a radiant church, without stain or wrinkle or any other blemish, but holy and blameless. In this same way, husbands ought to love their wives as their own bodies. He who loves his wife loves himself. After

all, no one ever hated his own body, but he feeds and cares for it, just as Christ does the church—for we are members of his body. "For this reason a man will leave his father and mother and be united to his wife, and the two will become one flesh." This is a profound mystery—but I am talking about Christ and the church. However, each one of you also must love his wife as he loves himself, and the wife must respect her husband. EPHESIANS 5:21-33

Ephesians 5 is a particularly rich marriage passage, and we will examine it in other contexts in this book. For now, let's look at Paul's advice about how marriage partners can enhance the beauty of their spouses.

The beauty that is really important is not physical beauty but spiritual beauty. Physical beauty is only skin deep. It not only can hide a nasty disposition, but it also always disappears with time. Paul draws our attention to the beauty that lasts forever, the beauty that really unites two people in relationship.

Two verbs are highlighted in this passage; both are keys for enhancing the beauty within a marriage relationship: "submit" and "love."

MUTUAL SUBMISSION IS THE ONLY WORKABLE PATH TO A STRONG MARRIAGE.

Submission has received undeserved criticism in our contemporary society, but the church is partly to blame. If we examine a number of contemporary Bible translations (for instance, the NIV), we see that verse 21 is separated from verse 22. Verse 22 commands a wife to submit to her husband, and that is usually the extent of the advice to Christian couples when they get married. It is good advice, but it needs to be complemented by what precedes it: mutual submission. Not only must the wife submit to her husband, but the husband must also submit to his wife.

Such mutual submission does not compromise the headship of the husband; it enhances it. Indeed, mutual submission is the only workable path to a strong marriage.

After all, what is submission? Submission is the giving up of one's own will and agenda for life for the benefit of another person. It is putting oneself in alignment to the greater good of the other. Submission is not obeying another; it is putting oneself under the other to serve the good of God for that person's life. Therefore, if a husband orders a wife to commit a clear sin, then she is to look submissively for ways to love him boldly rather than merely doing what he says.

SUBMISSION IS NOT OBEYING ANOTHER;
IT IS PUTTING ONESELF UNDER THE
OTHER TO SERVE THE GOOD OF GOD
FOR THAT PERSON'S LIFE.

In marriage two people become one. No longer is there room for one of the two to call all the shots. The husband needs to live for his wife more than for himself, and the wife needs to live for her husband more than for herself.

The second important verb of the section is "love," which provides the motivation for submission. What good reason could there be for renouncing one's own desires anyway? Love.

How does love manifest itself? Love seeks the best for our spouses, and it even defines what is best: to be like Christ—to be "holy and blameless." The goal of marriage is this moral and spiritual beauty, the beauty of being like Christ, the beauty of displaying the fruit of the Spirit.

We tend to load the term *holiness* with all kinds of connotations. What does it mean to be holy? To many people it means don't drink, don't smoke, don't dance, and don't hang out with those who do. To be holy is to bear the shining splendor of the glory of God. It is to be blameless and perfect.

THE COMMAND TO LOVE OUR SPOUSES AND MAKE THEM HOLY IS THE COMMAND TO ENCOURAGE THEM IN THEIR SPIRITUAL MATURITY SO THAT THEY BECOME MORE AND MORE LIKE CHRIST.

Only God is inherently holy. He defines holiness, and we become holy by coming into his presence, by avoiding sin, and by becoming more and more like him. As Christians our model of holy behavior is Christ himself. Thus the command to love our spouses and make them holy is the command to encourage them in their spiritual maturity so that they become more and more like Christ. It is to be fully human in such a way that we invite others to thirst and hunger after righteousness. What does that look like?

WHAT IS THE GOAL OF OUR MARRIAGE?

God ordained marriage as the starting point of family. From the start the plan was for Adam and Eve to fill the earth with their children. It is hard in this day of talk about overpopulation and scanty resources to imagine it, but the earth was a vast, empty place anticipating the birth of many children to inhabit it.

Filling: Marriage as the Source of Family

Unless the Lord builds the house,
its builders labor in vain.
Unless the Lord watches over the city,
the watchmen stand guard in vain.
In vain you rise early
and stay up late,
toiling for food to eat—
for he grants sleep to those he loves.
Sons are a heritage from the Lord,
children a reward from him.
Like arrows in the hands of a warrior
are sons born in one's youth.
Blessed is the man
whose quiver is full of them.
They will not be put to shame
when they contend with their enemies in the gate. PSALM 127

When Solomon composed this psalm, the word "house" likely had a rich meaning. During much of Solomon's early reign he was occupied with building the most important "house" of all—the temple. But the second half of the psalm clearly demonstrates that he had in mind something a little more ordinary. Solomon the wise man is using the image of builders building a house to refer to the effort that goes into making a family. The building stands for the family, and Solomon's crucial teaching is that the Lord must be at the center of the family for it to prosper. Putting it negatively and to the point, a family that does not have the Lord is doomed to meaninglessness. It may prosper from a human perspective, but in the end, it is and accomplishes nothing.

As mentioned, it is the second half that confirms Solomon's concern with marriage. He states what every ancient Near

Eastern couple knew: sons are a heritage from the Lord. Many contemporary translations of the Bible, concerned about the sexual bias of the psalm, translate "children" rather than "sons," and they rightly capture the spirit of the psalm as we appropriate it in our own time. But Solomon specifically here does praise sons. In an ancient Near Eastern society, the physical prowess of sons was necessary for the assurance of justice for the father in his old age. He wouldn't be taken advantage of as long as his sons were around to look after him.

Today, we thank the Lord for all our children, and as a matter of fact, the second half of verse 3 ("children [are] a reward from him") intentionally expands the reference beyond sons to include all the offspring (Hebrew is literally "fruit of the womb").

But as we stand at the end of the second millennium, we wonder about our duty to fill the earth. With billions of people now living and with dwindling resources, we wonder about the urgency of having children. God asked humans to fill the earth, and we did. This may be the only divine commandment that we have obeyed to the letter!

Nonetheless, the psalm does tell us that the children we do have are gifts from him. They are a creative expression of our marriage unions. As the second half of the psalm indicates, they become allies with the man and the woman in the battle of life.

Children are to be raised with the perspective of war; we want them to have good, productive, happy lives, but we more deeply want them to have lives for service, lives for fighting a war for the King.

Filling: Marriage as the Source of New Birth

The fruit of a marriage ought to be children. In certain cases, the fruit may not be physical children. But every marriage is called to produce spiritual heirs. "Then Jesus came to them and said, 'All authority in heaven and on earth has been given to me. Therefore go and make disciples of all nations, baptizing them in the name of the Father and of the Son and of the Holy Spirit, and teaching them to obey everything I have commanded you. And surely I am with you always, to the very end of the age'" (Matt. 28:18-20).

The great commission was given to us through the disciples. Like Genesis 1:28, where God gives basic and crucial commands to all people through Adam and Eve, so Jesus here gives his marching orders to Christians. This is what they are to devote their lives to. Genesis 1:28 is often called the cultural mandate. With that in mind, we can call Matthew 28:18-20 the gospel mandate. It is the mandate to subdue the earth with the gospel. We are the voice of the Lord on the earth. After all, "How can they believe in the one of whom they have not heard?" (Rom. 10:14).

We as individual Christians must understand that we are not only to fill the earth with biological children but also to fill it with spiritual children. Specifically, the great commission calls us to a life of ministry, a life of evangelism and discipleship.

CHRISTIANS WHO ARE MARRIED SHOULD HAVE A VISION FOR A LIFE OF MINISTRY TOGETHER.

In the same way that we have seen that the cultural mandate involves struggle and warfare in a post-Fall world, so does the gospel mandate. After all, those who are not for Christ are against him. If someone is not in the kingdom of God, that person is in the kingdom of Satan. Evangelism is warfare, but warfare in the New Testament sense—that is, spiritual warfare conducted with spiritual weapons.

Although the call to ministry goes out to all Christians, husbands and wives form a unique, intimate alliance in fulfilling the gospel mandate. The New Testament couple Priscilla and Aquila give us a glimpse of a couple who are intimate allies in spiritual warfare of teaching. They are a teaching team, always mentioned together in the Scripture. "Meanwhile a Jew named Apollos, a native of Alexandria, came to Ephesus. He was a learned man, with a thorough knowledge of the Scriptures. He had been instructed in the way of the Lord, and he spoke with great fervor and taught about Jesus accurately, though he knew only the baptism of John. He began to speak boldly in the synagogue. When Priscilla and Aquila heard him, they invited him to their home and explained to him the way of God more adequately" (Acts 18:24-26).

A CHRISTIAN MARRIAGE SHOULD BE
THE FRAMEWORK FOR A BOLD
MOVEMENT TO BRING GOD'S
BEAUTY AND SALVATION TO A DARK
WORLD OF CHAOS.

This brief glimpse of one married couple does not mean that every married Christian couple should do everything together. Also, ministry is not limited only to the professions of minister or seminary teacher. The point is that Christians who are married should have a vision for a life of ministry together. They may be doing different things: she may be a doctor and he a teacher. But they should think of their lives as jointly consecrated to the Lord. They should talk and communicate about where they will put their time and money. They should dream and plan and act in unison toward the goal of seeing spiritual fruit as a result of their union.

A Christian marriage should be the framework for a bold movement to bring God's beauty and salvation to a dark world of chaos.

QUESTIONS FOR REFLECTION AND CONVERSATION

1. Where is the chaos in your life? How do you normally react to it? Do you ignore it, flee, or fight? What is your spouse's pattern of response to chaos? What would your spouse say is his or her response to chaos? What would your spouse say is your response to chaos?

2. In what ways is your life like a battleground?

3. How would you characterize your speech with your spouse? In what ways do your words give life? In what ways do they kill? How does your spouse feel about your words to him or her? If you have never asked for feedback about your speech, ask your spouse or close friends how they see the impact of your words on others.

4. In what ways are you conscious of the effect your words have on your spouse?

5. Would you label your speech with your spouse "wise" or "foolish"?

6. When your spouse hurts you with words, how do you react? Do you lash back? repress it? calmly discuss it with your spouse?

7. When you are in conflict with your spouse, do you tend to heighten the battle, flee the argument, or seek a solution? What factors prevent the latter?

8. Do you have a sense of control over what and how you speak?

9. Are you forgiving in your relationship with your spouse? When do you find yourself withholding forgiveness?

Under what circumstances do you think your spouse withholds forgiveness?

10. Do you keep a list of past offenses with your spouse? Do you use it as ammunition against your spouse?

11. What personal goals do you have? What goals do you have for your marriage? If you have never discussed these goals with your spouse, arrange a time to do that.

12. After sharing your goals with each other, do several specific things to help your spouse move toward his or her personal goals and do several specific things to move toward your goals as a couple.

8

JACK AND MARTHA DISCOVER AN INTIMATE ALLIANCE AGAINST CHAOS

Jack was fired from his job a month after his big presentation. It was a day that began like almost every day—from what he ate, to what he wore, to the route he drove to work, and to the way he greeted his secretary. But it was a day designed by God from eternity to give Jack the opportunity for life. It was a disaster that became a severe mercy—a beastly wound that would require more than God's balm to salve. It would require a radical turn in life direction if Jack was not only to survive but also to thrive.

The blow came in the form of a memo. It was direct. At least Jack could say that about his boss—he was direct. The memo said:

Jack,

As of 9:00 A.M. I am relieving you of your responsibilities as vice president. The new direction you have set for the corporation is unacceptable. You will be given three months' severance pay; your stock options can be sold at current market value, or they may be held for later sale. All this is stated in your contract. If you have any questions, I will be available today from 10:00 to 10:30.

Martin Bark, President

Jack read the memo over again and again. Mr. Bark was not a man to jest or play practical jokes. It was a simple exit. In one five-sentence memo Jack felt eight years of hard work, travel, planning, sweat, and tears torn out from under him.

The meeting with his boss was officious. Transition plans had been in operation for two weeks; all his travel and activity had already been funneled to the people he had trained. He could barely look at them when he went to pack his briefcase. His only request was to wait until the weekend to clean out his office so that no one would be present to see him depart in shame. Mr. Bark had little heart for sentimentality, but even he understood the reason for the Saturday move out. He granted it without hesitation.

TWO WEEKS LATER. Jack and Martha went into hiding. They missed church; they canceled dinner engagements. Jack suffered the first major depression of his life; Martha watched helplessly—her words bounced off his despair like a .22 bullet off the hull of an aircraft carrier. But once or twice, in a way that was different from before, they had conversations that were neither angry nor polite.

They both felt a desperation that simply went beyond the current loss. Jack's loss of a job was for him the loss of his future, his dreams, his reason for getting up in the morning, his sense of value, and his basis for walking through other struggles with confidence. He was successful, and he had the car, the house, and the clothes to validate it. And now not only were they in danger, but his ability to provide was shattered. He knew he had failed as a father and a husband, but at least he had provided for his family opportunities and possessions that seemed to be a small payoff for his guilt. Now even that was lost.

One morning Martha asked Jack the question she had mulled over in her mind for months: "What has happened to our dreams?" She said, "Jack, do you recall the night we prayed that God would use our marriage to bring a blessing to others? What has happened to our lives that a loss of a job makes us both wonder if we are going to survive?"

Slowly, Jack looked at her. For the first time in many, many years he looked at his wife with both intrigue and sorrow. He had not looked at her as an ally, an advocate for the things of God, in over a decade. She was tender, and she was bold. She was his friend—not a co-worker, not an enemy who was waiting for him to fail. Tears began to fall from his eyes, and he felt the first stirrings of terror-filled hope.

ONE MONTH LATER.   Jack began to meet regularly with a man from his church. Jack had noticed Larry at meetings and Sunday school. He was quiet, and when he prayed, he seemed to be talking to someone he believed not only heard him but also was close enough to touch. The first meeting was awkward. Jack laid out his situation—his ongoing unemployment and his sense of dis-ease in his soul.

The only thing Jack recalled after the meeting were the questions that unsettled him in their simplicity and allure. Larry had asked him, "How do you want your children to remember you? What would they remember today if you were to die?" As Jack talked over the questions with Martha, they haunted him. Jack knew the answer to the second question: his children would recall how tired, busy, and irritable he seemed. They also might remember the vacation to Cancún where he was deathly ill and vomited for three days. Not much of a legacy.

TWO MONTHS LATER. Jack eventually found another job. It involved a 30 percent cut in pay, and it felt like a real blow to his heart to take it. But he either had to go to work or borrow money from his mother.

The night he made the decision to take the job, he talked with his kids and his wife about what he wanted to provide for them. The weeks of reflection prompted by Larry's questions had formed in him a desire for a different legacy. It was a simple desire: He wanted to live a life that commended Jesus as the God of his heart and the God of the universe. He told his children this with anticipation and hope.

His older daughter, who had grown accustomed to the life of upper-middle-class wealth, frowned and said, "Dad, what is wrong with making the kind of money you used to make? I won't be able to go to a good college; we won't have nice vacations. We are going to be poor."

The years of seeing her father pursue the values of wealth and success were more powerful than a few Bible lessons and youth group meetings about what is important in life. Jack felt his heart sink and his anger rise. He wanted to dash her arrogance to the ground, not because it offended God, but because it exposed his past failure and his current job humiliation. He felt trapped and horrified. But he felt rise within him words that felt like seeds to be planted on an apparently hardened, untilled field. He said to his daughter, "Sweetheart, I have much to confess to you. Your words reflect the kind of fear and values that I have lived with for most of my life. I can't tell you it is wrong to make money. And I hope the future holds the opportunity to make even more than I have in the past. But I want my life to matter for eternity far more than I want to drive a European car or live in this nice neighborhood. I want the same for your life. And my example has made it very hard for you to have a good picture of what that would mean. Forgive me."

The conversation did not go well. She stormed out of the room, slammed her door, and was surly and uncooperative. Martha was overwhelmed with fear and discouragement. For the first time, Jack felt real sorrow for her. He did not try to pick up the pieces. Instead, he listened and prayed. He was beginning to sense what he could offer his wife and family.

Jack learned that a local church was hosting a Family Life Marriage Conference. Jack read one of the conference leader's books and decided this man offered something that went beyond merely having a better marriage; he offered the opportunity to picture what he could become as a man so he could plant a garden in the name of Christ. Jack was excited. Martha was terrified. The seminar and his meetings with Larry established a path that invited Jack to envision and plant a work of God.

Jack did not know what it would mean or where it would go, but he picked up his old tennis racket and challenged his wife to a match. He knew she would win. He had quit years ago. It was simply too impractical to spend time in such an activity. But he began to imagine and pray about spending time with his wife and family. And then he began to envision what it would mean to meet local league couples who played because they were empty and bored. The thought dawned on him: No field is too barren for the seed of the gospel. He began to feel that life might actually be fun.

Part Three

HOW WILL WE WORK TOGETHER AS HUSBANDS AND WIVES?

9

Jeremy and Sue:

The Couple Who Didn't

Need Each Other

Sue looked at the clock and knew the church board meeting was not going well. But then it never did. Sue thought about praying for her husband, but it seemed pointless. God could divide the Red Sea, but to break Jeremy's heart seemed beyond hope.

Jeremy had been an assistant pastor for eight years, and he had gotten along with nearly everyone. He called himself a peacemaker. He was gifted in the pulpit; he knew what to say, how to say it, and he did it well. He was honored with accolades and finally an advancement to a growing suburban church, where he had been the senior pastor for almost three years now.

Jeremy was the spark that was needed to propel growth, vigor, and a new building program. The elders wanted a dynamic young pastor who would attract the baby boomers, not alienate the older folks, and connect even to some of the baby busters. Demographically, Jeremy was a natural.

Sue looked at the clock. She knew it was pointless to wait up for him. It would be another night alone, another night pretending she was supportive and happy. In fact, she was mindlessly supportive and numbly happy to the degree that she only vaguely remembered that she was a liar. But the world rewards liars, and she had a nice home, a relatively new car, free tuition for the kids at a Christian school, enough acquaintances to while away a few lunches every week, and a one-month paid vacation for her family every year. It was not an awful life.

She looked into the mirror and was startled to see a woman who looked more like her mother than she had ever before noticed. Her mother was an efficient, no-nonsense manager who guided her family through school, work, marriages, babies, and choice of detergent.

Sue was the middle child, the second girl. Angie, her older sister, was an aggressive and successful lawyer who had just started her family and hired live-in help. Sue had never worked as hard in school as Angie had. Sue did not aspire to greatness or success in a career. She received neither the criticism nor the praise that fell Angie's way.

Sue knew she was petite and pretty, but she was surprised to see that the lines above her eyes were beginning to crease just as her mother's did. She wondered if she frowned as much as her mother did. It didn't seem fair. *Angie ought to be the one aging like Mom, not me,* she thought.

From the time Sue was a young girl, she had lived in a private world that was quiet and kind. Her mother yelled; Sue's inner world had very little noise. Her mother was critical; Sue's world was populated by children and animals. It was like a private world made up of Disney, Shirley Temple, and reruns of *Father Knows Best.* No one knew of Sue's safe place, and she did not flee to it often. But it was always available when she was lonely and hurt.

Sue felt herself drifting to one of her favorite daydreams: she was a bride, wearing a lavish white gown shimmering with sequins; on her head was a straw hat adorned with lace. She walked through the forest, feeling as if the trees were holding their hands together in anticipation. The animals stood quietly in wonder as she walked down the tree-lined aisle in an elegant, slow promenade. There was no bridegroom, no preacher, and no pews holding expectant family and friends. She was alone, adored, and beautiful.

The phone rang, and Sue surprised herself when she audibly swore. It was Jeremy. He never called to tell her he was going to be late, so she knew that he must be having trouble at the meeting and that he had wanted to escape from making small talk when they took a ten-minute break.

The board meeting was not going well. A decision needed to be made about a fund-raising consultant, and Jeremy studiously avoided offering his opinion. Jeremy never volunteered his thoughts or offered to state the opposing sides of an opinion in order to move the discussion to a resolution based on a consensus of thought. He simply sat, waited, and hoped against hope the board members would get tired enough either to quit or to decide. But it seldom happened. The board members always seemed indefatigable, resolute to argue, and committed never to decide. Jeremy was the ringmaster of a cacophonous circus. He hated this part of his job. The elders resented his unwillingness to lead.

His call to Sue was both a flight from hobnobbing with his antagonistic elders and an effort to let his wife know how easy she had it. He knew it was not easy to get two wild boys to bed, but at least she didn't have to corral a bunch of frustrated businesspeople who couldn't order their boss around but who felt God called them to be his boss. He hated their "business" mind-set. He was a theologian, a culture shaper, a big-idea person, and they wanted him to raise money, press flesh, and rally the troops around the building program.

But Jeremy had never vocalized his concerns. It wouldn't be polite or expedient. He bore their ruminations with political savvy, postponing all the potentially divisive decisions by suggesting more study and by siding with the views of the most powerful elders. Jeremy was a competent and capable man who knew that integrity could be defined as either living by conviction or succeeding by craft. He chose success.

Sue gently hung up the phone. She recalled Donna Reed putting the phone on the hook with elegant, tender regard, as if she were holding a living thing. She liked that picture. But her brow was furrowed. *How dare he tell me how easy it is to cocoon with the kids,* she thought angrily. She felt herself stand on a precipice, ready to return to her downy forest world or to swear again. She swore.

NEXT MORNING

Sue: "How did the meeting go last night?"

Jeremy: "Well. I think we have postponed the decision on a fund-raiser for at least a few more weeks. I think I can find someone who will not put too many expectations on the staff for fund-raising."

Sue: "Staff? I thought that would be mostly your job."

Jeremy: "No. It's a new day. It is not just the CEO's job to advance the kingdom; every person, staff included, must bear responsibility. It's like us: You make decisions that I don't even know or care to know about. And it all works out. But if I had to do it all, we both would be frustrated. Right?"

Sue: "I guess. But you seem to leave on my shoulders a lot of things I wish you would handle. And I bet you . . . . Never mind."

Jeremy: "No, go ahead. What were you going to say?"

Sue: "Only that you seem to be frustrated after every meeting. It just seems that the board members want you to lead more than you want to."

Jeremy: "Sweetheart, you have never been in meetings like that. Let me give your innocent heart an education. They want me to lead only to find fault with whatever I decide. It's part of the leadership game. I let them wrangle, and then I basically frame the direction toward the goal I want anyway."

Sue: "Do you do that with me too?"

Jeremy: "Don't be funny. I don't need to do that with you. You always go along with what I want. (Laughs.) Why should I beat around the bush at home?"

Sue: "Did anyone ever tell you that you are condescending?"

Jeremy: "No. What's your point?"

Sue: "Nothing."

Sue turned from the sink to get more milk from the refrigerator. Instead, she kept walking out of the kitchen and went upstairs to wake the kids. She scurried them out of bed with an inviting voice; she loved to be gentle with them. They were rowdy boys, sometimes disrespectful, but they loved her, and she loved them. She finished herding them off to the bathroom and went to her mirror to put the finishing touches on her happy face.

The book she was reading about love sat near her sink. She hated the cover and was not real fond of the content either, but she felt compelled to think about what it might mean if she were to love Jeremy, really love him. She had never thought that she did not love him: she was a Christian; she was submissive; and she did her best to support his ministry. She had even taught a six-week Bible study about being all God wanted a woman to be for her husband. It had made her a little uncomfortable to teach about something she knew was not true of her own life. But she could not confess her situation to the women in the Bible study. After all, their marriage was a model for many couples in the church, and she didn't want to disappoint Jeremy by telling the truth.

But that ugly book stared back at her as she put on her makeup. One sentence kept ringing in her ears: "Love changes the human heart." She tried to put it in her own words. "If the person you love has not changed—that is, if the person has not grown more tender through brokenness or more arrogant and hard as the offer to repent has been rejected—then it is a clear indication you have not loved that person. Love changes a person—always. The status quo—life today as it was, relationship as it always has been—indicates a failure of love."

The thought passed through her mind: *How dare God ask me to love a patronizing man?* Then another thought ripped through her mind: *It's dangerous to be a woman with a man who looks good but hides a cruel heart.*

It nearly floored her to hear the thought break into her orderly inner world like the shrill sound of a biting wind. She felt herself shudder. She looked in the mirror and felt her eyes soften with tears. To love Jeremy, let alone love him as a woman should, seemed more overwhelming than bearing up under the boredom and loneliness of her day.

The door opened, and Jeremy sauntered over to the closet to get his sport coat. He barely looked at Sue and said: "I resent that you called me condescending. That was a low blow after what I went through with the elders last night. If you have criticism, I would appreciate your setting up a time to let me know rather than springing it on me out of the blue."

Sue looked at her frightened husband in the mirror and felt a wave of sadness for him. She had never noticed how his pompous air hid his timidity. He was a man on the run, a man who was not used to being caught undressed in any situation. It was the first time she realized he was not really a man—beyond being an adult male. She finally faced the fact that Jeremy used his competence, sophistication, and congeniality to keep people from seeing both his sin and his desperation. A man admits his failure and is unashamed of his weakness; Jeremy had never in his life honestly admitted his harm of others or his need for grace.

She realized that she never really wanted to be a woman. To be a woman to Jeremy, Sue knew she would have to risk conflict, loneliness, and rejection. She had never been willing to do so; the price was simply too high. She was feminine, but she had been unwilling to be a woman. It was too dangerous to be a woman around judgmental mothers and critical men.

Sue looked at her husband with different eyes; she did not feel unkind when she said: "How about tonight after dinner?"

10

RE-ENTERING EDEN:

LEAVING, WEAVING, CLEAVING,

AND BECOMING ONE FLESH

Marriages grow glory when each spouse invites the other to become more like Jesus Christ. We are to shape the still-unformed beauty of each other's soul to reveal God's character more fully. When I shape my wife, my goal is for her to become a more glorious woman. When my wife shapes me, her goal is for me to be a more glorious man. We are distinct and unique, and our Christlikeness will reveal itself in ways consistent with being made in the image of God—male and female.

The path of growth is no different for a man than it is for a woman, but the results will be different to the degree that God intends for a man and a woman to be distinct. We either live with an awareness of and draw forth the uniqueness of being a man or a woman, or we ignore and destroy the distinctiveness of gender. We have a choice: We can either delight in diversity or destroy distinctions. Tragically, this can be done without any awareness of denying the distinctiveness of man and woman.

WE HAVE A CHOICE: WE CAN EITHER DELIGHT IN DIVERSITY OR DESTROY DISTINCTIONS.

It may seem too radical a premise, but I believe that no man (except Christ) and no woman have ever fully enjoyed being male or female. Why? Let me remind you that we are made in the image of God as male and female. Somehow gender reflects something about God. A man reflects something about God's character that is different from a woman and vice versa. The rest of the chapter will attempt to put words to these differences. But for the moment, let me ask, "Why do we struggle with being men and women?"

Gender reflects something about the glory of God. And God's enemy, Satan, wishes to destroy glory. The evil one cannot destroy God; therefore he tries to destroy the reflection of God: man and woman. His prime way of attempting to destroy glory is to make it too frightening to be truly a man or a woman and to offer counterfeit routes to live out gender. The rest of the chapter is an effort to answer why we are afraid and how we refuse to live out our calling as men and women.

This was true for Sue and Jeremy. He was a man's man—handsome, adept, competent, successful—but the way he avoided conflict and disdained intimacy indicated he was not comfortable being a man. Sue was lovely, feminine, engaging, generous, but she cowered from the call to love her husband boldly. She knew the requirements and complied with the expectations, but she offered few people a heart that longed to see Christ birthed in them. Sadly, the person she least perceived to need her love was her husband.

What is required for each of them to change as a man and as a woman? What will it mean for each of them to draw forth the beauty of the other's gender?

What does it mean to be male and female? What does it mean that God made Adam and Eve to work together? How do we work together as husbands and wives to fulfill the creation mandate to fill, subdue, and rule creation?

HOW ARE WE TO WORK TOGETHER TO FULFILL OUR ROLES?

Imagine what it would have been like for Adam after God created him. He was in the Garden of Eden; all of his needs were met. He was in God's new and beautiful creation, filled with flowers, trees, and all kinds of animals. Most amazing of all, he was in intimate communication with God himself.

GOD CREATED ADAM FOR RELATIONSHIP.

But he was lonely. "The Lord God said, 'It is not good for the man to be alone. I will make a helper suitable for him.' . . . So the Lord God caused the man to fall into a deep sleep; and while he was sleeping, he took one of the man's ribs and closed up the place with flesh. Then the Lord God made a woman from the rib he had taken out of the man, and he brought her to the man" (Gen. 2:18, 21-22).

The force of this point can hardly be reckoned. God created Adam for relationship; he created Adam for another person who was neither his master nor his inferior, but his equal. And without intimacy with an equal, Adam was lonely—even with creation and the Creator.

God does not exclusively fill the human heart. He made humankind to need more than himself. The staggering humility of God to make something that was not to be fully satisfied with the Creator and the creation is incomprehensible.

Who is this God? What is he like? If we are made in his image, then who is the being that we reflect? God has revealed himself through the Scriptures to be Trinitarian: Father, Son, and Holy Spirit. The three are not simply different functions lived out by the same person; they are three different persons of the same, equal being. And they live to glorify—to enjoy and honor—one another.

A MARRIAGE IS MADE UP
OF TWO EQUAL BUT PROFOUNDLY
DIFFERENT BEINGS; EACH REFLECTS
THE CHARACTER OF GOD IN WAYS
THAT GIVE A UNIQUE PICTURE
OF HIS CHARACTER.

One implication of the Trinitarian nature of God is that the core of the universe is relational. We reflect God as we relate to others in a way that mirrors his character. Why male and female? Why two different persons who are equal in being? The answer is perhaps simple. God is three persons and the same being; man and woman are two different persons and equal in being. We reflect God in his unity and diversity. Male and female are equal, but if they were identical—physically and internally—then the marriage would not reflect God's diversity.

146

A marriage is made up of two equal but profoundly different beings; each reflects the character of God in ways that give a unique picture of his character. The differences are neither obvious nor insignificant; great overlap exists. But the union of the two different parts creates both the fruit of filling and the energy to subdue and rule.

Put simply, our marriage is to give glory to God; we glorify God as we fill, subdue, and rule; and we do so uniquely as male and female. What can we learn from this passage about the nature and scope of what it means to be male and female?

INTIMACY WARS AGAINST LONELINESS

God created Eve, a woman, to be Adam's companion. While Genesis 1 gives the first narration of this part of creation, Genesis 2 retells the story, this time filling in the gaps and revealing more about the relationship between Adam and Eve.

This creation passage teaches us many things about the relationship between the sexes, particularly in a marriage relationship. Although the word *marriage* is not used, we are surely to understand the relationship between Adam and Eve as that of a married couple. Both the reasons why God created Eve and the way he created her instruct us about the relationship between a husband and wife.

God created Eve in order to address Adam's loneliness; said differently, God created Eve to free Adam's heart neither to bow nor to rule, but to receive and to give as one. No one has said it better than Matthew Henry when he stated that Eve was "not made out of his head to top him, not out of his feet to be trampled upon by him, but out of his side to be equal with him."[1]

God made Eve to be "a helper suitable" to Adam. It is wrong to understand this phrase to indicate a lack of equality between men and women. Some interpreters, predominantly male, understand the word "helper" here to be a close synonym to *servant.* That is, a woman is to help a man achieve his goals. On the other hand, other interpreters, predominantly female, assert that the helper is superior to the man because he is too weak to handle life.

These interpretations are unfortunate because they miss the clear teaching of the passage. The word "helper" is used primarily of God. It is used more often than not to reflect his heart to rescue, to protect, and to sustain life. The following two verses point toward a helper as a warrior who is committed to his people:

> Blessed are you, O Israel! Who is like you, a people saved by the Lord? He is your shield and helper and your glorious sword. Your enemies will cower before you, and you will trample down their high places. DEUTERONOMY 33:29

> But you, O God, do see trouble and grief; you consider it to take it in hand. The victim commits himself to you; you are the helper of the fatherless. PSALM 10:14

A woman is no stronger or weaker than a man; she is a helper who is jointly to engage creation and enter into relationship to bring glory to God. But her calling is to do so as a warrior of relationship, a guardian of truth in relationship, one who is made to uniquely reflect God's heart for relationship and his hatred of loneliness.

THE UNIQUENESS OF MALES AND FEMALES

Adam and Eve are equal but unique. How so? It is obvious beyond words that Adam and Eve are physically different. It can be seen not only anatomically but also in other categories. But are they different in other more inherent ways? Are males and females made with creational differences? We answer: yes. But the arguments for inherent differences are based on implication and cannot be argued from a mentality of proof texting. Therefore, our attitude for reflection must be irenic and open rather than dogmatic.

It is also important in this highly controversial issue to reveal gradually the thinking process that shapes our opinions. Let's explore two categories of thought: exegetical and scientific.

Exegetical
Three questions, minimally, need to be considered:

1. Why did God make Adam first and give him the prohibition about the tree of the knowledge of good and evil before Eve was created?
2. Why did God have Adam name the animals without Eve and realize in the process that he had no helper suitable for him?
3. Why does God bring different curses for man and woman?

In the ancient Near East, it was common to look at all formal relationships from the standpoint of a covenant. A covenant was a legally binding agreement that clarified the relationship between one great kingdom or king and a lesser or vassal kingdom. The rules were spelled out in a treaty between the great king and the vassal king. Then the vassal king would make those rules of relationship known to the rest of his kingdom.

The treaty had provisions of blessing and curse. It specified what punishment would occur if specific stipulations were broken. If any rebellion occurred in the vassal kingdom, then the vassal king was responsible to the great king because he was the leader—that is, he was the first to sacrifice on behalf of all the inhabitants of the kingdom.

Adam is the vassal king of Eden. He heard the great king's rules, and he was the one to tell Eve. He was given authority over naming the animals. When God sought out Adam and Eve after they had sinned, God spoke to Adam. It should be apparent that

Adam had more of a direct role in subduing and bearing responsibility for the direction of the kingdom. It would be foolish to say that Eve was not responsible for her sin or that she had no role in subduing and directing their activities in the Garden. Adam is simply the one who is called first to move into the unshaped creation and first to bear responsibility to sacrifice.

Adam is called to engage the chaos in the world more directly than Eve is. This seems further apparent when we look at the Curse (see part 5). We can presume the Curse was meant both to punish and to provide the humbling context for redemption. It would be an error to assume that the Curse was directed against a trivial or incidental element of our being. In fact, it was directed against and for the core of Adam and Eve in order to provide the context for the Savior to be born and the serpent to be destroyed.

THIS SEEMS TO IMPLY THAT ADAM WAS CREATED WITH THE PHYSICAL AND INTERNAL MAKEUP TO ENTER, CREATE, AND SHAPE FORM OUT OF CHAOS.

The curse given to Adam involved his work: all his shaping of chaos would be fraught with futility. He would succeed but not without sweat, blood, and sorrow. Even his success would be fleeting. This seems to imply that Adam was created with the physical and internal makeup to enter, create, and shape form out of chaos.

The curse given to Eve involved relationships: all her birthing of life would be laced with pain and loneliness. She would bring forth a child but not without sweat, blood, and sorrow. And she would be in conflict with her husband. The curse indicates, "Your desire will be for your husband, and he will rule over you" (Gen. 3:16). The word "desire" in this context implies ravenous absorption (see part 5 for more detail). In her loneliness, the woman will desire to absorb, to swallow the man to fill her emptiness, and he will fail her with base withdrawal or violent assault. This seems to imply that Eve was created with the physical and internal makeup to receive, gestate, and shape relationships out of the beauty of form.

THIS SEEMS TO IMPLY THAT EVE WAS CREATED WITH THE PHYSICAL AND INTERNAL MAKEUP TO RECEIVE, GESTATE, AND SHAPE RELATIONSHIPS OUT OF THE BEAUTY OF FORM.

Unfortunately, this seems too abstract and impractical. What does it mean to be a man or a woman? Sexually, a man plants his seed, and a woman slowly incubates the mysterious union of egg and sperm; together they create a human being. A man is a planter, a pursuer who is to enter the world with a strength and courage that form a new being. A woman is a nurturer who brings creation to life through the tender interconnectedness of her body and soul with the unborn child. What does this tell us?

A man reflects a godly dimension that is different from what a woman reflects. A man is to mirror strength—a man plants. A woman is to reflect tenderness—a woman nurtures. And what does this reflect about God? Human strength is an analogue of God's love of order, righteousness, and wrath. Human tenderness is an analogue of God's love of mystery, tenderness, and mercy.

Let me restate the point. A man is to plant his stamp on ideas, objects, and institutions. His creation is meant to propel the kingdom of God into new territory. A woman is to incubate relationship. She is to make connections. A man takes chaos and forms it into a distinct, different, ordered idea, object, or institution; a woman takes his work and draws it into a context that honors the higher principle of love. A man courageously creates, and a woman creatively shapes his creation into a lovely, relationally enhancing beauty.

A MAN COURAGEOUSLY CREATES, AND A WOMAN CREATIVELY SHAPES HIS CREATION INTO A LOVELY, RELATIONALLY ENHANCING BEAUTY.

It is imperative not to miss a crucial point. Males and females are not one-dimensional: a man is also made to nurture relationship, and a woman is equally made to till the earth. It is neither a compromise nor a contradiction for each to be involved with forming and filling. Nevertheless, a man slightly more reflects God's character of order, law, and justice; and a woman slightly more reflects God's character of mystery, grace, and mercy. One without the other is a grave distortion—male moving to violence and female gravitating to absorption. Order without mercy is authoritarian; mystery without form is hedonism. Male and female operate in a precarious balance between life and death.

Scientific
Recent studies done without the philosophic distortion of radical feminism indicate a fundamental rather than merely sociological difference between men and women. Carol

Gilligan, in a landmark work, *In a Different Voice,* notes that men and women reason, communicate, and choose differently based on one fundamental difference: the priority of task versus relationship. Men define maturity in terms of separating from relationship and accomplishing a great dream; women view maturity in light of the qualities of care, connection, and interdependence.

Gilligan's interviews with young professional women indicated, "Identity is defined in a context of relationship and judged by a standard of responsibility and care. Similarly, morality is seen by these women as arising from the experience of connection and conceived as a problem of inclusion rather than one of balancing claims."[2]

In her interviews with men, Gilligan found that identity is based on a different set of perceptions. "For the men, the tone of identity is different, clearer, more direct, more distinct and sharp-edged. . . . The male 'I' is defined in separation. . . . Instead of attachment, individual achievement rivets the male imagination, and great ideas or distinctive activity defines the standard of self-assessment and success. . . . Power and separation secure the man in an identity achieved through work."[3]

Other studies indicate that men are more perverse and violent than women. Males are seven times more likely than females to be sexual abusers.[4] And almost 82 percent of all sexual perversions are perpetrated by men.[5] On the other hand, women are four times more likely to be depressed and eight times more likely to struggle with bulimia and codependency.[6] All these symptoms point to emptiness and absorptive tendencies. Even in the symptoms of sin, men and women differ.

Gender Warning

But a great warning needs to be sounded. Do these conclusions mean that men are not to be engaged in relationship, that they ought to be out working full-time in the workplace? And do they imply that women should not be engaged in the workplace, that they ought to be running the home? *No.* It is a cultural error to organize calling into rote tasks that pigeonhole men as physicians and women as nurses.

It is more important to see task in the context of character. A woman is to reveal a tad more of God's mercy; a man is to reveal a tad more of God's holiness. Does that mean a man should be a lawyer and a woman a physician? Again, no. It means that a female lawyer will see justice in more relational, contextual terms, and a male lawyer will see relationship in more rights-oriented terms. A female business partner will see a decision in the light of its impact on the community; a male will see the decision in view of its effect on the corporation.

> A STRONG HUSBAND WILL DRAW
> FORTH THE STRONG TENDERNESS OF
> HIS WIFE, AND A TENDER WIFE
> WILL BIRTH THE TENDER STRENGTH
> OF HER HUSBAND.

A husband's strength must not only protect but also enhance his wife's tenderness. A wife's tenderness must not only draw forth her husband's desire to be a godly man but also energize his initiative to move into the terrifying world of relational chaos. Even more, a husband's courage ought to strengthen his wife's heart to fight; and a wife's care ought to tenderize her husband's heart to suffer.

When a man is weak, he denies the holiness and strength of God; when a woman controls, she denies the mercy and tenderness of God. But it need not be that way. When both husbands and wives labor to grow into the likeness of God as men and as women, they will equally grow and shape the other: a strong husband will draw forth the strong tenderness of his wife, and a tender wife will birth the tender strength of her husband. And the result will fill the earth and subdue it to God's character.

Summary for Marriage: Our spouses are equal but unique reflections of God. Adam is the father of form. His hands bring forth order out of chaos. He tills the earth and draws forth its fruit. He hunts the land and brings forth its meat. He moves into the chaos of unshaped matter and returns with the goods that will sustain life. He uniquely reveals God's power and holiness.

Eve is the mother of relationship. Her womb gives and nourishes life. She uniquely grows the seed of love into the fruit of intimacy. She is to join her husband in faithfully seeing the Word of God implanted in the heart to draw forth the indwelling glory of each person. She uniquely reflects God's tenderness and mercy.

A husband should strongly awaken his wife's tenderness; a wife should tenderly arouse her husband's courage. If a husband moves into chaos to create order, his wife shapes order into a connected beauty that reflects the relational heart of God. A wife is also to be strong, and a husband is also to be tender; for either person to lack what the other uniquely reveals is a perversion.

A husband and wife individually reflect God, but together they bear a splendor that cannot be found in either person alone. Their relationship dispels loneliness and offers the one and only truly equal relationship found on earth.

Our only option in living as husbands and wives is either to delight in diversity or to destroy distinctions.

QUESTIONS FOR REFLECTION AND CONVERSATION

1. "A view of maleness and femaleness requires an openness to distinctions without rigidity about roles." In what ways do you agree with this statement? In what ways do you disagree? Do you and your spouse agree? Discuss your perspectives together.

2. The relationship between male and female is marked by equality yet distinctiveness. But many people find it easier to live either by blurring or absolutizing distinctions. On which side of the error does your marriage more regularly fall? How? And with what results?

3. Where does your husband fail to be strong? Where does your wife fail to be tender? Describe times when your spouse's strength and/or tenderness meant the most to you.

11

SUBMITTING TO EACH

OTHER IN LOVE

God in his wisdom and grace created human beings with both the capacity and the need for relationship with one another. Genesis 2:18-22 in its context makes it clear that Adam would not, could not, make it on his own. As Adam helped God shape creation by naming the animals, he became increasingly aware that none of the animals would fulfill his deep longing for intimate fellowship. He was lonely and needed someone. God created Eve to be an equal but distinct and different being. Eve is one to whom Adam could relate, but she also would always retain a sense of mystery to him.

The Bible does not give us much detail about the relationship of Adam and Eve in the Garden of Eden. We can only speculate about how they related to one another and how their complementary gifts and talents worked together to continue the task of shaping creation.

We get no indication of the passage of time as we move from Genesis 2 to Genesis 3. We know some time passed, but whether it is a matter of days, months, or even centuries, we do not know. But when the day of the fateful decision arrives, we see that their relationship and their tasks undergo a dark transition. After they sin, they no longer shape a good creation into something even better; instead, they battle a hostile and dangerous chaos.

What particular contributions do males and females make to the battle? As we examine the passages that present a biblical picture of males and females and their relationship, we will see that their contributions to the battle to push back chaos are complementary. Their contributions are equal yet unique.

AS MALES AND FEMALES WE ARE SIGNIFICANTLY AND INTRIGUINGLY DIFFERENT. . . . THE DIFFERENCES INVITE FASCINATING, UNENDING EXPLORATION.

This is what makes the marriage relationship so wonderful. Husbands and wives form a union with an equal but different being, a union that avoids a somewhat monotonous symmetry. As human beings we share so much in common; as males and females we are significantly and intriguingly different. The similarities are such that we can have a basic understanding of each other; the differences invite fascinating, unending exploration. It is an exploration that must lead to humbling awe and grateful praise to the God who thought up such wild diversity. Unfortunately, the differences often lead to exasperation and contempt. But there are other basic problems with the idea of gender.

The problem with most attempts to define gender is that they do away with the mystery to achieve a kind of precision that just is not possible. When we draw up lists to define the female "role" and the male "role," we create a breach in the mystery of the relationship of gender. The results are stifling and artificial. On the other hand, a radical egalitarianism that does not allow for differences between the sexes ignores the obvious, even if the obvious cannot be closely defined. Ultimately we must succumb to the mystery of gender by not defining it too closely and precisely.

We can, however, talk about certain traits as feminine and others that are masculine, but these traits are not and should not be considered mutually exclusive. These traits reflect dimensions of the character of God.

The Scripture passages we will explore highlight strength as a masculine characteristic and tenderness as a feminine one. We must constantly remember that one is not better than the other. Also, and perhaps even more critical, we must not forget that these traits overlap. The male should have a tender strength, and the female should have a strong tenderness.

ULTIMATELY WE MUST SUCCUMB
TO THE MYSTERY OF GENDER
BY NOT DEFINING IT
TOO CLOSELY AND PRECISELY.

Indeed, the relationship between Jeremy and Sue illustrates a strength that is hollow and a tenderness that is a pretense. Jeremy's strength has little compassion, especially as it is expressed toward his wife. Sue's tenderness shrinks back from confrontation. The result of their union is a strength that hurts Sue and a tenderness that allows Jeremy to continue along the path to self-destruction.

Further, a woman tends to be more relational than a man. The common stereotype of a quiet, lone man and a woman who is frustrated after years of reaching out has a measure of truth to it. Women are more likely than men to cultivate relationship both inside the marriage with their spouses and as a couple with other people.

But once again this can be easily, though wrongly, caricatured. Men also desire relationship, or they would not get married in the first place. Women also have a sense that they need to preserve their individual boundaries. Once again, it is a matter of emphasis, not a matter of difference in kind.

THE DIFFERENCES THAT MEN AND WOMEN BRING TO A RELATIONSHIP MAKE THE INDIVIDUALS MORE THAN THEY COULD EVER BE ALONE.

The differences that men and women bring to a relationship make the individuals more than they could ever be alone. A strong, individualistic man would never experience the pleasures of blessing and serving others. An overly tender, relational woman would find herself absorbed, losing her own identity. A marriage relationship pushes the two partners into realms that may initially bewilder or frighten them. But stepping out with an intimate ally gives them the courage to experience new pleasures and to endure difficult trials.

But once again, it is foolhardy to press definitions. In the end we will plead that genders involve a similarity and a difference that are ultimately shrouded in mystery.

After all, gender is a revelation of God, who is also protected by mystery. We have already seen that God created both male and female in his image. The image of God is particularized into gender. God's character cannot be captured by his human image bearers, but each gender typically accentuates certain aspects of God's character. God is king, but he is also mother (Ps. 131; Isa. 66:13). The former highlights his strength, while the latter emphasizes his compassion. Gender thus throws perspective on the character of God. Neither gender is closer to God than the other; their own character strengths relate to different aspects of God's nature because they are attuned to them. However, since a husband's strength helps him resonate God's strong qualities, he can help his wife understand that aspect of God's being more clearly by incarnating it, even though he does that imperfectly. On the other hand, a woman's tenderness and compassion can increase her husband's awareness of God's mercy (1 Pet. 3:1-2).

GOD'S CHARACTER CANNOT BE CAPTURED BY HIS HUMAN IMAGE BEARER, BUT EACH GENDER TYPICALLY ACCENTUATES CERTAIN ASPECTS OF GOD'S CHARACTER.

By way of a caveat, we must say that marriage is not the only way to learn about God's character. We are creatures gifted with intelligence and imagination. Even if we are not married, we can imagine from reading the Scriptures and from observing individuals and couples. We can also enjoy meaningful and deep relationships with people of the other gender without being married to them. Marriages that are marred by conflict or a profound lack of communication can also be more of a block than a help to knowing God. Just as we can learn from the metaphor of God's fatherhood, even if our own father is dead, absent, or negligent, we can learn about God's nature through gender, even if we are single, divorced, or in a bad marriage.

NEITHER GENDER IS CLOSER TO GOD THAN THE OTHER; THEIR OWN CHARACTER STRENGTHS RELATE TO DIFFERENT ASPECTS OF GOD'S NATURE BECAUSE THEY ARE ATTUNED TO THEM.

THE SPLENDOR OF MALENESS AND THE BEAUTY OF FEMALENESS

A vivid portrait of the beauty of maleness and femaleness is provided in Psalm 45. As we have already observed in chapter 3, Psalm 45 is a wedding song. In verse 1 the poet expresses his excitement at the wedding that unfolds before his eyes. As he paints a picture of the scene by means of his word craft, he describes the splendor of the groom and the beauty of the bride. His words begin our quest through the Bible for portraits of maleness and femaleness in marriage.

My heart is stirred by a noble theme
as I recite my verses for the king;
my tongue is the pen of a skillful writer.
You are the most excellent of men
and your lips have been anointed with grace,
since God has blessed you forever.
Gird your sword upon your side, O mighty one;

clothe yourself with splendor and majesty.
In your majesty ride forth victoriously
in behalf of truth, humility and righteousness;
let your right hand display awesome deeds.
Let your sharp arrows pierce the hearts of the king's enemies;
let the nations fall beneath your feet.
Your throne, O God, will last for ever and ever;
a scepter of justice will be the scepter of your kingdom.
You love righteousness and hate wickedness;
therefore God, your God, has set you above your companions
by anointing you with the oil of joy.
All your robes are fragrant with myrrh and aloes and cassia;
from palaces adorned with ivory
the music of the strings makes you glad.
Daughters of kings are among your honored women;
at your right hand is the royal bride in gold of Ophir.
Listen, O daughter, consider and give ear:
Forget your people and your father's house.
The king is enthralled by your beauty;
honor him, for he is your lord.
The Daughter of Tyre will come with a gift,
men of wealth will seek your favor.
All glorious is the princess within her chamber;
her gown is interwoven with gold.
In embroidered garments she is led to the king;
her virgin companions follow her
and are brought to you.
They are led in with joy and gladness;
they enter the palace of the king.
Your sons will take the place of your fathers;
you will make them princes throughout the land.
I will perpetuate your memory through all generations;
therefore the nations will praise you for ever and ever. PSALM 45

The Groom: Warrior against Chaos

As the poet sees the king-groom appear on his wedding day, he exclaims that the king is "the most excellent of men." His excellency is never described in terms of his physical appearance. It is true that his clothing is splendid, but it is really his worth as a king and a warrior that is praised here.

Indeed, his lips and hands are the only parts of his body that are even mentioned. His lips are mentioned because his speech is gracious. When he speaks to those around him and also those who are under his leadership, he speaks life-words, not death-words. His lips bring healing and wholeness, not destruction and chaos.

His hands "display awesome deeds," deeds of battle and victory. The king of Israel was faced with many battles of a physical sort. The forces of chaos that ranged against him were the physical, national enemies of Israel, and it was the king's job to keep them at bay to allow God's beautiful order to enrich his kingdom.

THE CONTEMPORARY CHRISTIAN
GROOM SHOULD SHOW UP
AT HIS WEDDING ARMED,
BUT HIS WEAPONS ARE FAITH, PRAYER,
AND THE WORD OF GOD.

Today's groom is usually dressed in a tuxedo, with no sword in sight. But the battle that awaits him is no less real, and certainly it is no less dangerous. We have mentioned in the previous pages that life is a war, a spiritual battle that has physical manifestations. Our weapons are not physical but spiritual. The contemporary Christian groom should show up at his wedding armed, but his weapons are faith, prayer, and the Word of God.

Like the vassal king, the husband is to be the first to bleed on behalf of the person whom he has been called to protect: his wife. The husband must protect her, serve her, and train her in the art of warfare as they both seek to shape a hostile world to the glory of God. The husband is to win his wife far more by how he straps on and uses the weapons of spiritual warfare than by how he straps on and uses his yard tools or business sense.

LIKE THE VASSAL KING, THE HUSBAND IS TO BE THE FIRST TO BLEED ON BEHALF OF THE PERSON WHOM HE HAS BEEN CALLED TO PROTECT: HIS WIFE.

The Bride: Internal Beauty

As the poet turns to the bride, he almost needs to shield his eyes from her overwhelming beauty. But again, her beauty is not explicitly attached to her physical appearance. No part of her body is mentioned. Her magnificent wedding clothes are suitably costly and splendid. But at a key point, her beauty is shown to be an inward and not an outward beauty. "All glorious within is the princess; her gown is interwoven with gold" (Ps. 45:13).[1]

The NIV misunderstands this verse by adding to the first line the words "her chamber," which is not in the Hebrew. The passage is not saying the princess is beautiful inside her room, but that her beauty is an inner beauty. As Peter Craigie so aptly explains, "He has little to say about her physical beauty, but indicates again how the extravagantly beautiful garments worn for the occasion symbolize the inner honor and integrity of her person."[2]

As part of the spiritual beauty, the poet exhorts the new bride to submit to her husband: "The king is enthralled by your beauty; honor him, for he is your lord" (Ps. 45:11).

The queen's beauty has this powerful man mesmerized. She could use it to win her own way if she chose, but to do so would render him completely powerless. Her inner beauty draws and captures. But her beauty is not a cage to entrap but a glory to free and empower others. She draws forth delight that increases one's desire to sing to the glory of her Creator. A man is to go forth to defend good and destroy evil. A woman is to draw forth delight and to put aside other loyalties.

A MAN IS TO GO FORTH TO DEFEND
GOOD AND DESTROY EVIL.
A WOMAN IS TO DRAW FORTH
DELIGHT AND TO PUT ASIDE
OTHER LOYALTIES.

The poet reminds the queen that her husband is, to use the New Testament term, the "head" of the household (1 Cor. 11:3). This controversial topic will be treated in what follows.

The Fruit of Their Union

At the end of this wedding song, the bride and groom leave the crowds and go off alone. They have left their individual pasts and now have embarked on a new life together.

The psalm ends with a blessing. In the Hebrew clearly it is the man who is being directly addressed again, although now he is being addressed as the head of a household and not as an individual. The couple looks forward to a living memorial. The fruit of their union, their children, will stand as a memorial to the far distant future.

THE IDEAL WIFE: PROVERBS 31:10-31

Proverbs gives us glimpses of various women. On the one side, Proverbs describes women of dubious character: the "strange" woman, the adulterous wife, and most notably a woman named Folly (9:13-18). On the other, more positive side, Proverbs describes the wife of one's youth, the faithful woman, and Lady Wisdom (9:1-6). Why such a preoccupation with women in the book of Proverbs? Its original audience, the group to which it is immediately addressed, is made up of young men who need to hear about the dangers and wonders of the opposite sex.

The ideal woman portrayed in Proverbs 31 is a culmination of all the descriptions and teachings about women in the earlier chapters of the book. In particular we are to see the association between the ideal woman and Lady Wisdom along with a contrast to promiscuous women and Lady Folly.

The contrast between these two types of women is drawn most clearly in Proverbs 9. Wisdom and Folly are both standing on high ground calling to those simple young men who are walking along the road of life. They are inviting them in for a meal, enticing them to form a relationship. Their call is the same: "Let all who are simple come in here!" But the results are radically different. Those who go to Wisdom gain understanding, and those who go to Folly end up dead.

Who are these women? The location of their homes is the key. Only gods and goddesses lived on hills in the ancient Near East. Folly stands for all the false gods that lured Israel from true worship, while Wisdom is God himself. His wisdom is here personified as a woman with whom we can establish an intimate relationship.

In the book of Proverbs unfaithful, promiscuous, loose, foolish women are the tools of Folly, the symbol of false gods; faithful, god-fearing women are the servants of the true God. Proverbs 31 is a hymn of praise to the wise woman who mirrors the Lord.

> *A wife of noble character who can find?*
> *She is worth far more than rubies.*
> *Her husband has full confidence in her*
> *and lacks nothing of value.*
> *She brings him good, not harm,*
> *all the days of her life.*
> *She selects wool and flax*
> *and works with eager hands.*
> *She is like the merchant ships,*
> *bringing her food from afar.*
> *She gets up while it is still dark;*
> *she provides food for her family*
> *and portions for her servant girls.*
> *She considers a field and buys it;*
> *out of her earnings she plants a vineyard.*
> *She sets about her work vigorously;*
> *her arms are strong for her tasks.*
> *She sees that her trading is profitable,*
> *and her lamp does not go out at night.*
> *In her hand she holds the distaff*
> *and grasps the spindle with her fingers.*
> *She opens her arms to the poor*
> *and extends her hands to the needy.*
> *When it snows, she has no fear for her household;*
> *for all of them are clothed in scarlet.*
> *She makes coverings for her bed;*

she is clothed in fine linen and purple.
Her husband is respected at the city gate,
where he takes his seat among the elders of the land.
She makes linen garments and sells them,
and supplies the merchants with sashes.
She is clothed with strength and dignity;
she can laugh at the days to come.
She speaks with wisdom,
and faithful instruction is on her tongue.
She watches over the affairs of her household
and does not eat the bread of idleness.
Her children arise and call her blessed;
her husband also, and he praises her:
"Many women do noble things,
but you surpass them all."
Charm is deceptive, and beauty is fleeting;
but a woman who fears the Lord is to be praised.
Give her the reward she has earned,
and let her works bring her praise at the city gate.

PROVERBS 31:10-31

These verses form a hymn of praise for God's gift of a wife. The content of the psalm does not flow smoothly from one topic to another, partly because the song is an acrostic, a poem in which each line begins with a successive letter of the Hebrew alphabet. The effect is the impression that we are reading the ABCs of married womanhood.

The poem opens with a question that sets the agenda for the rest: "A wife of noble character who can find?" The answer to this question is not totally obvious. On one level, especially after reading the description, the answer might be, "No one. There are no such women!" Perhaps, though, the expected answer has been anticipated in Proverbs 19:14: A good wife is a gift from God. But it is also true that no woman will fit this picture perfectly.

All marriages experience difficulties and all spouses have faults. But this profile of a godly woman rescues us from many naïve and tragic stereotypes that have been constructed in Christianity. We often think of the man as the ruler and the wife as the "little" woman who serves his purposes by quietly keeping house.

Recall Jeremy and Sue's story. Jeremy had built around his relationships protective walls that let him keep up the façade of strength. He was master at home, condescending to his wife. He was the focal point at church, playing a political game to avoid conflict rather than getting involved in the nitty-gritty of life. Jeremy's strength was a pretense because he did not wrestle with the reality of his own heart.

A GODLY WOMAN ENGAGES IN THE BATTLE OF LIFE WITH AS MUCH COURAGE AND VALOR AS HER HUSBAND. BUT HER FOCUS IS LESS ON DEFENDING AGAINST EXTERNAL ENEMIES AND MORE ON TEACHING HER FAMILY ABOUT THE HIGH CALL OF RELATIONSHIP.

Sue's avoidance of his arrogance may have appeared as support, but it was anything but love. We will soon see that a godly woman engages in the battle of life with as much courage and valor as her husband. But her focus is less on defending against external enemies and more on teaching her family about the high call of relationship. If Sue had pursued that call of femininity, her marriage may not have devolved into the tragic paradigm of the arrogant husband and the weak wife.

The wife of Proverbs 31 is a woman from a social level shared by only a few women. In a word, this woman is wealthy. The ideal woman is pictured as wealthy because the original audience of Proverbs was made up of privileged young men training for governmental service. The principles enfleshed here, however, apply to all of us.

We must remember one other important interpretive principle as we bridge the gap from the passage's original Old Testament setting to our own setting at the transition to the third millennium A.D. The picture of the ideal woman in Proverbs is an ancient woman, a woman from Palestine. Just stating that, however, reminds us how incredibly revolutionary this poem is. The woman of Proverbs 31 is remarkably independent and aggressive in ways that many Christians think are thoroughly modern and suspiciously unbiblical. It is imperative to grasp that God's vision of a woman is quite different from the views held currently in the Christian culture.

We will explore this passage topically, not sequentially, reflecting on this woman as one who shapes her world, as one who relates to her family, and as one who loves her God.

THE NOBLE WOMAN SHAPES AND PLUNDERS HER WORLD. T h e first thing that impresses the reader of this passage is how energetic and outgoing the noble woman is. Indeed, it is exhausting to read about all her activity. This woman is not a meek, retiring, demure ornament. She is a dynamic, outgoing, aggressive contributor to the battle of daily life. Interestingly, she is called "strong," though clearly her strength is inspired by her compassion toward her family.

As many scholars have noted about this passage, the description of this woman as a warrior is just under the surface. Most English translations blunt this, but it can be seen in the word that is translated "noble," which in the original language is normally used of war heroes. But most interesting is the phrase that is translated "lacks nothing of value." This translation does not come close to the Hebrew, which says, "She does not lack plunder." The image is that she is out there battling in daily life, pushing the chaos of a fallen world back, and returning victorious with the plunder of her enemies.

SHE IS A DYNAMIC, OUTGOING, AGGRESSIVE CONTRIBUTOR TO THE BATTLE OF DAILY LIFE.

Today we rarely use martial imagery to describe daily activity, but we can surely see how it applies. A woman rises in the morning to a series of challenges that demand her physical, emotional, intellectual, and relational energies. In this fallen world, those challenges are rarely morally or spiritually neutral. Whether the challenge is cleaning a floor, dealing with a difficult client, or both, modern women need to think of their lives in battle terms.

The poem describes the woman's many activities. She has started a cottage industry; she is a seamstress and a merchant. Many people try to restrict the woman's activity here by saying that her labor was simply domestic, but then again most male occupations in ancient Israel were also domestic. A modern application might be a wife who is a teacher, a lawyer, or a corporate executive.

But the woman's shaping activity is not only commercial and economic. She is also a teacher: "She speaks with wisdom, and faithful instruction is on her tongue." She is an educator, and in this way she also forms the minds of those who listen to her.

172

THE NOBLE WOMAN CARES FOR HER FAMILY. The godly woman of Proverbs 31 does not single-mindedly pursue her own happiness and career goals. Her efforts have as their goal the betterment of her family. Her husband benefits from her labors: "She brings him good, not harm." She gets up early to prepare breakfast for her family and the servants. She is always thinking of the future, so that when any trouble might come, she is prepared.

The effect of her labors allows her husband to thrive at his work as well. The middle of the poem shows him praising her at the city gate. The city gate is roughly equivalent to today's city hall. It was the center of the administration of a town or village. The point is that he is successful at what he does, and he sees his wife as a colaborer in the struggle of life. He gives his wife the praise that she deserves. Indeed, at the conclusion of the poem her children join him in their thanks to her. They know she has taken good care of them and supported them.

THE NOBLE WOMAN LOVES GOD

Charm is deceptive, and beauty is fleeting;
but a woman who fears the Lord is to be praised.

These words are among the last of the whole poem and really provide the foundation for the rest. The consistent teaching of the book of Proverbs, starting with the first chapter, is that the fear of the Lord is the foundation of all success and achievement in life. Here we see that this is also true of marriage.

The hymn places charm and beauty in their proper perspective. Human beauty is not evil, and charm does not always have to be deceptive. But when they are, they should be scorned. Indeed, female beauty and sincere charm should be admired, but only for what they are. Without faith, beauty and charm are totally worthless; they are repulsive.

Proverbs 31:10-31 is thus a hymn to a noble woman, a godly woman. While the picture is presented with vividness by presenting a woman from a particular social class, her character of strong compassion, her courage as she reaches out to a torn world, and most important, her deep trust in God are goals for all women and all wives.

THE FAITHFUL MAN: PSALM 112

Psalm 112 is a counterpart to Proverbs 31. The latter praises the godly woman; this psalm praises the godly man.

It is true that much of this psalm can apply to the godly woman as well as the godly man, and in its modern application we may think of its opening line as, "Blessed is the person who fears the Lord." But there is little question but that the ancient author and the original audience understood this psalm to apply first to males.

Like Proverbs 31, Psalm 112 is an acrostic poem; in this case, every half-line of the poem begins with a successive letter of the Hebrew alphabet. As Proverbs 31 gave us the ABCs of godly womanhood, Psalm 112 gives us the ABCs of godly manhood.

Praise the Lord.
Blessed is the man who fears the Lord,
who finds great delight in his commands.
His children will be mighty in the land;
the generation of the upright will be blessed.
Wealth and riches are in his house,
and his righteousness endures forever.
Even in darkness light dawns for the upright,
for the gracious and compassionate and righteous man.
Good will come to him who is generous and lends freely,

who conducts his affairs with justice.
Surely he will never be shaken;
a righteous man will be remembered forever.
He will have no fear of bad news;
his heart is steadfast, trusting in the Lord.
His heart is secure, he will have no fear;
in the end he will look in triumph on his foes.
He has scattered abroad his gifts to the poor,
his righteousness endures forever;
his horn will be lifted high in honor.
The wicked man will see and be vexed,
he will gnash his teeth and waste away;
the longings of the wicked will come to nothing.

In chapter 9 we saw Jeremy present himself as a fearless man; he feels in control of the situations around him and sees the elders and others as objects he can handle. But deep down we can sense that he keeps people at a distance precisely because he is afraid of what others can do to him. He shields himself from conflict because he is afraid of what the consequences might be. This attitude reveals a lack of the one and only fear that Psalm 112 informs us is legitimate: the fear of the Lord. In the light of the fear of God, all other fears fade into insignificance. The godly man fears no one or no thing except God. Cowardice is a flight from the one true fear to fear something that ultimately has no real power. Whenever a man fears anything but God, his wife will live with a quiet terror and discontent.

The psalm continues with an associated trait: the one who fears the Lord also loves his commands. The opening of Psalm 112 is similar to the beginning of Psalm 1: both begin with the expression "Blessed is the man" and then describe a person who obeys God's law. Even though we New Testament Christians see these verses through the eyes of grace, the law still plays an important role in our lives. It expresses God's will for us. In plain language, the law of God, as expressed in the Ten Commandments, tells us how to live in a way that pleases him. So the law becomes the guideline to us for a life of gratitude. God has saved us from our guilt and from the judgment for breaking the law. In grateful response, we try to live lives that are pleasing to him.

Psalm 112 describes such a grateful man. He is in relationship with God and expresses his thanks by joyful observance of God's law. A godly man is a Word-centered man. He loves the Word of God and draws his ethics, passion, and hope from what is revealed in the Scriptures.

The godly man has an unflappable confidence in the future. This is the case even though the psalm also recognizes that life is a battle. The man is a warrior who goes out into daily life ready to encounter the forces of darkness that seek to undo him and those around him. However, he is secure because he knows that God will bring him the victory at the end.

> THE MAN IS A WARRIOR WHO GOES OUT INTO DAILY LIFE READY TO ENCOUNTER THE FORCES OF DARKNESS THAT SEEK TO UNDO HIM AND THOSE AROUND HIM.

Few men have this type of confidence today. We feel our world is more dangerous, complex, and difficult than the world of Israelite men. In some ways perhaps this is true, but not in others. Ancient Israelite men had many forces that threatened their existence and the safety of their families. Famine could hit without warning. War was a near-constant phenomenon in the ancient world. Disease could ravage the countryside, and corrupt but unchecked government officials could destroy his life. Nonetheless, the godly man of Psalm 112 had "no fear of bad news," because his fear was in the Lord. Notice that the psalm assumes that life will bring him bad news. It will bring him trouble, but his confidence in the Lord is what keeps him going.

Because he lacked fear and was confident in the future, he is no miser with his own wealth. Like the godly woman, the godly man is generous with the poor. The result is that his glory will be enhanced, or in terms of the psalmist's metaphor of the proud ox, that "his horn will be lifted high in honor."

Neither Psalm 112 nor Proverbs 31 is exhaustive in its description of maleness or femaleness, but together they provide a window on what it means to be a godly man and a godly woman. Interestingly, these two poems talk little about the godly man and woman in relationship. With that in mind we turn now to the New Testament and a series of passages that give further insight about men and women in their relationships with one another.

MUTUAL SUBMISSION: THE KEY TO A SUCCESSFUL MARRIAGE

Man and woman are two equal but distinct creatures. Their union presents many opportunities for joy as well as conflict. If life is a battle, then various threats will confront a married couple. How they cope with these threats will determine whether or not their marriage will be a success.

Success can be defined in a number of ways. Success in the minds of many people means uninterrupted happiness, riches, and fame. That is not the biblical view. The biblical view of life is that glory shines in suffering and service. Wealth, fame, and happiness are not bad, but they are fleeting. Marriage is successful when two spouses care for one another and stay committed to each other through the intense heat of the battle. When they hurt, they know who will listen and care. When they rejoice, they have someone to laugh with. They are indeed intimate allies in the battle against the chaos of the world.

MARRIAGE IS SUCCESSFUL WHEN TWO SPOUSES CARE FOR ONE ANOTHER AND STAY COMMITTED TO EACH OTHER THROUGH THE INTENSE HEAT OF THE BATTLE.

It is similar to our relationship with God. When we become Christians, God does not promise that our worries and struggles are over. No, the conflict still wages. But in the midst of the struggle, God gives us glimpses of joy, reminders of the incredible happiness we will enjoy in his presence in the afterlife.

Married life has bursts of brilliance in the midst of the struggle. The key to continued care and commitment is an attitude of mutual submission and love. Let's again look at a few verses from Ephesians 5.

> Submit to one another out of reverence for Christ.
> Wives, submit to your husbands as to the Lord . . .
> Husbands, love your wives . . .
> Each one of you also must love his wife as he loves himself,
> and the wife must respect her husband. EPHESIANS 5:21-22, 25, 33

We look at Ephesians 5 first because the other passages will focus more exclusively on the need for wives to submit to their husbands. We do not know why the focus is as it is; perhaps in the particular occasions represented by the letters, the women needed a special reminder. But Ephesians reminds us that the overarching command is for mutual submission. Husband and wife need to submit to one another.

Remember from earlier discussions that submission is yielding one's individual will for the good of another. Husbands and wives can respond to mutual submission in one of four ways. Some couples reject mutual submission altogether and find themselves in disastrous marriages. These couples rend a one-flesh union to shreds.

Some spouses retain an independent will. Each does what he or she wants to do, regardless of what the other spouse wants. The result is two ships passing in the sea. They have no union, just association.

AS A HUSBAND I AM TO SACRIFICE MY WILL TO SUCCEED FOR THE SAKE OF BEING MY WIFE'S COMPANION, THE ONE WHO UNIQUELY DISPELS LONELINESS IN HER LIFE.

Other couples struggle with relational totalitarianism: one of the spouses exerts a dominant will, while the other obeys. We are not made to co-exist in this way. A man who always does what his wife wants or always lets her call the shots will hate her. The same is true for a woman who has no say in the direction of the relationship. This does not prohibit one of the two from taking initiative in some areas of the relationship, but a continual dominance in the name of submission will damage the union of two equal beings.

Still other couples find the joy and wholeness of true mutual submission. Mutual submission means we will lay down our lives for our spouses' glory. As a husband I am to sacrifice my will to succeed for the sake of being my wife's companion, the one who uniquely dispels loneliness in her life. As a wife, she is to sacrifice her loyalty to any other—including parents, children, and friends—for the sake of being my equal in shaping and ruling creation.

Mutual submission in marriage is simply an outgrowth of the general Christian principle of relationship enunciated by Paul in Philippians 2:3-4: "Do nothing out of selfish ambition or vain conceit, but in humility consider others better than yourselves. Each of you should look not only to your own interests, but also to the interests of others."

AS A WIFE, SHE IS TO SACRIFICE
HER LOYALTY TO ANY OTHER—
INCLUDING PARENTS, CHILDREN,
AND FRIENDS—
FOR THE SAKE OF BEING MY EQUAL
IN SHAPING AND RULING CREATION.

THE QUALITIES OF GODLY HUSBANDS AND WIVES

We now turn to several other New Testament passages that discuss the qualities of godly husbands and wives. We look first at Paul's letter to Timothy. "Although I hope to come to you soon, I am writing you these instructions so that, if I am delayed, you will know how people ought to conduct themselves in God's household, which is the church of the living God, the pillar and foundation of the truth" (1 Tim. 3:14-15). These words from the end of Paul's letter give the context for the teaching he included in earlier parts of the letter. Specifically, and this is pivotal for proper application, Paul says that his instructions are related to how men and women ought to relate in "God's household, which is the church of the living God." Paul focuses his teaching on men and women who are part of the church.

What else does Paul have to say about husbands and wives in the church? Let's look at several key passages: 1 Timothy 2:8–3:14; Titus 1:5-9; 2:1-8; 1 Peter 3:1-7.[3] While some of these passages are specifically directed to the church, they have relevance here because they enumerate the godly qualities of people who will be leaders in the church. These passages describe the ideal godly husband and wife, the role models for all Christian husbands and wives.

The Godly Husband

How would you describe the ideal man? The ideal man in the eyes of the broader culture appears to be young, well muscled (or at least lean), rich, sensitive (or at least casual), and cosmopolitan. He will talk, but not too much. His appearance is tough, a little grizzled, but consciously so. His attitude is inviting to friends, especially beautiful women, but he also communicates a warning that he is someone who should not be messed with. He has influence, but he does not make a big deal of it, unless he has to.

This is the media's picture of the ideal man. But what are most real men like? Here the variety is staggering. Men vary from handsome to repulsive, but most are passably good looking. They are thin, fat, too well muscled, and occasionally in excellent physical shape, at least for a moment of their lives. Some are strong to the point of violence; others are weak and the prey of others. Many would like to know a beautiful woman, or any woman at all, and as for taste and influence—few have either.

What does the Bible see as the ideal man? The following passages give us a picture of a role model for godly men.

I want men everywhere to lift up holy hands in prayer, without anger or disputing. 1 TIMOTHY 2:8

Here is a trustworthy saying: If anyone sets his heart on being an overseer, he desires a noble task. Now the overseer must be above reproach, the husband of but one wife, temperate, self-controlled, respectable, hospitable, able to teach, not given to drunkenness, not violent but gentle, not quarrelsome, not a lover of money. He must manage his own family well and see that his children obey him with proper respect. (If anyone does not know how to manage his own family, how can he take care of God's church?) He must not be a recent convert, or he may become conceited and fall under the same judgment as the devil. He must also have a good reputation with outsiders, so that he will not fall into disgrace and into the devil's trap. 1 TIMOTHY 3:1-7

Deacons, likewise, are to be men worthy of respect, sincere, not indulging in much wine, and not pursuing dishonest gain. They must keep hold of the deep truths of the faith with a clear conscience. They must first be tested; and then if there is nothing against them, let them serve as deacons. 1 TIMOTHY 3:8-10

A deacon must be the husband of but one wife and must manage his children and his household well. Those who have served well gain an excellent standing and great assurance in their faith in Christ Jesus. 1 TIMOTHY 3:12-13

The reason I left you in Crete was that you might straighten out what was left unfinished and appoint elders in every town, as I directed you. An elder must be blameless, the husband of but one wife, a man whose children believe and are not open to the charge of being wild and disobedient. Since an overseer is entrusted with God's work, he must be blameless—not overbearing, not quick-tempered, not given to drunkenness, not violent, not pursuing dishonest gain. Rather he must be hospitable, one who loves what is good, who is self-controlled, upright, holy and disciplined. He must hold firmly to the trustworthy message as it has been taught, so that he can encourage others by sound doctrine and refute those who oppose it. TITUS 1:5-9

You must teach what is in accord with sound doctrine. Teach the older men to be temperate, worthy of respect, self-controlled, and sound in faith, in love and in endurance. TITUS 2:1-2

Similarly, encourage the young men to be self-controlled. In everything set them an example by doing what is good. In your teaching show integrity, seriousness and soundness of speech that cannot be condemned, so that those who oppose you may be ashamed because they have nothing bad to say about us. TITUS 2:6-8

Husbands, in the same way be considerate as you live with your wives, and treat them with respect as the weaker partner and as heirs with you of the gracious gift of life, so that nothing will hinder your prayers. 1 PETER 3:7

First, one quality is striking by its absence. Nothing is said in these passages about the man's physical appearance. The Bible cares about what is important about a man, and his physical attractiveness is not among the traits it considers important. We must be quick to say, however, that the Bible is not completely oblivious to the physical. In later chapters we

183

will look at sections from the Song of Songs, where we will see a sensuality that clearly encompasses the physical.

If it is not beauty that makes a male attractive, what does? In a word, it is spiritual maturity. And this spiritual maturity comes to expression in certain directions of life. It also signals the absence of other personality and behavior traits.

What does it mean to be a mature male? It means, first, to be a man of faith and prayer (1 Tim. 2:8; Titus 1:9). Unfortunately, what is usually evoked by this is the image of a man who retreats from the world and finds his solace in the prayer closet. Such a view of life is unattractive, even cowardly, and it is not the biblical view of faith and prayer.

As we have seen clearly in past sections, life is a battleground. The battle takes many forms, and our role in the battle differs from person to person. We can see it in our relationships; we feel it in our jobs. The battleground for a lawyer who is dealing with issues of societal justice is different from that of an elementary school teacher who is informing his students about God's world, which is different from the doctor who fights against the forces of chaos as they rage against the body.

FAITH IS WHAT PROPELS US
INTO THE BATTLE.

Faith is what propels us into the battle. Faith gives us perspective and hope that our work is not meaningless. But since God is ultimately in charge, our work is invested with eternal significance. Faith is a weapon in the battle against the forces of evil according to Ephesians 6:16: "In addition to all this, take up the shield of faith, with which you can extinguish all the flaming arrows of the evil one."

Prayer is another divine weapon against the chaos of life

(Eph. 6:18). Prayer is not a passive attitude toward life; rather, prayer uses words to ask God to shape the world and our lives to his glory. It is a weapon we use to engage life head-on with confidence and vitality.

A man of faith and prayer will be a man of confidence and vitality as he interacts with a dangerous and hostile world. His confidence emanates from his knowledge that God is in control of his world.

A MAN OF FAITH AND PRAYER WILL BE
A MAN OF CONFIDENCE AND VITALITY
AS HE INTERACTS WITH
A DANGEROUS AND HOSTILE WORLD.

As a result, he has a strength that other men do not have. This strength gives him the power to "manage" his family. The word "manage" can be better translated "care for." The word translated "manage" in 1 Timothy 3:4 is the same word used to describe the action of the Good Samaritan, who sacrificed himself to provide for the care of another. When a husband manages his family, his management is not primarily an activity of scheduling and delegating; it is serving by being willing to sacrifice first on behalf of his family.

Because the godly husband sacrifices for others, he is also a leader in his community (1 Tim. 3:4-5, 7, 12; Titus 1:6). He has a good reputation in the community; he is honored, not shamed, at home, in the church, or in the broader society (1 Tim. 3:7).

His faith, which undergirds his strength, gives him the substance that enables him to teach. The mature Christian man can teach others by example and by word. This teaching does not necessarily or usually take the form of preaching in church or teaching Sunday school. All of us are engaged in teaching others either consciously or unconsciously by our good or bad example.

Every Christian man should aspire to be a mentor to someone less mature and have a mentor who is more mature than he. Timothy, Titus, and other early Christian leaders could look to Paul as an example. Paul himself looked to Jesus (1 Cor. 11:1).

Teaching is a weapon against the forces of chaos. As Paul points out to Titus, the mature Christian man must teach in order to silence the "many rebellious people, mere talkers and deceivers" who are trying to infiltrate the Christian community with false teaching (Titus 1:10-16).

Paul also warns Christian men to avoid certain behavior. He puts it positively when he says that men should be pure, holy, above reproach, and self-controlled.

The apostle Paul goes further and applies these general areas to specific concerns. It seems clear that he does this in order to highlight certain areas where men are especially vulnerable. For instance, men need to avoid certain addictions. Paul clearly states that men need to exercise care in their approach to money, alcohol, and sex. Not that any of these three are evil in and of themselves, but they each have a powerful attraction that can lead to obsession and turn a strong, faithful man into a nonentity.

Paul's warnings about money and alcohol are clear enough, but his warnings about sex are more subtle. In 1 Timothy 3:2 and Titus 1:6, Paul insists that an overseer be the husband of one wife. Now certainly this verse stands as a guard against bigamy, having more than one wife, which was still a danger in the first-century society in which Paul lived. However, even at that time this warning had a wider meaning. Paul is stating that the mature Christian man's sexuality is focused exclusively on the one to whom he is formally committed. An overseer who had one wife legally but also had a mistress or two would not conform to Paul's description of the overseer or deacon.

Paul also warns men not to be angry or violent (1 Tim. 2:8; 3:3). We believe that Paul specifically warns men about anger because that is a special temptation to the male psyche. Unrighteous anger is strength gone awry. Anger is also the result of an ungodly perspective of the world. It lashes out at chaos but with the attitude that God is not ultimately in control. The result is that such anger does not push chaos back as much as contribute to it.

But Paul also puts this positively. Men should not be angry, but they should be gentle, peace loving, even hospitable (1 Tim. 3:2-3). Only men of strong faith and prayer can consistently exhibit these qualities in a fallen world.

CHRISTIAN MEN ARE NOT TO BE ABUSERS; THEY ARE TO BE CONSIDERATE TO THEIR WIVES.

And interestingly, Peter applies the quality of gentleness specifically to marriage when he tells Christian men to "be considerate as you live with your wives" (1 Pet. 3:7). The first observation to be made on this passage is that this implies a form of submission on the part of the man toward his wife. Although the specific word for submission is not used here, to be considerate toward another means to bend one's will and desires to the desires of another. When I am considerate, I take into account what my wife needs, not what would make my life easier.

The second observation flows from Peter's motivation for this special charge to Christian men. He tells them to be considerate because wives are the "weaker partner" in the relationship. It is too easy for modern men and women to jump all over this phrase as a sign of the Bible's primitive values or for some Christian men to use it to justify their false view of women. In the context Peter is saying that women are generally weaker in terms of their physical strength, which makes them more socially vulnerable than men. In other words, women are not psychologically, intellectually, or emotionally inferior to men, but they are often weaker physically, and that has allowed certain cruel men to push, batter, and abuse women in their relationships. Peter is telling his readers that Christian men are not to be abusers; they are to be considerate to their wives.

Men are not only to avoid abusing their wives but also to treat them with honor and respect. They are to glorify their wives, as we discussed in chapters 2 and 3. After all, according to Peter, men are to treat their wives as joint heirs "of the gracious gift of life" (1 Pet. 3:7).

The Qualities of a Godly Wife

In spite of the efforts of certain women's groups, the media's picture of the ideal woman at the end of the twentieth century is still defined in predominantly physical terms. And the neuroses of many modern women confirm the tensions that they experience from the expectations of society.

What is the ideal woman in our society? She is trim, thin, lithe. Her hair is full, and her complexion is soft and lovely. She dresses well and smells like a garden. Her attitude toward men is seductive.

Our diverse society reflects variety in the image of the ideal woman, but whether she is pictured as an aggressive, competent businesswoman or a sultry, sexy siren, physical attractiveness is a constant standard for women to achieve and for men to desire. The tragedy, of course, is that not all women can meet the standards erected by movies, ads, and television. Many of the stresses of modern women can be traced to a feeling of failure to live up to the modern ideal.

But society places an additional demand on modern women. Not only should they be pretty, but they also need to excel at their careers. Indeed, we should applaud recent progress in opening up access for women in areas that they formerly were prohibited from entering. But now the predominant pressure has reversed itself. Women who do want to devote their lives to home, church, volunteer work, or noncareer work feel as if they are second-class women because they have not entered the professional workforce.

The pressures on all women in our society are intense. The choices have expanded, and the voices that urge decisions have increased.

But what is the biblical picture of a godly woman? The Bible will not specifically answer all the questions we want to ask it. For instance, as we have already observed in Proverbs 31, the Bible does allow for women to carry on a professional life, but that does not mean that every woman should. It does not demand that a woman work outside the home, and the final choice is one that each woman must make in relation to her family.

However, the following passages provide an important lens through which we should view the pressures on women today. And the first two passages affirm the perspective expressed in Proverbs 31:30: "Charm is deceptive, and beauty is fleeting; but a woman who fears the Lord is to be praised." The principle that stands boldly against modern standards is that physical beauty pales in significance next to spiritual beauty.

> I also want women to dress modestly, with decency and propriety, not with braided hair or gold or pearls or

expensive clothes, but with good deeds, appropriate for women who profess to worship God.

A woman should learn in quietness and full submission. I do not permit a woman to teach or to have authority over a man; she must be silent. For Adam was formed first, then Eve. And Adam was not the one deceived; it was the woman who was deceived and became a sinner. But women will be saved through childbearing—if they continue in faith, love and holiness with propriety. 1 TIMOTHY 2:9-15

Wives, in the same way be submissive to your husbands so that, if any of them do not believe the word, they may be won over without words by the behavior of their wives, when they see the purity and reverence of your lives. Your beauty should not come from outward adornment, such as braided hair and the wearing of gold jewelry and fine clothes. Instead, it should be that of your inner self, the unfading beauty of a gentle and quiet spirit, which is of great worth in God's sight. For this is the way the holy women of the past who put their hope in God used to make themselves beautiful. They were submissive to their own husbands, like Sarah, who obeyed Abraham and called him her master. You are her daughters if you do what is right and do not give way to fear. 1 PETER 3:1-6

Both Paul and Peter stress that spiritual beauty is more important than physical beauty. The apostle's tirade against braids, jewels, and expensive clothes should not be seen as some kind of puritanical hatred of beauty, but rather as a slap in our faces to make us wake up and see what is important.

Indeed, we have to understand their comments about physical beauty as hyperbole, because elsewhere in Scripture, most notably in Song of Songs, sensual physical beauty is celebrated. In other words, compared to what is really impor-

tant—namely our character and our relationship to God—
physical beauty is insignificant.

And that is good news for men and women alike. No longer
is our ultimate worth connected to how thin we are, how tall
we are, how sexually attractive we are. What matters is our
relationship to God and our spiritual maturity. By faith we see
that physical beauty is but a mere metaphor of a greater, more
compelling beauty—a heart given to God.

PHYSICAL BEAUTY IS BUT A MERE METAPHOR OF A GREATER, MORE COMPELLING BEAUTY— A HEART GIVEN TO GOD.

The issue of submission appears in the two passages listed
above as well as in the passage listed below. We have already
pointed out that this command must be understood in the light
of the mutual submission commanded by Paul in Ephesians
5:21. We have also seen that Peter urged men to a submissive
attitude toward their wives when he told them to "be considerate" toward them (1 Pet. 3:7). Nonetheless it is true that women
are told more often and more directly that their attitude toward
their husbands needs to be marked by submission, a bowing of
their will to the will of their husbands.

> Likewise, teach the older women to be reverent in the way
> they live, not to be slanderers or addicted to much wine,
> but to teach what is good. Then they can train the younger
> women to love their husbands and children, to be self-
> controlled and pure, to be busy at home, to be kind, and to
> be subject to their husbands, so that no one will malign the
> word of God. TITUS 2:3-5

Perhaps no other teaching in the Bible is more resisted than the practice of submission within marriage. We suggest a few reasons for this.

First, our society sees people as sovereign individuals. American rugged individualism teaches that we have an inherent right to be completely independent of anyone else. We rail against the idea of submitting to anyone.

However, such an attitude on the part of either the husband or wife is totally unbiblical and will kill the joy of marriage. The truth is that we are all interdependent creatures. We all ultimately submit to God, and we must submit to each other to have anything like an interpersonal relationship.

Second, we resist the idea of submission because a misunderstanding of the concept has led to much abuse. For example, some people envision submission as a one-way street. The wife must submit to the husband in everything and in every way. Marriage turns out to be a form of dictatorship.

TO BE THE HEAD IS TO LEAD BY SACRIFICING FIRST FOR THOSE WE ARE CALLED TO SERVE.

While it is true that the husband is the "head" of the wife, he is the one who is ultimately responsible to die on behalf of his wife first (1 Cor. 11:3; Eph. 5:25-27). To be the head is to lead by sacrificing first for those we are called to serve. This is the picture Jesus gives us: He, the head of the church, suffered and died for the sake of washing her in blood and water. He did this to enhance her beauty (Eph. 5:25-30).

Obviously then, headship is not to be understood as the dictatorship of the husband wielding his own will over the rest of the household. The male is not superior to the female any more than God the Father is superior to the Son, who is equally God and said to look to the Father as his "head" (1 Cor. 11:3).

But why are wives called to submit to their husbands more directly and more often than husbands are commanded to submit to their wives? Partly the answer is because the husband is the head of the household, and as unpopular as that concept is in our contemporary and authority-less society, it is still true and important. In any kind of organization—and a family is a social organization—someone must assume leadership. In the family, according to the Bible, that someone is the husband.

The other part of the answer appears when we view the wife's submission in the context of first-century culture. As Peter Davids points out in his commentary on 1 Peter, the encouragement to submit was "necessary in that in the church women found a freedom in worship under the influence of the Spirit that they did not enjoy elsewhere in society and that led some of them to a rejection of their husbands' authority, deeply embarrassing both the men and church."[4]

Before men and women embark on the incredibly intimate relationship of marriage, they need to hear the clear message that marriage involves submission. Before they enter into a marriage, a man and a woman should ask themselves these questions. Am I willing to give up some of my freedom, my independence, to another person? Am I ready and willing to submit myself to this particular man or woman? Do I think this person is willing to submit himself or herself to me?

Of course, the answer to these questions at best will be "as God gives me the grace to do so." None of us expects to do so perfectly.

It is incredibly fascinating that Peter chooses the relationship between Sarah and Abraham as a model of a woman who has submitted well to her husband (1 Pet. 3:5-6). As we go back and read the story of Sarah, we do not get a model of a quiet, passive, submissive woman. Sarah at times might be called cantankerous in her attitude toward Abraham and even toward God (Gen. 16:1-8; 18:12). Nonetheless, Sarah sticks by her husband even during the mounting disappointments of their life together, so that together they could rejoice in the birth of Isaac in their extreme old age (Gen. 21:1-7).

A man who struggles to engage chaos to shape it to the beauty of God's glory will desperately need a wife who believes in him, who envisions what he could become, and who sets her heart to serve him. A woman who struggles to see her family transformed into the character of Jesus Christ will desperately need a husband who will sacrifice for her and their children in order to provide the context for mercy and forgiveness. When a man is godly, his family will feel safe to move into the unknown to claim it for glory. When a woman is godly, her family will move into the unknown with a passion to reveal glory in relationship.

QUESTIONS FOR REFLECTION AND CONVERSATION

1. In what ways is your spouse different from you? As you think about the ways the two of you think, act, feel, or desire, think about whether or not these are gender differences. Be kind to each other.
2. What is distinctly male or female about your spouse?
3. As you view the future, how would you describe your attitude toward life? Are you hopeful, confident, troubled, despairing, indifferent? What does this tell you about your fear of God?
4. *Submission* is a highly emotive word. It evokes strong feelings whether we speak about it or leave it out of the discussion. Indeed, it is even controversial to talk of "mutual submission." Discuss together how you presently handle submission in your marriage. How would you like to see submission at work in your marriage?

5. What does submission mean to you? What is your response to this definition: "the yielding of one's individual will for the good of the other"?

6. How does a husband submit to his wife? How does a wife submit to her husband?

7. Would you describe your marriage as successful? In what way(s)?

8. What qualities do you most prize in your spouse? What do you feel is lacking? How balanced are your spouse's physical, emotional, and spiritual qualities? What can you do to bring more balance to your spouse's life?

9. In what ways do you and your spouse use faith and prayer as weapons in fighting the battle of life? What would you like to see change in these areas? What are the external factors (time, busyness, different prayer habits) that impede your spiritual life together? What are the internal factors (fear of praying out loud, differences in level of maturity, boredom, or lack of passion for God) that affect your spiritual life?

10. How is your leadership style (headship) related to sacrifice and servanthood? Be concrete. In what way does your decision-making style violate sacrifice and servanthood?

11. Husbands: Does your wife encourage your ability to relate to other people?

12. Husbands: What do you fear about being a man? What things would your wife say you fear about being a man?

13. Wives: What do you fear about being a woman? What things would your husband say you fear about being a woman?

14. Wives: Does your marriage strengthen you as a person?

15. Wives: Does Proverbs 31 match your vision of what it means to be a woman? Where does it make you feel

burdened? In what ways does it invite you to be free?
How do you comprehend those two different feelings?

16. Wives: What restrains you from reaching your potential
as a woman, wife, and friend?

17. Husbands: Does Psalm 112 match your vision of what
it means to be a man? Where does it make you feel
burdened? In what ways does it invite you to be free?
How do you comprehend those two different feelings?

18. Husbands: What restrains you from reaching your
potential as a man, husband, and friend?

12

Jeremy and Sue Become
Intimate Allies in Helping
Each Other Grow

Sue prayed most of the day with a dear friend who knew
more about her marriage than Sue had ever shared. It was not
too hard to see the pattern. Jeremy was a successful, person-
able, competent man who had little time for his family,
friends, or even physical exercise. Sue was a quiet, caring, shy,
busy wife who had too little time with her husband.

Jeremy looked like a man's man; Sue was the epitome of
Laura Ashley femininity. Both were well-groomed counterfeits
who successfully hid their cowardice and flight from reality.
Sue was aware of her flight from being a woman; Jeremy did
not have a clue that he did not enjoy being a man. Jeremy
never really thought about being a man; it was what he was.

But the evening changed all that. It was an evening that Jeremy would later say arrived at his door like an asteroid hitting the earth. He had said to Sue, "If you have criticism, I would appreciate your setting up a time to let me know rather than springing it on me out of the blue." Lifted by the Spirit of God to see a vision of what her husband was, what he could be, and what her part might be in the transformation from one to the other, she had suggested they talk that evening.

Jeremy looked surprised, but he regained his composure, said he would look forward to their talk, and would be home by 7:00. The first sign of a very different heart came when Sue said, "No, be home at 6:00. We have too much to talk about to start that late. I will arrange to have a quiet night." He looked at her blankly and said he would be home by 6:00.

Later that afternoon after prayer, Sue did something she had never done in her life. She called the church secretary and told her to cancel all of Jeremy's appointments the next day. Mrs. Matthison was taken aback and said she needed to talk to Jeremy. Sue was direct and firm: "No. I have made plans that he does not know about, and if you talk with him, you will ruin the surprise. I will take full responsibility." She arranged baby-sitting for the night and called a downtown hotel for a room. Then she wrote out a battle plan. Later the paper was framed as a memorial that seemed as important as the vows they had made at their wedding. The battle plan hangs today next to their wedding picture in her private study.

LOVE PLAN—WAR PLAN

Prayer: O Lord, my Savior, my Shield, my Glory, the one who raises my head, I pray for your heart to be raised in mine. I pray I will be firmly in your hand and securely in your will. I know my marriage is far from your desire for us. I know I have been unwilling to offer my heart, my soul, and my body to Jeremy for your glory. I have been a dutiful, bland wife, and I have failed to offer him the passion I have saved for my fantasies. They are wrong. The stronghold of my inner world must crumble under your holy hand. I pray for wisdom, O Lord, to speak of both my failure to be a woman and his reluctance to be a man. I pray for big things, Father. I pray that you will break my heart and use my tears to soften Jeremy's heart as well. I pray for what you desire in our lives. I ask you to speak through me for the sake of our love, our marriage, your church, and your children. Amen.

Plan: Have the bags packed and in my car when Jeremy arrives home. Tell him that we are driving downtown for dinner. Once we arrive, let the doorman take our bags and pick up the key at the desk. Go straight to dinner so that Jeremy does not get the wrong idea about the evening. Tell him about my sin. Tell him about him. Ask him to pray with me, for me, for us, for himself. Hope and hope and hope and hope.

Things I want to say:

1. I have failed you as a loving wife. I have been weak, voice-less, and disengaged from my pain and sin as well as from your struggle and sin.
2. I have refused to ask you questions, not only about your day but also about your life. I know you so well, but so very little. I don't know why you avoid conflict to the point of sacrificing your integrity. I don't know why success is more important than honor and love. I don't know what your heart really knows and desires from God. I want to pledge to you my curiosity, my pain, my dreams for you.
3. I have never asked you what you find unlovely about me. I have never invited you to speak into my life honestly. I am afraid to hear what you will say, but I cannot live with

unseen cancers, unsaid secrets, that will continue to rot away our heart for one another and for our Father.

4. I have never asked you if you really want a different, better marriage. And when we have come even close to discussing what we want, I have settled for your quick assurances and religious patter. I have never asked for your heart. I will not live in this marriage without your heart—a broken, contrite heart at that.

5. I want to ask you to see someone—a friend, a prayer partner, or a counselor—with whom you can talk and pray and envision what we were meant to be. I will not settle for cheap commitments; I would rather end the charade if you want nothing more than a façade for your self-righteous, patronizing heart. I want you, not what you have used to survive.

Commitment: I will not quit. I will not harden. I will not flee to my forest.

Prayer: Be with me, O God. Be with Jeremy. Be with us. Amen.

When Jeremy returned home that evening, he was stunned to see a baby-sitter, the car packed, and his wife dressed to go out to dinner. For the obvious reasons, he forgot the purpose for their evening conversation. He noticed only the suitcase, and his mind raced foward to images of the sensual evening ahead.

The bags were delivered to the room, and for some strange reason Sue insisted on going straight to dinner. After initial small talk, he saw her take out a white piece of computer paper. He had learned to read upside-down long ago, and he strained to see the heading and any print. But she coyly slid it behind her plate.

She began by lightly touching him on the shoulder: "I want to tell you I have committed serious sins. And I am here tonight to confess to you and talk with you about the future of our marriage." Jeremy's heart began to pound. Nothing in their twelve years of marriage had jolted him more than her first sentence. Before the evening was over, however, it would be eclipsed by words that were beyond his comprehension.

It is impossible to describe the next hour and a half. For Jeremy, the meal lasted for years. For Sue it passed in an instant. Sue made it through the first two points—and then some. Jeremy heard the first few sentences, and then everything became a blur.

He retorted. He guffawed. He became pompous, hostile, then sullen. The conversation had spurts and starts, but it ended when Sue asked him if he wanted to deal with his sin and pray with her about her failures.

She had never felt so feminine, so alive, and so bold. She was neither hostile nor demanding. When he mocked her and tried to instruct her in his condescending tone, she said, "Jeremy, this is what I mean by condescending. You are a wonderful teacher, and your words are true. But your teaching is not a gift of love; it is an attempt to silence me. I love you, and I will not flee from you again. Do you want me, or do you want a hollow shell for a wife?"

Her beauty and tenderness unnerved him. All his preemptive strikes to silence and shame her only further exposed his cowardice. He could feel himself losing ground, and he felt hard and cruel. When she vocalized what she saw as a growing meanness and arrogance, he felt alone and helpless. If violence was not going to work, if withdrawal was seen only as proof of cowardice, then he was stuck.

Finally, he stood up and walked out of the restaurant and out of the hotel. She was stunned. She had never, never thought he would simply walk out on her. Where would he go? How long should she sit at the table waiting for him?

She sat for a half hour, then she signed for the meal and went back to the room. She could feel the terror rising and the tug inside her to return to the world of caring trees and adoring animals. But she felt even more drawn to pray. For the first time in a long while, perhaps ever, she felt connected to God. She wanted to pray. And she felt fear, but far more she felt a desire to engage, to connect with Jeremy. She knew it might be the end, but she also knew she was giving birth to a very different marriage. She was his helper, and she was not going to refuse him the opportunity to become a man.

Jeremy returned about two hours later. He was furious. He knocked on the hotel door and entered without a word. Sue desperately wanted to ask him where he had been, what he was thinking, what he was going to do with her words. After a long time, he finally asked to see the piece of paper. She gave it to him, and he read the page slowly over and over again. He stared at the paper for twenty minutes.

He put it down and said: "If you want a divorce, I will grant it to you. But if you want to stick it out and give me a chance to digest what you have fed me tonight, then please wait until I know what to say. I have never been more dumbfounded and speechless in my life."

Never in her life had he asked her for anything other than to carry out a task. He had never before admitted being helpless. She felt a surge of pride for him for the first time. He would not comprehend for years how safe she felt with him at that moment. But she felt at rest.

On the other side of the bed, he felt shame and bursts of rage. He knew she loved him. He knew she did not want to harm him, but he also knew that for the first time in their marriage, he was dealing with a woman. And it pleased him. He could not help but smile, and his smile prompted a taste of strength that was different from any of his pompous shows, angry tirades, or politicizing contortions. The thought stirred in his mind: "Perhaps I will have to become a man to handle a woman like Sue."

Part Four

HOW DO WE EXPERIENCE THE DEEPEST, MOST PROFOUND INTIMACY OF BODY AND SOUL?

13

CLAY AND KAREN:

THE COUPLE WHOSE SEX

LIFE WAS DYING

The day did not begin well. Clay awakened, put on his seersucker Cardin bathrobe that made him feel more wealthy than he was, and made his way downstairs. Before he got to the kitchen, his wife, Karen, stopped him in the hallway and said, "The sprinkler system is broken. I can't get the automatic timer to work, and I just noticed a burned section of lawn in the backyard." No good-morning greeting. Not even a hello. The hassle was like a cloud that threatened to darken the day.

But Clay rose above it. He thought to himself: *A day doesn't have momentum in itself. I can make it a bad day, or I can make it a good one.* Clay could not have been more wrong.

His day was a disaster at nearly every turn. His first appointment didn't show up. He sat in the man's office for half an hour, alternately fuming and wondering whether to wait or leave an irate message. His second appointment, with his best salesman, was brief. The salesman told him he had been offered a better job and would be leaving in a week.

At each juncture of descent into a hellish day, Clay thought, *It can't possibly get any worse.* It did. Disappointment was followed by insult. Insult was deepened by insincere comfort. And insincere comfort was smothered by patronizing advice. Then Karen called to ask if he would pick up the kids and bring home some dinner; she was exhausted from a three-hour lunch appointment.

He grunted yes and didn't finish the call with a good-bye. He hung up and stared out the window. It was common for him to stare out the window and think of Maureen.

He had met Maureen several years ago at a sales convention. And he always began his fantasy with the memory of their first encounter.

Clay considered himself average in looks, demeanor, and about everything else. He fit in. He did his job well, and he was respected as another cog in the wheel of industry; another person who filled up a seat in church. He was conventional, hardworking, and moral. He was a good boy—the kind that had made his mother proud even when he was in the first grade. He was also lonely, but only in an average way.

Maureen had sat next to him in the large convention hall. She had turned to him and smiled. Her words had stunned him: "Hi, I am not usually so forward, but would you mind if I sat with you during these tiresome replays of what we already know?"

He had immediately felt like a coconspirator in the genteel art of mocking meetings. He had laughed and said: "I would be delighted." He had felt warm. Frightened. Alive. They had exchanged knowing looks when the speaker announced the day's schedule of meetings.

When Clay had picked a workshop on Inventory Cataloging, he noticed that Maureen had checked the same box. She had done the same for every other meeting he would attend during the day.

In a lucid moment, he had realized that he and Maureen would eventually have an affair if he were to allow it.

They had attended the first meeting. He had watched her jet-black hair move freely on her shoulders. He could see the light outline of her bra, and he had allowed his eyes to drop from her shoulders down to the rest of her body. The war was intense. He could have her. She had made that clear. Why him? Why now? He had been married for only two years, and he loved his wife. He was a Christian, and he knew an affair was wrong. But he felt not only the growing arousal, but even more he felt the tingle of anticipation.

Sex with his wife was initially good. In fact, it was fabulous. But over time she had had an increasingly difficult time having an orgasm. It took so long. It seemed so short. And frankly, it didn't seem to be worth all the work. Masturbation was easier. He had succumbed to masturbating several times a week and having sex with his wife now and then.

But Maureen was a woman of passion. He could feel it. She was not a vixen, a come-on artist. In fact, after their initial encounter she had seemed shy and far more comfortable listening than talking. She had an intensity, a desirability that his wife, who was far more attractive, never seemed to exude in her pleasant, cool helpfulness. His resolve had seemed to cloud as he had continued to stare at her delicate and lithe body.

During one of the breaks, Maureen had gotten up to get a glass of juice at the refreshment table. Clay had turned his eyes from her, and before he had realized what he was doing, he had grabbed his notebook and walked out the door. He had kept walking. He had walked out of the convention center and out into the city. Ten blocks later he had stopped at a little diner tucked between two large skyscrapers. He had gone in, needing some caffeine to clear his head.

He had seen her again late that afternoon. She had been talking with a few other acquaintances. Their eyes had connected. She had been neither furious nor interested. She had looked at him when he had passed by for a moment, and then she had turned back to her conversation.

It had been one of the hardest, most cruel moments of his life. He had known he was doing the right thing. But when she had turned away, he had felt a loss that seemed worse than any other rejection he had ever felt.

He could have had her. And he now was nothing, utterly nothing to her but a passing face that drew neither rage nor desire. He had realized that he was just another average face that people notice without noticing. He had felt dead.

That night he had masturbated with the fantasy of what could have been. He did so nearly every time he fantasized after that for years.

Clay felt like a moral fool. He felt more like a coward than a hero. He endured his choice with quiet resolve, but he could never forgive himself for walking out of that convention room for a lousy cup of coffee.

Clay was not obsessive; he did not think about Maureen during most days. But when he felt alone and ignored or pressured and unappreciated, he felt the urge to fantasize. Maureen was always there to grant him the moment he had lost.

Clay had never told his wife about his encounter with Maureen. It didn't seem to affect his relationship with Karen other than to diminish the number of times he might have initiated sex with her. The encounter was private and shameful, but it was his. No one could take it away.

During most of Clay's life he had served the will of the

greater good. He didn't do drugs; it would have killed his mother. He had joined the youth division of a club in which his father was involved. His only rebellion had been to attend a church youth group that was not part of his parents' liberal, mainline denomination. He had attended their church every Sunday. But on Sunday night, when no respectable Presbyterian would be doing anything other than watching *60 Minutes,* he had walked to a small Baptist church that had a thriving youth group. It was in the youth group that he had met Karen, and it was at a youth meeting that he had received Jesus as his Savior.

Life had changed after that. He had found new friends and a new purpose. In time he had won Karen's admiration, respect, and passion. Karen was a whiz kid. She was smart, perky, and deeply sincere. She was an all-American girl who still looked good wearing her hair in little-girl braids when she was in college.

Clay did not know it, but Karen had her secrets as well. In all their years of marriage she had never told him about the incident.

It had only occurred once, with her brother, who was six years older than she. One weekend night soon after his twelfth birthday, when their parents were at a church party, her brother had slid into bed with her and had made her touch him until her hand was wet and sticky. She had screamed and run out of the room. That night she had fallen asleep in the bathroom with the water running and the door locked. Her parents had never asked. Her brother had never said anything to her about the incident. Karen had stayed equally silent.

Karen enjoyed sex with Clay—that is, she enjoyed the touch and some of the foreplay. She usually didn't feel too frustrated that Clay couldn't stay erect for long after entering her. He felt awful. She felt guilty. She continually reassured him that she loved him, and she enjoyed feeling close to him.

One night at a party Karen had overheard Clay telling a male friend who was about to get married, "Sex is great, but it is only a small part of a good marriage. You need to give up the illusion that sex is all about romantic fireworks and scorching passion. You'll learn to enjoy each other even without it." She had felt proud of him, but something she could not put into words had tugged at her. They had a good sex life. It was in order. They had perspective about its place. And they loved each other without demanding more.

Karen felt a quiet ache that never seemed to go away. She felt something was wrong, but she couldn't give the feeling a face or a name. She just felt a haunting fear that something lingered in silence, something that might someday tear at the comfortable fabric of their lives.

Clay was diligent, faithful, but distant. He kept his secret. He could no more voice it than he could recreate the event that haunted him. Clay took life like a series of tests that he couldn't bear to fail; but he had no hope that he would pass with honors. Things seemed fine. Karen was busy with her law practice. He was moderately successful in his career. They loved the Lord. They loved their kids. And they waited for each day to end.

14

RE-ENTERING EDEN:

FINDING ONE-FLESH INTIMACY

God created marriages to bring forth a harvest of fruit. The fruit involves not only children but also changes in character, passion, and purpose. The process God instituted to create children and to bring about a change in character is sexual union. Sex changes the heart. It brings forth either a chorus of praise, wonder, and joy or a song of sorrow and harm.

Sex is not incidental to marriage. While sex was never meant to be the heart of intimacy, it is the music of marriage. And when marriage partners experience disharmony in other areas of their lives, the cacophony will inevitably crowd out the sweet trills of sexual passion.

A husband and wife either participate in the mystery of sexual union as a taste of intimacy with God, or they see it as nothing more than a momentary pleasure. And for some people the pleasure is so webbed with fear, disgust, or anger that it has lost even its sensual delight. Sex draws the heart toward either greater intimacy or a deeper sense of abuse and harm.

A HUSBAND AND WIFE EITHER PARTICIPATE IN THE MYSTERY OF SEXUAL UNION AS A TASTE OF INTIMACY WITH GOD, OR THEY SEE IT AS NOTHING MORE THAN A MOMENTARY PLEASURE.

Clay and Karen had personal histories of sin and sorrow that stole the harmony from their sexual intimacy. Even more tragic, they were unwilling to talk about their dissatisfaction. Their silence instilled greater emptiness; their emptiness propelled them to either look elsewhere or to remain busy and disengaged from their shame and anger.

Clay was haunted by his near fall into adultery. Karen was haunted by her past sexual abuse. Their histories conspired against the present; they were barriers that kept them from bringing forth a rich harvest. They were meant to enjoy more. But their refusal to risk exposing their shame for the sake of potential wholeness and joy denuded the pleasure of their intimacy. It was the silent chasm that separated Clay and Karen. The risk, however, felt more terrifying than the potential pleasure.

THE GLORY OF SENSUALITY

Deep body-and-soul intimacy with another person is rare. We all desire it. We yearn for someone to know us and then desire to know even more. We long for someone to know us beyond the perceptible to the depths of what even we do not comprehend. We want a person with whom we can be "naked," a person who will not judge us and who will find in our presence an unreserved delight.

Such a relationship was God's gift to Adam and Eve. God responded to Adam's loneliness by creating Eve. And he created her so that they would literally fit together as a unity in diversity. He meant them to be a union without loss of uniqueness. He gave them an intimacy that drew their hearts not only to each other but also to delight in and desire God more passionately.

What is God's purpose for sex? What are we to find as the joy in our sexual relationship to our spouse?

God gave us sex to arouse and satisfy a hunger for intimacy. Sexuality arouses a desire for union. Sexual consummation satisfies the desire, but it also mysteriously creates a hunger for more—not only for more sex, but also for a taste of ultimate union, the final reconciliation with God.

IT IS A GREAT MYSTERY HOW THE FLESH CREATES A DESIRE FOR THE SPIRIT.

It is a great mystery how the flesh creates a desire for the spirit. God designed pleasure. He gave us the capacity in abundance to taste, touch, smell, see, and hear. Each sense mediates both pleasure and pain. Sensuous pleasure—the smell of baking bread, the taste of Toblerone chocolate, or the touch of the soft nape of our lover's neck—tingles and tantalizes our senses. The allure beckons us to want more. And the enjoyment of more eventually leads to a moment of cessation when our desire is satiated, and for a moment we rest.

Arousal moves to desire; desire energizes the choice to engage; and intercourse leads to rest. And rest, the quintessential taste of heaven, lasts for only an instant. The moment of peace is but a mere glimpse of what lies ahead. All rest, in other words, rekindles a desire for what cannot be found in any other way or place but heaven.

WE MUST LOOK AT SEXUALITY AS AN IMPORTANT WINDOW INTO THE HEART OF GOD.

Tragically, we use sex more than any other part of God's creation to attempt to find a way to re-enter Eden. Clay resorted to sexual fantasy leading to a near affair to escape the frustrations and boredom of life. On the other hand, Karen attempted to escape from sex in order to find a way back to Eden. She struggled with the memories of past sexual abuse, and for her, sex was a re-entry into the horror of an earthly hell. She turned from fantasy and sensuality to work, busyness, and stiff accommodation to her husband's efforts to please her. This couple allowed their past pain and shame to block their enjoyment of a gift God gives for our current pleasure and our anticipation of eternity.

Consider the loss if a person is frightened or disgusted by pleasure, especially sexual pleasure. Far more is tarnished than the mere erotic. When sexual pleasure is viewed with uneasiness or contempt, husbands and wives lose not only their passion for each other but also their passion for heaven. This loss is no small matter. If God created sex for more than mere physical and relational pleasure, then we must look at sexuality as an important window into the heart of God.

God's plan is for us to pursue and know him in and through

the sexual intimacy we have with our spouses. Spiritual intimacy and delight are not opposed to sexual intimacy; spiritual intimacy is actually found in the midst of the relational, fleshly delight of reunion. A taste of the character of God is found in sexual foreplay, heightened arousal, orgasm, and quiescence. God is a God of passion. He adores joy, and he delights in our delight in glory.

Imagine God's anticipation as he waited for Adam to awaken from the birth-sleep and see the person that arose from his side. How did God feel when Adam saw Eve? Perhaps the level of Adam's delight may give an indication. "The man said, 'This is now bone of my bones and flesh of my flesh; she shall be called "woman," for she was taken out of man.' For this reason a man will leave his father and mother and be united to his wife, and they will become one flesh" (Gen. 2:23-24).

GOD'S PLAN IS FOR US TO PURSUE AND KNOW HIM IN AND THROUGH THE SEXUAL INTIMACY WE HAVE WITH OUR SPOUSES.

What a picture of passion! When Adam first sees Eve, he breaks out into song. He cannot contain his joy, and he sings an erotic hymn. This is no small point. Something deeply poetic in the heart of every man sings with a depth of passion for his beloved. The first hymn is not overtly directed to God, but it is an indirect praise to God through proclaiming the anticipated joy in erotic love. Eroticism is God's playful creation, his delight in delighting the erogenous heart of his creatures.

Adam exclaims that he and Eve may look like two persons, but they are really one. Eve, after all, was originally a part of him. She is even called by a name that indicates this essential unity.

Interestingly, the English words *man* and *woman* reflect the kind of wordplay we find in the Hebrew. In Hebrew *man* is *'ish*, while *woman* is *'ishshah*. Another pair of words could have been used—for instance, the Hebrew words for *male* and *female*. But no other words would have reflected the essential unity and union between the man and the woman. They are not two, but one.

Once again, this passage is misread if either Adam's statement or Eve's derivative creation is understood to mean that the woman is subordinate to the man. The man is not in any way better, superior, or closer to God than the woman is. Indeed, the passage could not be clearer: the man needs the woman as much as the woman needs the man.

This passage immediately establishes biblical marriage as monogamous. In other words, marriage is between two persons, not three or four or more. We need to see that the biblical ideal at the creation of the human race is one husband, one wife.

We live in a country where monogamous marriage is the law. Bigamy is punishable by fine and imprisonment, not to speak of social ostracism. But, if well-known statistics are correct, then many Americans practice serial polygamy. Many people have a bevy of "lovers" as they have affairs; many people have a succession of "spouses" as they divorce one spouse they don't quite like to couple with another and then another and then another.

The teaching of Genesis 2:23-25 is that the kind of intimacy described here can be found only in the marriage of a husband and a wife.

And what an intimacy it is! Verse 24 generalizes the first

marriage for all marriages. A woman was made from man, and it is with a man that she finds a union that she can find in no other relationship. For that reason, both a man and a woman are to leave their families and be united in an intimacy that is called one flesh. John Bettler, the head of the Christian counseling program at Westminster Theological Seminary, described this threefold progression as leaving, weaving, and cleaving.

LEAVING

Leaving is perhaps the hardest step for most couples, and it is one that leads to many problems later in married life. Both husband and wife must move away from their parents—and the past that defined who they are and what they do—in order to move toward their spouse with new freedom and openness.

Before we qualify this, recognize that this move away from parents and the past was at least as awesome a step in ancient biblical times as it is today. Parents, as a rule, were more honored in the past than they are in contemporary Western society. The verb translated "leave" is an extremely strong one; elsewhere it is translated "forsake."

LEAVING MEANS STARTING A WHOLE
NEW RELATIONSHIP IN WHICH
THE CORE LOYALTY IS NOT TO
PARENTS' PRIORITIES, TRADITIONS, OR
INFLUENCE BUT TO AN ENTIRELY NEW
FAMILY THAT MUST SET ITS OWN
COURSE, FORM, AND PURPOSE.

Of course, this does not mean that husbands and wives should cut off communication with their parents. It does not even prohibit a couple from physically moving in with one set of parents for a while under special circumstances (though this has many dangers). And it does not presume that we can easily wipe away our past and start utterly anew with our spouses.

But it does mean starting a whole new relationship in which the core loyalty is not to parents' priorities, traditions, or influence but to an entirely new family that must set its own course, form, and purpose. For example, Clay was a "good" boy. He would never have rebelled because he feared destroying his mother. His relationship with her may have kept him out of trouble, but it also may have established a dependency on a strong woman rather than allowing him to develop his own convictions about who he is and what he desires to be.

THE FAILURE TO SHIFT LOYALTY FROM PARENTS TO SPOUSE IS A CENTRAL ISSUE IN ALMOST ALL MARITAL CONFLICT.

Leaving also means being aware how the past might have shaped us both. For example, Karen lived with the struggles of past sexual abuse. Although we can never fully or legitimately cut off the past, we can begin to see and separate from the darker secrets that rule our passions. To leave means to take a step from our parents and the past in order to move closer to our spouse.

Our greatest delight cannot be in the opinions or desires of a parent but only with the one with whom we have joined to form a new family. The failure to shift loyalty from parents to spouse is a central issue in almost all marital conflict. Men and women come into marriage knowing that no one will ever love them as their parents did. When a parent fails and sins deeply against a child, it is even more damaging than if anyone else were to commit the same sin. The reason is simple: no one else reflects God to a child the way parents do. And even when parents are terrible failures, they offer a unique image of sacrifice and perseverance that will not and cannot be found in the first few insecure years of marriage.

Consequently, when misunderstanding, sin, and loneliness arise, it is highly predictable for one or both marriage partners to realign their loyalties with the old coalition—their parents. But intimacy cannot occur if other people hold equal or greater access to the hearts of husbands and wives. Leaving requires radical faith. It is a journey toward a horizon of hope from the safe harbor of our home. When storms arise, the tiller naturally swings to restore equilibrium by returning to the old port. Leaving means permanently turning from the safety of home to pursue the task of cutting out our corner in the new world. And only a radical vision of what is required and why it is required will buoy the faith of the spouses who set out on this journey—for hardship is a certainty. Leaving is the ground for establishing the kind of intimacy that weaves two separate persons into a tapestry of beauty.

WEAVING

Intimacy cannot happen unless husbands and wives jettison their original family loyalties. The husband cannot live to prove to his parents that he is successful. The wife cannot manage the household hoping finally to gain her parents' blessing through her children. But what is the intimacy that is available for those who truly leave home? The new relationship is to be like strands of silk and gold that are woven into a tapestry of enduring, delicate creation.

Weaving—the intercourse of heart and word—involves the making of stories in order to make love. Making stories is far more than sharing common experience; it is much more than being together in a moment. Making stories is being trans-formed by the moment together.

Recently, my wife and I (Dan) were counseling good friends who were about to be married. They were embroiled in a terrible fight that tore at the tenuous fabric of their new love. The woman shook with fear. Dread filled her eyes as she saw their love shrouded in rage.

As the four of us spoke together, I recalled a terrible fight Becky and I had had only two days before our wedding. The details are not important, but in the midst of my fury, I had slammed my hand down on the frigid dashboard of my old car. A thick root system of cracks spread through the plastic dashboard. My wife-to-be sat in horror and disgust. I was consumed in carnivorous shame. It was not a happy event. We owned the car for three more years, and each time we rode in it, we were reminded of our tumultuous beginning.

As our friends smoldered in heartache, I turned to Becky and said, "Does this remind you of anything?"

She smiled and said, "Green Plymouth Duster. Dashboard." We laughed.

MAKING STORIES IS BEING TRANSFORMED BY THE MOMENT TOGETHER.

Our friends at first were chagrined. We told them our tragic story, and we all laughed with tears and joy. Our friends love each other, but they had failed to join hearts in the midst of their conflict. Our story gave them hope. Our story gave us hope. It united us in the mystery of how any two sinners can join and stay joined longer than the time it takes to consummate the sexual act. Animals join for a moment, but it is solely for procreation and the relief of primitive organic urges.

Man and woman join to procreate. They consummate to quell deep stirrings of their organic beings; but far more, sexual intercourse pictures a union of stories that mark the journey of encountering God. My wife's refusal to remain disgusted and horrified shamed my shame and further opened my heart to godly sorrow. It marked our early days with the paradox of graceful wholeness in the face of shattering sin.

The "green Duster" is a woven moment that ought to have been tragic, but it was redeemed through the irony of grace. Many other moments have been far less dramatic but equally transforming. The weaving of lives is really the interpenetrating of stories that not only give us a glimpse of each other and ourselves but also offer a taste of the mystery of God's work in human relationships.

THE WEAVING OF LIVES IS REALLY
THE INTERPENETRATING OF STORIES
THAT NOT ONLY GIVE US A
GLIMPSE OF EACH OTHER
AND OURSELVES BUT ALSO OFFER A
TASTE OF THE MYSTERY OF GOD'S
WORK IN HUMAN RELATIONSHIPS.

But a warning must be sounded. We don't gain the intimacy of weaving by passively watching events unfold, as if we were sitting silently together in the same theater. Weaving requires speech, exposure, vulnerability, and honesty. It requires the wrestling of souls before spouses can experience the harmony of bodies. Clay and Karen avoided the verbalization of secrets. They kept their inner worlds private and off-limits to the other.

Clay never shared his sexual fantasies or his frustrations with his failure to satisfy Karen sexually. Karen never verbalized her disappointment in Clay or her history of past abuse.

Certainly not every event of the past or every passing sinful thought needs to be shared. But if our life stories are going to unite our hearts, we must offer to each other the private conversations of our souls.

Without shared stories that link both hearts to the pursuit of mystery, sex will be a hollow mockery of intimacy. It will be a marriage without word, a physical groping for pleasure that curses the very union on which it rests its entire pleasure. But where stories weave hearts together in a mysterious union of awe, surprise, gratitude, and joy, then sex is the crowning affirmation of mystery, the physical joining of two beings into a new being.

A husband and wife become one. Notice that this is a restoration of the original situation. The biblical picture of Eve's creation indicates that something was taken out of Adam to form Eve. The two of them together were an original unity. Husbands and wives yearn for this reunification.

It happens in marriage when a husband and wife weave their lives together. Their lives are now inextricably bound together in a single strand. Their separate activities and pursuits should always reflect the joint glory of their union: a husband ought to be more confident because his wife delights in him; a wife ought to be more secure because her husband glories in her presence. The husband and wife, then, reflect the mystery of the Trinity. They are different and yet share the same being. They are one and yet unique. Again, God's character is made known in flesh.

CLEAVING

Finally, husbands and wives are to cleave together. They become one flesh. We should not jump too quickly to the obvious sexual overtones of this phrase. As we have seen, the lives of the husband and wife are interwoven together in a single fabric. They are closer than any other human relationship, including all other kinship relationships.

But this one-flesh unity is expressed most dramatically in the act of sexual intercourse. Sexual intimacy is the culmination of the leaving and weaving process. Therefore, it is the pinnacle of intimacy that assumes true leaving and cleaving. When leaving is incomplete, weaving will be disjointed. When weaving is mere proximity and not interpenetrating of hearts, then cleaving will be stained with fear, anger, and disgust.

SEXUAL INTIMACY IS THE CULMINATION OF THE LEAVING AND WEAVING PROCESS.

Put simply, married sexuality will always be fraught with more problems, tensions, and disappointments than immorality. Why? Because more is at stake; more can go wrong when leaving and weaving is incomplete. Immorality attempts to do an end-run around the problems of relationship. And for a time, usually short, it works with fewer complications than marital sexuality. No wonder fantasies are preferred to the frustrations and inevitable incompleteness of failed leaving and inadequate weaving. Sin works for a season, but the wages of immorality are always more disastrous than the recurrent struggles of a growing and struggling marital union.

Strangers can have sex, but that act is not true intimacy. An angry or distant couple can have sex, but it is not one-flesh intimacy. The physical act happens, and a type of physical satisfaction may be experienced, but the spouses do not experience the same type of glory that is experienced when sexual intercourse is the result of a solid marriage based on leaving and weaving.

The Creation story in Genesis ends with an intriguing note that both culminates the ecstasy of the first union in the Garden and anticipates the dark turn ahead. "The man and his wife were both naked, and they felt no shame" (Gen. 2:25).

Adam and Eve stood before one another naked, and they felt no shame. They were completely vulnerable in each other's presence, and they felt no self-consciousness, no guilt, no shame.

Their state of erotic innocence is in sharp contrast to the tragedy that lies ahead when eroticism is shattered with violence, and innocence gives way to shame.

Summary for marriage: Husbands and wives long for the delight of union, for erotic nakedness, and for a heartfelt vulnerability—all without shame. We are called to put aside anything that hinders us from being one flesh. Our only option in our relationship as husbands and wives is either to enjoy union or to abuse pleasure.

QUESTIONS FOR REFLECTION AND CONVERSATION

1. Most marriages struggle with leaving the pressures and loyalties of the families in which they grew up. Where do you see the baggage of the past influencing the present?
2. What traditions and values from your childhood family have become a delightful part of your new family?
3. In what ways have you and your spouse left your families? In what ways may that leaving still be incomplete?
4. In what ways do you and your spouse weave your lives together? How can you both work on weaving your lives

together even more? Discuss times when your weaving of stories has brought you intimacy.

5. In what ways do you and your spouse experience one-flesh intimacy? What can you do to increase that intimacy? Describe times when you felt the deepest intimacy with your spouse.

6. All marriages struggle with shame and nakedness. Few couples find it easy to talk about the joys and sorrows of their sexuality. Without speaking specifically about sex, talk about what would enable you to feel less shame and more safety in talking about that area.

GLORYING IN SEXUALITY

AND SENSUALITY

Sexuality is an area of significant struggle. It is the one marriage component most influenced by factors as diverse as sexual abuse, past immorality, family influences, relational tensions, fear of performance, body image, and physical exhaustion. And add to that list the cultural issues of sexual obsession and idolatry, which contrast with the church's history of ambivalence.

Many of these struggles tore at Clay and Karen's relationship. Sexuality, whose purpose is to unite the two partners deeply, was actually driving Karen and Clay further apart. In many ways, sexuality is a barometer of the weather of a marriage relationship. When areas of spiritual and relational intimacy are lacking or troubled, then sexual intimacy as God designed it will be affected as well. Couples have not only their own histories to address but also the church's history.

ATTITUDES ABOUT SEXUALITY

Early in the history of the church a hostile attitude toward sensuality infiltrated the Christian community. Celibacy was esteemed, and sexual longings were discouraged and even punished in certain instances. The great leaders of the early church incarnated this disdain for the flesh in their writings and their lives. Origen (c. A.D. 185–c. 254) interpreted the highly sensual Song of Songs in an allegorical, spiritual manner, doing to that book the same thing he did to his body when he took a knife and castrated himself. While not many people took this radical approach to their struggles with lust, others did their best to flee the temptations of sex. Augustine (A.D. 354–430) converted from a promiscuous lifestyle and retreated from fleshly contact with the opposite sex. He equated sexuality with his pagan past and decided it was something to avoid. Jerome (c. A.D. 347–c. 420) would throw himself into thorny brambles so that the pain would overwhelm his desire for the female body. When this method failed him, it is said that he took up the study of Hebrew! Apparently that managed to distract him from sexual thoughts.

These early struggles with sensuality may strike us as odd or ancient, but they are important to us because their root cause still infects the thinking of Christians today.

Many of the first leaders of the church converted to Christianity from the pagan GrecoRoman world. In certain major strands of the secular philosophy of their day, most notably stemming from Plato, the body and the soul were severely separated. The soul was the eternal part of a human being, while the body was a prison that would be thrown away at death.

Some of Paul's language about the body, soul, and spirit was vulnerable to a misreading based on these secular philosophies. The Old Testament, which provides the background for Paul, makes it clear that human beings are whole beings and not the result of a casual and temporary connection between our body and our intangible souls. When Genesis says that we human beings are created in God's image, it means our bodies and our souls. God created us as whole beings and pronounced that our creation—including our bodies—is "good."

Plato's spirit still hovers over the church, denigrating the body and its sensual delights. We still have a sense that the body is really not very important. At times, it is a part of us that is in periodic uproar and needs to be quelled. Or equally difficult for many, their bodies struggle with dormant desire that does not respond. Most people conclude that the spirit is what really counts.

Even if we are not repulsed by the body and its desires, we are still suspicious and anxious about intimacy and physical pleasure. Our delight in sensuality is part of our emotional life, and Christians are notoriously afraid of emotions. We can be swept up in our emotions, and certainly strong sexual urges can seemingly compel us to do things we should not.

If your thinking reflects any of these hesitations, your world is about to be shaken to the core by the Bible. Certainly the Scripture does not advocate or permit an unbridled sensuality, but it encourages a delight in sensual intimacy within the bounds of marriage. Indeed, the oneness that married couples experience in the act of sexual intercourse becomes a biblical symbol for the oneness we experience in our deeply intimate relationship with God. Many problems arise in the marriage relationship due to an inability of the husband and wife to leave, weave, and climactically cleave. The failure to leave and weave often damages a healthy sexual relationship between husband and wife.

A man and a woman often enter marriage with tremendous ambivalence about sex. On the one hand, most are excited with tremendous anticipation about their wedding night. They cannot wait for the wedding ceremony to be over so that they can escape to their honeymoon and a week of uninterrupted sexual bliss. This excitement, though, is often tinged with fear and foreboding or at least nervousness. In order to experience the joys of sexual pleasure, the two must become physically, emotionally, and spiritually vulnerable to each other in ways that expose them more fully than they have been accustomed in their past relationship. The result is that couples discover that finding sexual pleasure is more elusive than they had originally thought. Often couples take years to grow comfortable with each other in terms of their sexuality. Worse still, some struggle with their sexuality throughout their whole married life.

THE ONENESS THAT MARRIED COUPLES EXPERIENCE IN THE ACT OF SEXUAL INTERCOURSE BECOMES A BIBLICAL SYMBOL FOR THE ONENESS WE EXPERIENCE IN OUR DEEPLY INTIMATE RELATIONSHIP WITH GOD.

In the case of Clay and Karen, their sex life began well. As newlyweds it was an exciting new adventure. But as time went on, the rest of life crowded in on them, and their desire, especially Karen's, began to wane. They took each other for granted. Sex was another task to be performed, not a mysterious expression of their union. As their passion slowly dissipated, Clay found himself slowly becoming vulnerable to secret fantasies and other relationships.

Both Karen and Clay refused to struggle with what sex meant to the other and with what it meant to themselves. For every couple, sex is more than sex. Not only is sex a weapon that sometimes punishes, demeans, and divides, but it also bears the baggage of the past and the fears of the future. To assume that the honeymoon pleasure will last is to deny the heavy weight that sexuality brings to every identity and every marriage.

BARRIERS TO SEX AS GOD INTENDED IT TO BE

Every couple faces three great enemies to desire, arousal, and climax: *anxiety, disgust,* and *anger. Anxiety* is often due to a fear of performance. Contrary to locker-room humor or slumber-party boasts, sexual expertise is learned over time, after repeated trial and error. It is God's intention that sexual experimentation—through trial and error—occur in a bonded marriage relationship, where inexperience and awkwardness have the safety net of covenantal commitment and love.

Disgust is often related to parental and/or church shame that has impugned the desirability and delight of sexuality. Of course, parents are right to teach their children that sex before marriage is wrong, immoral, sinful. The Bible is clear that sex is reserved for the commitment of marriage.

Nonetheless, concerned parents often communicate more than they intend in their warnings. Parents themselves are frightened for their children as they grow up in a promiscuous society that idolizes sexuality. In their worry, they spend much more time talking about the dangers and problems of sexuality than its splendor, more about its heartaches than its delights.

But parents need to set their vision higher for their children. They should not only hope and pray that their children abstain from sexual intercourse outside of marriage but also that when they do get married, they will have a biblical view of the joys of sex so that they can fully enjoy this divine gift. Parents need to teach their children the wonders and joy of their sexuality.[1]

Another factor leading to disgust is the shame related to past sexual abuse or even past immorality. The commingling of arousal and contempt (for oneself and/or for others) is a potent barrier that taints the gift of sexuality. The sexual abuse Karen experienced may have contributed to a later ambivalence about sex even within marriage. The fact that she has never talked with Clay about that abusive incident only deepens her anxieties.

A third area of blockage is *anger*. Anger arises when one or both spouses feel used. It is not uncommon for one spouse to feel as if the other wants to avoid leaving and weaving but definitely wants to enjoy the intimacy experienced through cleaving. When a person feels as if his or her body is being used and soul ignored or denigrated, then anger, subtle or obvious, will block the enjoyment of God's plan. In one sense, the sexual arena is a prime warning signal that something is awry both in the heart and in the corporate bond of the relationship. Sexual dissatisfaction is a sensitive indicator that God's plan for marriage is off track.

SEXUAL DISSATISFACTION IS A SENSITIVE INDICATOR THAT GOD'S PLAN FOR MARRIAGE IS OFF TRACK.

Today's husbands and wives enter marriage with more baggage than those who lived during the biblical period. People in ancient cultures married in their early teens, while people today get married much later in life. Think about this for a moment. God made our bodies so that they were physically ready to enjoy sex in their early teens, but now we wait for well over a decade after we are sexually mature to get married. This places tremendous sexual pressures on the young.

Once again, abstinence is the only biblical path outside of marriage. God gives his people the strength to refrain from sexual activity, no matter how strong the urge. But this does not nullify the fact that Christian men and women have entered the marriage relationship after years of associating their sexuality with feelings of guilt, prohibition, and mixed messages. This becomes another obstacle to healthy enjoyment of sex.

SEXUAL INTIMACY: THE MIRROR OF OUR RELATIONSHIP TO GOD

But the good news of the Bible is that within marriage, husbands and wives are free to struggle and grow in enjoying each other's bodies. We are invited to reach ecstatic heights of joy that may be superseded only by our delight in union with Christ.

BUT THE GOOD NEWS OF THE BIBLE
IS THAT WITHIN MARRIAGE,
HUSBANDS AND WIVES ARE FREE
TO STRUGGLE AND GROW IN
ENJOYING EACH OTHER'S BODIES.

And indeed, once again we see why our sexuality is such an apt analogy for our relationship with God. Just as we experience deep joy as we lose ourselves and merge into oneness with our spouse at the moment of sexual climax, we experience ultimate joy as we become one with Jesus Christ in a union that leads to incomprehensible joy. Marital intercourse mirrors our relationship to God and causes us to worship him for giving us this good gift.

In *The Mystery of Marriage,* a book that offers a powerful and visionary grasp of marriage, Mike Mason writes about sexuality:

> It is to experience a feeling that behaves in many ways like fear, except that it is indescribably delicious. Of all the sensations we can experience with our physical senses, surely this is the one that comes closest to the Lord's Supper in being an actual touching of the source of our being, of our Creator. . . . He made sex, we have cause to suspect, specifically so that it would be difficult for the mind of man to conceive of anything more earthy, more humiliating, or more desirable, and so to be a constant reminder to him of his true nature. But it was also to instruct him in a higher nature, and in his destiny. For in touching a person of the opposite sex in the most secret place of his or her body, with one's own most private part, there is something that reaches beyond touch, that gets behind flesh itself to the place where it connects with spirit, to the place where incarnation happens.[2]

To enjoy the fruits of our marriage, we must be prepared to leave the encumbrances of the past and embrace the present and the future with hope. Our marriages must be characterized by a growing intimacy and an experience of sensuality and delight. The Scriptures themselves encourage us in these directions.

We now turn to the biblical texts that guide us toward proper delight in the intimacy that leads to sensual delight. We include here only a sample of the texts that teach and model the wonders of leaving, weaving, and cleaving.

Leaving

The marriage relationship is an exclusive one. It requires an intense union that changes the quality of previous relationships. Husbands and wives need to hear the biblical command to leave their parents as the command to move their loyalties from their parents to their spouse. Let's look at three biblical passages that enhance the clear teaching of Genesis 2:24 to leave father and mother.

RUTH AND NAOMI. The book of Ruth gives us a powerful glimpse into a story of leaving behind one's family loyalties to embrace a new relationship. While Ruth is not leaving her own family to weave and cleave with her husband, Ruth's words demonstrate the selfless devotion spouses should give to each other.

Ruth was the daughter-in-law of Naomi, whose husband, Elimelech, had taken his family from Israel to Moab to find relief from a famine. When Naomi's husband and two sons died, she decided to return to Israel to be close to relatives. She encouraged her two daughters-in-law to stay with their families in Moab. While the one daughter-in-law chose to stay, Ruth moved her loyalties from herchildhood family to the family of her dead husband.

Ruth gave voice to her intent to leave her native land and weave her life with Naomi's.

> But Ruth replied, "Don't urge me to leave you or to turn
> back from you. Where you go I will go, and where you stay
> I will stay. Your people will be my people and your God my
> God. Where you die I will die, and there I will be buried.
> May the Lord deal with me, be it ever so severely, if anything
> but death separates you and me." When Naomi realized that
> Ruth was determined to go with her, she stopped urging her.
> RUTH 1:16-18

Ruth wholeheartedly commits not only to leaving her family but also to leaving her country and even her god in order to embrace Naomi, Israel, and the God of Israel. This transference of basic loyalty from her childhood family to the nucleus of a new family is utterly crucial to a healthy marriage, and that is why Ruth's words are so appropriately spoken during a marriage ceremony.

THIS TRANSFERENCE OF BASIC LOYALTY FROM THE CHILDHOOD FAMILY TO THE NUCLEUS OF A NEW FAMILY IS UTTERLY CRUCIAL TO A HEALTHY MARRIAGE.

It should be clear when these words are read in the shadow of Genesis 2:23-25 that this is a mutual not a unilateral commitment. Leaving the childhood family is not something that the wife alone or the husband alone agrees to do. Both the man and the woman agree before God that their marriage relationship is now the most important human relationship in their lives.

Ideally, couples should talk to their parents about this. Wise and loving parents will be supportive and not suffocate their child's marriage relationship. Short of complete neglect or evidence of abuse, parents should learn to keep their distance. The best relationship is usually one in which the parents of the bride and the groom show themselves ready to help, to give advice, to support—with no strings attached. Paradoxically, the parents who give their children the room to "leave" are the ones that enjoy the healthiest relationships with their married children.

Ruth's words, though spoken to an older woman and not to her spouse, are a wonderful expression of the transference of loyalty from the original family to the new family.

THE KING AND HIS BRIDE.   Psalm 45, which we examined in chapter 3, is a wedding song. It is interesting that the first advice the poet gives the bride reflects the command in Genesis 2. "Listen, O daughter, consider and give ear: Forget your people and your father's house. The king is enthralled by your beauty; honor him, for he is your lord. The Daughter of Tyre will come with a gift, men of wealth will seek your favor" (Ps. 45:10-12).

He tells her to forget her people and her father's house. This advice seems harsh. It sounds as if he is telling her to disregard her parents, who raised her and sacrificed for her. What he is telling her, however, is crucial to a healthy marriage. She needs to break her primary loyalties to her parents in order to turn them over to her new husband. When she makes decisions about her life and actions, she is not to ask herself how her father or mother would react but how her husband would react. How do her actions affect her husband's life?

Her sacrifice is motivated by her husband's love for her. He is enthralled by her beauty; he is deeply in love with her. She is to reciprocate his love with her own, which is permeated by deep respect for him.

Further, as she moves from the role of daughter to the role of wife, she receives great reward, including newfound respect. Verse 12 indicates that she will be the recipient of gifts and will be the focus of the attention of important people.

Why does this psalm treat the woman's responsibility to leave her childhood family more explicitly than the man's responsibility? Many scholars find indications within the psalm that the bride is of foreign origin. Her potential for homesickness was thus much higher than the groom's. But this psalm may be expressing a gender issue as well. Women often, though certainly not always, have a greater difficulty leaving their parents than men do.

Lest we find this strange, we must remember that the Genesis command to leave is specifically addressed to the man.

Perhaps it is best to consider Psalm 45:10 the female complement to the Genesis command.

However, even within the psalm itself we see hints that the king also is shifting loyalties. The king no longer looks to the past, to his father, but to the future, to the sons that he will create with his new wife (Ps. 45:16).

A PASSIONATE LOVE SONG.   The Song of Songs is a poem of the most passionate love. People misunderstand it when they transport the language too quickly into the divine sphere. First and foremost, it is the language of desire between two human lovers—the woman, whose voice dominates the book, and her husband. They desire each other more than they desire any other human being. Whereas after the Fall, Adam and Eve stood in front of one another and felt shame, in the Song of Songs the unnamed husband and wife stand in the garden and revel in the other's naked body.

IT IS DAMAGING TO THE EXTREME
TO ALLOW THE IMPORTANT
THEOLOGICAL TEACHING OF THE SONG
TO OBSCURE THE EQUALLY IMPORTANT
MESSAGE OF EROTIC LOVE.

While the book has a powerful divine dimension, which we will explore later in the epilogue, it is damaging to the extreme to allow the important theological teaching of the Song to obscure the equally important message of erotic love. When we speak of topics like marriage, sensuality, and lovemaking in the Bible, the Song of Songs becomes the center of our discussion.[3]

Let's look at three poems that call the beloved to leave in order to weave and finally to cleave.

The first poem begins the book. The woman gets right to the point. She desires the passionate embrace of her husband, her king. Her invitation is accompanied by references to the senses. She desires his touch, which she values above the delightful taste of wine. His scent draws her to him. All her senses are attuned to him, and she desires to be totally absorbed.

> Let him kiss me with the kisses of his mouth—for your love is more delightful than wine. Pleasing is the fragrance of your perfumes; your name is like perfume poured out. No wonder the maidens love you! Take me away with you—let us hurry! Let the king bring me into his chambers. SONG OF SONGS 1:2-4.

But this union requires their separation. She calls on him to come to her and take her away. They need to leave their present setting to seek the seclusion of the king's bedroom.

The second poem also comes from the woman's point of view. She is in her home, apparently gazing out of her window toward the hills in the distance. We can feel her excitement as she spots her lover coming toward her with the intention of taking her away. His virility is captured by the comparison to a gazelle or a young stag.

Her husband approaches her and entices her to enjoy the winter thaw with him. The warm spring season, with its flowers and blossoming vines, has arrived. He wants her to come away with him to enjoy the smells, sights, and sounds of the garden, which throughout the Song is the place of passionate lovemaking. She must leave the house in order to enjoy the delights of her husband.

> Listen! My lover! Look! Here he comes, leaping across the mountains, bounding over the hills. My lover is like a gazelle or a young stag. Look! There he stands behind our wall, gazing through the windows, peering through the lattice.

My lover spoke and said to me, "Arise, my darling, my beautiful one, and come with me. See! The winter is past; the rains are over and gone. Flowers appear on the earth; the season of singing has come, the cooing of doves is heard in our land. The fig tree forms its early fruit; the blossoming vines spread their fragrance. Arise, come, my darling; my beautiful one, come with me." SONG OF SONGS 2:8-13

The third poem appears in the midst of the lengthy song that describes the woman's body in erotic terms and that is a prelude to lovemaking. In the midst of this enticing description, he calls on her to go away with him, to leave her present setting and be with him.

Come with me from Lebanon, my bride, come with me from Lebanon. Descend from the crest of Amana, from the top of Senir, the summit of Hermon, from the lions' dens and the mountain haunts of the leopards. SONG OF SONGS 4:8

The language, as is typical of the Song, is metaphorical. She is not in Lebanon literally. It would be physically impossible for her to be on top of the three mountains—Amana, Senir, and Hermon—at the same time. She is not literally in a cave with lions or leopards. These are symbols of her present location, places of grandeur but of some danger.

The king calls her from these harsh places into the beauty of the garden, where they can enjoy each other's God-given beauty. They can revel in the divine gift of sexual love. They can leave, in order to weave and cleave.

Weaving
The command to leave is clear. It is the first step to intimacy in marriage. But it is crucial that the bride and groom take the next step: They leave in order to weave. The diminishing of

old relationships has as its purpose the heightening of the new. The following passages describe the quality and intensity of weaving.

A LOVE THAT KNITS US TOGETHER.   One of the New Testament's most profound expressions of love is found in 1 Corinthians 13. This "love chapter" is often quoted in wedding ceremonies. While Paul was not thinking about marriage when he wrote these powerful words to the church at Corinth, we can see their usefulness to the marriage relationship.

In the chapter Paul describes what forces will build or destroy love. Paul's understanding of love works against everything within us. We often find ourselves valuing a relationship for what it provides us. We say that love is wonderful because it makes us feel good; it fulfills our needs. When love is not returned or is somehow disappointed, we say that love hurts.

THE ROUTE TO INTIMACY
IS A PARADOX: WE MUST CARE
LESS ABOUT OURSELVES
THAN WE DO ABOUT OUR SPOUSE.

The love that Paul describes is a love that lives to glorify the other. The route to intimacy is a paradox: We must care less about ourselves than we do about our spouse. If we enter a relationship to find someone who will labor for our glory, then we will violate and drain that person's capacity to offer life. But when we offer love, we open the heart to taste the rich purpose and joy of honoring another.

But the Curse is real, and the prospect of that kind of love is remote. We are caught by Paul's words. We want what he requires our spouse to offer us, but we are realistic enough to admit that we can seldom return the same love to our spouse.

Paul invites us to look at the heights of love under three headings: love is preeminent, love prizes, and love persists.

WEAVING: LOVE IS PREEMINENT

> And now I will show you the most excellent way.
>
> If I speak in the tongues of men and of angels, but have not love, I am only a resounding gong or a clanging cymbal. If I have the gift of prophecy and can fathom all mysteries and all knowledge, and if I have a faith that can move mountains, but have not love, I am nothing. If I give all I possess to the poor and surrender my body to the flames, but have not love, I gain nothing. 1 CORINTHIANS 12:31–13:3

The mind boggles at Paul's assertion: Love is more important than anything else in the world! Our piety might respond, "No, faith in God is more important." Paul responds by saying, in effect, "Faith without love is dead." Paul is saying that we must evaluate our heart toward God by the measure of how we love one another. They are not only inseparable, but even more radical, love for each other is the avenue for growing in love for God. To claim we love God and then to be indifferent, disconnected from others, is to live a lie.

Our skepticism might respond, "How romantic and mushy." But remember that here Paul is talking about love as the essence, the core purpose of life, not as an occasional emotional thrill.

If faith and the spiritual gifts are nothing without love, certainly marriage that exists for any purpose other than love is a charade. We are not merely to love one another; we are to live to let love grow, facing where it is threadbare and sometimes utterly absent. We cannot live to love unless we are willing to struggle with how far we are from the "Royal Law of Love."

What is the character of this intimacy that Paul describes? Since love is a heart that moves, we are not surprised to see that the apostle describes it by using a series of verbs. These verbs inform us that love moves away from the self and toward the other.

> Love is patient, love is kind. It does not envy, it does not
> boast, it is not proud. It is not rude, it is not self-seeking,
> it is not easily angered, it keeps no record of wrongs.
> Love does not delight in evil but rejoices with the truth.
> It always protects, always trusts, always hopes, always
> perseveres. 1 CORINTHIANS 13:4-7

The first two characteristics of intimate love are a complementary pair. Love is patient and kind. Patience is perhaps the most difficult of all. It calls us to move toward our spouse by not moving at all. It insists that we wait on our spouse.

Our natural tendency is to jump in with both feet. We want a problem corrected immediately. We want to remove annoyance in a second. Patience is a gift that says: "I will trust that God is up to something; I will not insist, demand, or expedite change. I will wait."

If patience is trust in God's good plan, then kindness is a taste of that plan, which can be seen in the Cross. Kindness is the gift of mercy. It seeks to transform our spouses by offering them what is undeserved and unexpected. A kindness can be as simple as a massage at the end of a hard day or a smile. Kindness shows understanding.

But kindness may ask for even bigger sacrifices. A husband who works obsessively to make ends meet may need to take two weeks off to vacation with his wife, while his wife may need to understand that his work is not purely selfish but indeed necessary for the good of the family or community.

Patience and kindness work hand in hand to produce a deep and abiding marital love. They allow the relationship to show what it means to trust God (patience) and what it means to know God is good (kindness).

By highlighting the traits of patience and kindness, Paul signals the key to intimate love: it cares more about the other than it does for the self. This rings true as Paul continues his commentary by telling us what love is not.

First, intimate love is not boastful. A boast is a claim to preeminence. Love does not magnify the self or belittle the other. Love lifts up the other person first.

Closely connected to boasting is pride. Pride is at the root of boasting. We demonstrate pride when we think that we are better than anyone else. Pride will kill a marriage. The assumption that my time, my pressures, my pain are more important than my spouse's needs will put our marriage in a stranglehold that will choke love.

The third trait that mars love is rudeness. Clay's day started badly because Karen treated him rudely, taking him for granted. Taking each other for granted is a major trap in marriage. To be rude is to demand with an implied or direct threat that the relationship will be tarnished if certain things are not done as we desire. We face the daily temptation to come to each other at the end of a day and plop into a chair, pick up the paper, and tune out. Rudeness is dishonoring; love cherishes the honor to enhance, not intimidate or punish.

Love also is not self-seeking. As Paul says elsewhere, "Consider others better than yourselves. Each of you should look not only to your own interests, but also to the interests of others" (Phil. 2:3-4).

Self-seeking attitudes often appear in our sexual relationship to our spouses. Many people, particularly men, enter into marriage thinking that they have come to the end of their sexual frustrations. They think, "Finally, I can have sex legally and morally anytime I want it!" Such an attitude is (and should be) quickly disappointed.

People rarely sustain the same level of sexual desire as their spouses. This imbalance can lead to considerable friction in a marriage.

Various factors can enter here. A husband may not want to satisfy his wife sexually because he is annoyed that she challenged one of his ideas at dinner. A wife may have no interest in playing around in bed; she prefers to sleep after dealing with a hectic day of appointments.

LOVE WILL LEAD US TO CARE MORE ABOUT OUR SPOUSES' NEEDS THAN ABOUT OUR OWN NEEDS.

Paul suggests that love will lead us to care more about our spouses' needs than about our own needs. Insisting on sex in spite of the exhaustion of your wife rarely leads to satisfaction. On the other side, a rejected husband may make it difficult for his wife to sleep! Seeking the other's good may not result in immediate rest and great sex, but as both husband and wife seek the good of the other, they will find that their hearts are knit together in need of Christ and in appreciation of one another.

The final trait that will prevent husbands and wives from weaving is anger. Two people who desire to be intimate must not be easily angered. Paul urges us to be tolerant toward one another. The two who are joined into one still retain their individual idiosyncrasies. We all know the stereotypical annoyances: cap off the toothpaste tube, toilet seats left up, socks on the floor. We think these are humorous—until we are married and the wife sits on the toilet in the dark for the first time.

Once again Paul concretizes the principle that we are to seek the good of the other, not ourselves. Why do people get angry? People get angry when they feel that their rights, their needs are not met. Anger is not always wrong, but a truly intimate married love should not be characterized by anger.

Many spouses think they are not angry people. They can take irritation after irritation with civility. But inside they seethe. Mentally they tabulate everything their spouse has done to wrong them. "She interrupted me three weeks ago while I was speaking." "He ignored me when I needed to talk to him."

We think we are not easily angered, but when that final or major breach in relationship comes, then the dam bursts, and a torrent of offenses flows in accusation. A manageable disagreement becomes a major blowup that takes hours or weeks to unravel and resolve.

However, love keeps no record of wrongs. They are brought to the surface, dealt with, and then canceled. To do otherwise is to deny the gospel, court relational disaster, and break the bonds of intimacy that lead to sensual delight.

Paul is not yet finished with his wise description of love. He continues with the observation that love does not delight in evil but rejoices in truth. Why would we rejoice in the evil of our spouses? In our warped thinking we sometimes believe that our spouses' sin justifies our failures toward them. And once we are off the hook, then it is up to our spouses to change.

Love always protects, trusts, hopes, and perseveres. Paul concludes his rich and profound description of love with four final verbs, the first and last of which urge us to constructive action, while the middle two urge a positive state of mind.

Love protects from harm. This protection on occasion may take the form of jealousy, but at core it is a willingness to bear pain on behalf of the other, to stand in the breach, knowing wounds will come.

Love perseveres. Not far into marriage most couples realize that the world is not easy, and their marriage is made up of two sinners. Married love needs to be a bold love right from the beginning.

As a result, love both trusts and hopes. To trust and to hope is not to be naïve. It is to believe that even in deceit and betrayal, God's Spirit is at work, convicting and conforming both spouses to a maturity that cannot be achieved without suffering and brokenness.

MARRIED LOVE NEEDS TO BE A BOLD LOVE RIGHT FROM THE BEGINNING.

In the words of Gordon Fee, these four verbs teach us that "love has a tenacity in the present, buoyed by its absolute confidence in the future, that enables it to live in every kind of circumstance and continually to pour itself out in behalf of others."[4]

WEAVING: LOVE PERSISTS AND NEVER FAILS

Love never fails. But where there are prophecies, they will cease; where there are tongues, they will be stilled; where there is knowledge, it will pass away. For we know in part and we prophesy in part, but when perfection comes, the imperfect disappears. When I was a child, I talked like a child, I thought like a child, I reasoned like a child. When I became a man, I put childish ways behind me. Now we see but a poor reflection as in a mirror; then we shall see face to face. Now I know in part; then I shall know fully, even as I am fully known.

And now these three remain: faith, hope and love. But the greatest of these is love. 1 CORINTHIANS 13:8-13

True love never dies.

Paul is a realist. We have already seen that he knows love will encounter obstacle after obstacle. But he can still affirm the imperishability of love.

What would Paul say to the countless couples who "fall out of love"? He would say they never loved each other in the first place. Perhaps they were infatuated with each other, but they were not really in love. Love is more than a feeling; it is a tenacious, courageous commitment. It is the courage to remain faithful when the cost seems greater than the reward. Love waits with hope for redemption even in the midst of the darkness of despair.

Paul has composed a beautiful and powerful statement about the wonders of Christian love. He presents a picture of a deep, compassionate, self-giving, other-affirming, never-failing love. Are any of us capable of giving this kind of love?

No. Not one of us is capable of loving in this way.

But Paul could still present this picture of love to us with a straight face because of Jesus Christ. Jesus is the one who incarnates this love perfectly. He loves us in this wonderful way. His example, his death, and his resurrection allow us, even us, to become one with him, to have a glimpse of this love in our relationships.

A LOVE THAT ENDURES. The Song of Songs paints a picture of a love that endures. Toward the conclusion of the Song the wife utters the most passionate words of love and commitment toward her husband. She in essence vows to him her undying love. She gives herself to him with utter abandon. "Place me like a seal over your heart, like a seal on your arm; for love is as strong as death, its jealousy unyielding as the grave. It burns like blazing fire, like a mighty flame. Many waters cannot quench love; rivers cannot wash it away" (Song of Songs 8:6-7).

Many Christians are afraid of strong emotions. They argue that emotions are irrational and can lead us astray. While some truth and reason for caution may be found in this observation, it can also lead to a lack of passion that stifles rather than frees true love. Love is more than a decision; it is more than a choice to commit. It is a yearning, a desire to be with someone, to merge two lives into one.

As the wife unreservedly commits herself to her husband, she first of all asks him to put her seal on his heart and his arm. In the Old Testament world a seal was like a signature. It was either a cylinder that would be rolled on a soft clay writing tablet or a stamp impressed on clay or papyrus with the effect of demonstrating ownership of something. The wife was saying, "You belong to me. You are mine alone."

We must be careful not to read too much into this simile. We rightly recoil at any idea that one individual owns another person in the sense that they can use or abuse that person for selfish purposes. By this time in the Song, we know that this kind of selfish thinking is far from the woman's mind. This love is a mutual love, which seeks the best for the other person. It is a mutual love, where the weaving of two lives issues in the repeated refrain: "My lover is mine and I am his" (Song of Songs 2:16; 6:3; 7:10).

The wife makes her claim on her husband because her desire for him is so strong. She compares her love for him to the seemingly unconquerable force of death. Although death seems to be the final foe, the woman knows better. She knows of a force that is death's equal, a force that can stare into the face of death and not flinch: her love for her husband.

She then describes the heat of her passion by comparing it to an intensely burning fire. This image for intense love speaks across the ages and culture. It is a hot passion that not even a deluge of water can put out. She loves her husband, and nothing can stand in the way of their love.

Cleaving

Even the metaphor of weaving is not strong enough to describe the intensity of the relationship between a husband and a wife. Genesis 2 describes marriage as a relationship in which two individuals cleave into one. The passion of sexual intercourse melds two bodies, souls, and minds into one and represents the climax of union. The Bible, particularly the Song of Songs, celebrates intercourse in beautiful, passionate, and vivid language.

The imagery is alien to us, but it is clear that we are reading the language of love. The man looks at his wife and cannot contain himself. He must tell her how beautiful she is.

Lover
How beautiful you are, my darling!
Oh, how beautiful!
Your eyes behind your veil are doves.
Your hair is like a flock of goats descending from Mount
    Gilead.
Your teeth are like a flock of sheep just shorn, coming up from
    the washing.
Each has its twin; not one of them is alone.
Your lips are like a scarlet ribbon; your mouth is lovely.
Your temples behind your veil are like the halves of a
    pomegranate.
Your neck is like the tower of David, built with elegance;
on it hang a thousand shields, all of them shields of warriors.
Your two breasts are like two fawns, like twin fawns of a
    gazelle that browse among the lilies.
Until the day breaks and the shadows flee,
I will go to the mountain of myrrh and to the hill of
    incense.
All beautiful you are, my darling; there is no flaw in you.
Come with me from Lebanon, my bride, come with me from
    Lebanon.
Descend from the crest of Amana, from the top of Senir, the
    summit of Hermon, from the lions' dens and the mountain
    haunts of the leopards.

*You have stolen my heart, my sister, my bride; you have stolen
my heart with one glance of your eyes, with one jewel of
your necklace.*
How delightful is your love, my sister, my bride!
*How much more pleasing is your love than wine, and the
fragrance of your perfume than any spice!*
*Your lips drop sweetness as the honeycomb, my bride; milk
and honey are under your tongue.*
The fragrance of your garments is like that of Lebanon.
*You are a garden locked up, my sister, my bride; you are a
spring enclosed, a sealed fountain.*
*Your plants are an orchard of pomegranates with choice
fruits, with henna and nard, nard and saffron, calamus
and cinnamon, with every kind of incense tree, with
myrrh and aloes and all the finest spices.*
*You are a garden fountain, a well of flowing water streaming
down from Lebanon.* SONG OF SONGS 4:1-15

The husband in the Song sings of his wife's beauty in images
that are both engaging and tender. He looks at his wife and he
describes her attractiveness from the head down: her eyes, her
hair, her teeth, her lips, her cheeks, her neck, her breasts, and
her pubic mound are all ravishing.

This intimate talk is a prelude to physical intimacy, to a
delicious cleaving. He requests entrance into her garden of
desires, and she invites him in. The chorus celebrates the ecstasy
of their union.

Beloved
Awake, north wind, and come, south wind!
*Blow on my garden, that its fragrance may spread
abroad.*
*Let my lover come into his garden and taste its choice
fruits.*

Lover
I have come into my garden, my sister, my bride;
I have gathered my myrrh with my spice.
I have eaten my honeycomb and my honey;
I have drunk my wine and my milk.

Friends
Eat, O friends, and drink; drink your fill, O lovers. SONG OF
SONGS 4:16–5:1

The husband and wife in this love song are not afraid to express their intense emotions. They model intimate passion.

Many men today can barely say "I love you," and they find it risky to express love and admiration to their spouses. After all, such openness might be greeted with detachment. Many men have distanced themselves to avoid the pain of disappointment. But in seeking to avoid pain in this way, men close themselves off from the joy of intimacy.

WE ARE TO RECLAIM THE PLEASURE
OF OUR BODIES AS MUCH AS
WE ARE TO RECLAIM THE PURITY
OF OUR SOULS.

The wife evokes other senses in her husband. Her fragrance is of the most exquisite perfume. Her lips taste of honey. She is soft to the touch. It is astonishing to fathom the sensual pleasure God intends for us to experience. The sight, smell, touch, and taste of pleasure are to invigorate our senses and draw our hearts to shout with gratitude and praise to God. No wonder Satan works to taint sensuality and sexuality and make it seem dirty and dangerous. We are to reclaim the pleasure of our bodies as much as we are to reclaim the purity of our souls.

The role of the woman throughout the Song is truly astounding, especially in the light of its ancient origins. It is the woman, not the man, who is the dominant voice throughout the poems that make up the Song. She is the one who seeks, pursues, and initiates. Here she boldly exclaims her physical attraction to her husband.

> *My lover is radiant and ruddy, outstanding among ten*
> *thousand.*
> *His head is purest gold; his hair is wavy and black as a*
> *raven.*
> *His eyes are like doves by the water streams, washed in milk,*
> *mounted like jewels.*
> *His cheeks are like beds of spice yielding perfume.*
> *His lips are like lilies dripping with myrrh.*
> *His arms are rods of gold set with chrysolite.*
> *His body is like polished ivory decorated with sapphires.*
> *His legs are pillars of marble set on bases of pure gold.*
> *His appearance is like Lebanon, choice as its cedars.*
> *His mouth is sweetness itself; he is altogether lovely.*
> *This is my lover, this my friend, O daughters of Jerusalem.*
> SONG OF SONGS 5:10-16

Many women, particularly Christian women, feel it is their place to receive and respond rather than to give and to instigate arousal. They feel more comfortable as the object of male desire than as the one who longs to be filled.

Some women lose their power of seduction and sexual playfulness in marriage because they misunderstand Christian morality, are exhausted by their daily work, or they simply fall into a routine. If their husbands did not pursue them, they would numbly continue to sustain their boring asexual lifestyle. Their husband's pursuit, frequently tinged with anger and selfishness, often leads to conflict, not mutual satisfaction.

The woman in the Song is a reminder to Christian women that an aggressive sexuality goes hand in hand with a healthy marital relationship. The woman in this poem of love simply drools over her husband's physical beauty. She considers him the most handsome man around.

THE WOMAN IN THE SONG IS A REMINDER TO CHRISTIAN WOMEN THAT AN AGGRESSIVE SEXUALITY GOES HAND IN HAND WITH A HEALTHY MARITAL RELATIONSHIP.

She begins her song by describing the striking splendor of his head and face. After commenting on his strong arms, she then describes a part of his body as polished ivory. Most English translations hesitate in this verse. The Hebrew is quite erotic, and most translators cannot bring themselves to bring out the obvious meaning. The smooth and expensively ornamented tusk of ivory is a loving description of her husband's erect penis. After all, this again is a prelude to their lovemaking. There is no shy, shamed, mechanical movement under the sheets. Rather, the two stand before each other, aroused, feeling no shame, but only joy in each other's sexuality.

Lover
Your stature is like that of the palm, and your breasts like clusters of fruit. I said, "I will climb the palm tree; I will

*take hold of its fruit." May your breasts be like the clusters
of the vine, the fragrance of your breath like apples, and
your mouth like the best wine.*

Beloved
*May the wine go straight to my lover, flowing gently over lips
and teeth. I belong to my lover, and his desire is for me.*
SONG OF SONGS 7:7-10

The man speaks first. He describes his wife's beauty, but this
time with a focus.

Using the power of the imagination, he likens his wife to a
palm tree. The object of his attention is on the heavy fruit of
the tree, which hangs above him, inviting him to slide his body
up its narrow trunk so he can fondle the fruit and suck its sweet
juice. The very aroma of her breath invites him to come closer.
He suspects that if he kisses her deeply, he will taste wine. Her
presence intoxicates him.

MARRIED SEXUAL EXPRESSION
IS A PARADIGM OF GOD'S INTIMACY
WITH HIS PEOPLE.

His wife responds by inviting her husband to share the wine
that is in her mouth. The poem ends with her ecstatic procla-
mation of their mutual intimate love.

It may be obvious given these erotic texts, but God loves sex.
Married sexual expression is a paradigm of his intimacy with
his people. And the pleasure of arousal and climax are pictures
of what God desires for his people not only in marriage but
also in worship and praise of him.

It should not be surprising, then, that Satan desires to

distort the rich wonder of God's design for married sexual passion through abuse, immorality, disgust, boredom, anger, and fear.

A marriage that grows in leaving, weaving, and cleaving that be able to handle the demands of such a glorious experience. Only husbands and wives who grasp what sex brings to love and what kind of love can bear the weight of sex will grow in their pleasure as well as their intimacy.

QUESTIONS FOR REFLECTION AND CONVERSATION
1. Reflect on your sexual relationship with your spouse throughout your marriage and at the present moment. In what ways are you satisfied? In what ways could your sexual relationship improve?
2. After achieving a level of safety in discussing sex with your spouse, discuss what you see as the strengths and weaknesses of your present sexual relationship. Discuss your perspectives in a nonthreatening, nonaccusatory manner.
3. Do you find sex beautiful? Explain your response.
4. Are you confused about sexuality? What factors in the past and the present may be involved in your current feelings?
5. Is the level of your sexual intimacy with your spouse improving as time goes on?
6. How did your parents view sex as you were growing up? How do your peers view sex? What was your level of sexual activity before you were married? How do you think these factors influence your sexual views and behavior today?
7. Do you enjoy your marriage partner? Do you enjoy his or her presence and conversation? Do you have many intimate (though nonsexual) conversations? What makes a conversation intimate for you?

8. Discuss with your spouse what you can do to explore your sexual relationship. Take turns sharing ideas. Be careful not to force conversation or behavior.

9. How can you help your spouse experience a deeper and more secure sexual life?

10. In what areas do you need the most help? Where will you look for that help? How can you and your spouse experience God's best for your intimate relationship?

16

CLAY AND KAREN BECOME INTIMATE ALLIES IN THEIR SEXUAL ONENESS

Clay felt a twinge of nervousness as he pulled out of the driveway that morning. He wasn't used to this. He prided himself on being a private man, not wearing his emotions or his problems on his shirtsleeves. He knew that it was stylish to be a sensitive man in the nineties, but it seemed like nothing more than media hype to him. Maybe it was better to keep all his emotions to himself; it was certainly much less messy that way.

Sure, he was outgoing—after all, he worked in sales. But that was different. Being an extrovert with business contacts was no problem as long as he didn't have to share what was going on inside of him. Not that he had major problems. He didn't. But ever since he had married Karen five years ago, it seemed that he couldn't keep the little problems so small any more.

Not that Karen was the problem. He loved her and was very happy to have married her. But he felt a distance between them, and it was growing more troublesome. What else should they expect? They were in their late twenties; they were both independent and unfamiliar with pain. They had tried for years to have children, and the growing specter of infertility was a problem their competence, education, and faith could not resolve.

Karen was a high-powered young lawyer who earned more money than he did. But that wasn't the problem. Just the opposite! Her income allowed them to do some pretty fabulous things, like that long weekend in Paris.

He smiled at the memory as he pulled onto the ramp to get on the highway.

But the problems were there. They were not huge, just there. Karen had suggested that he might find participating in a small group helpful. She was already part of one and found it benefited her a lot.

At the time, Clay resented the suggestion. He didn't like the thought that Karen wanted him to meet with more "mature" men. She hadn't said it, but he knew that it was the really "together" men who did this. After all, who else would get up so early to meet at a Bible study before work? That's just what he wanted to do—meet with some spiritual "giants" at 6:30 in the morning.

But he decided to do it. He met once a week with five men just to talk about how life was going. He figured that if the group was a bust, he could always drop out.

Surprisingly, these guys weren't so spiritual after all. They were dealing with a lot of the issues that he was, even more. He found himself opening up to them, telling them things he thought he never would, about himself, about Karen, and about their relationship.

Once again, he thought about how unusual this was for him. His parents weren't real talkers. For the most part, they were great. They were always there when he needed them, but he didn't always need them. So what if they were a little distant? That whole generation of parents was a little distant compared to today's "overinvolved" parents.

His mother always had the house clean, even if she had to stay up late at night, exhausted, to have it clean. And her food was always ready on time. The good old days, when wives could stay at home.

It seemed to him that the pendulum always swung too far one way or the other. If his parents' generation could be criticized as closed and private, his generation, the boomer generation, was too open and vulnerable.

Clay turned off the highway.

He decided he should go over what he was going to say to the group that morning. Once again, a wave of nervousness came over him. It was his turn to be "spotlighted." That is, while each of the men shared something each week, one person was assigned an extended time of sharing. Clay's topic for the spotlight was the specific issues that kept him from loving his wife well.

Clay wasn't about to tell them everything. He would tell them some of the struggles of his relationship, but not about the masturbation. He would not give up Maureen. And he wasn't going to say anything about his occasional worries that Karen was asexual. When he and Karen had sex, she seemed to enjoy it; occasionally she even had an orgasm. But maybe she was faking it. If so, she was a pretty good actress. He had read a magazine article about people who weren't hetero- or homosexual, just asexual. They cared little about sex.

But those thoughts came at the worse moments, when they had gone more than a couple of weeks without sex. He had read in another magazine how the average couple had sex at least twice a week. When he and Karen didn't have frequent sex, the pressure was just too great; he just needed some kind of harmless release.

But he then harbored some resentment toward Karen. Why didn't she want to get intimate with him? Was the problem with him or with her?

No, I'm not ready to get into all those issues with the group, he thought as he pulled into the parking garage. But he would ask for prayer that he could be more understanding of Karen. He really did love her, and he knew that she really loved him.

As he walked into the room and saw that Ken, Roger, and Trent were already there, his stomach went tight again. Yes, today was his day to share.

The sharing was about to bring about changes that he would never fully fathom. Even though he had not planned to share about the masturbation, he shared that he was feeling less and less desire for his wife. He shared that Karen seemed equally uninterested, but they were happy, and things were really fine.

One of the older men spoke with gentle directness: "Clay, it is not my desire to get you to share more than you want to share. And it is equally wrong for me to assume my experience with these issues is similar to yours. But when my wife and I struggle with the same issues, I am to some degree distant from her in my own secret fantasies and masturbation." The room grew somber and silent. Clay sat in the room and could feel his heart beat so hard that he feared the pounding would give him away.

Finally Clay spoke. "Yes. I own a fantasy that I don't want to tell. But I also don't want to live with it." He sank in his chair. He waited for the first blow; the first assault of patronizing self-righteousness. It did not come. Instead, the men remained deeply engaged but silent.

The older man finally broke the silence: "Clay, you assume

you are alone. You are not. You also probably assume that your shame and your angry expectation that we will judge you will keep us from waiting. It won't. We will stay with you until you decide what direction you want to choose."

That day Clay chose life. He did not share everything. But he decided not to accept a life of deceit, secret shame, and the arrogant possession of the power of fantasy. He opened up. He was invited to think about what his marriage, including their sexual relationship, might become if he was not distant, if he spoke with freedom and honesty. Clay began to think about what might be involved in his wife's reluctance to speak directly and passionately about her desires in the marriage, even though professionally she was articulate, confident, and passionate.

Clay went out of that small-group meeting a changed man. He began to talk with Karen about what he was learning. In time, their conversations unearthed the night Karen's brother had abused her sexually. They also talked about the ways Clay was influenced by his childhood home, which could not bear failure and which had no concept of grace. Clay and Karen talked about the ways they stole intimacy from each other. For the first time, they felt free to be together in pain and in passion and in pleasure.

FOURTEEN MONTHS LATER. Karen looked at her watch. It was 7:36. She set the timer to about a minute and a half and turned on the microwave oven. Sesame beef was Clay's favorite.

Clay had just called her on his cellular phone. He told her he was only a few miles away, coming from the mall where he had picked up a little gift for her. He was so thoughtful these days.

They had been married for more than six years now, but the last few months had been the best by far. Not that they didn't have problems. She knew Clay still struggled with the fact that she could be quiet and distant.

She rushed out to the garden in the backyard, picked a flower, and put it in the small vase on the table.

She had enjoyed sex since they were first married, but distance had been an insurmountable barrier. Her hectic life left her feeling too tired to be passionate; she still struggled with that. But the distance no longer felt like a chasm that kept them separated.

Now that she thought about it, perhaps that was the biggest change she had seen in Clay lately. He talked more. And not just about sex. Of course, she wanted more—talk that is—but this was a good start.

She quickly took her apron off as she heard the garage door opening.

Of course, maybe the change was the result of the small group. Clay had been enjoying that small group the past few months. They had been doing a Bible study about relationships. Maybe they had been encouraging each other in this direction.

She didn't really care what had brought about the changes. Clay talked to her in ways that both warmed her heart and unnerved her. For the first time in their marriage, he was unwilling to stop a conversation when she said, "I don't know." In the past, he viewed that line as a legitimate way to end the conversation in order to move to more desirable activities. Now he simply waited for her to think the matter over and then pursue the topic, regardless of her uncertainty.

She felt a new level of intrigue, openness, and energy in Clay when he pursued her heart. That energy was a sweet nectar that seemed to increase her desire for him. With the freshly plucked flower in a vase, she took in its color and shape and breathed in its rich bouquet. It was going to be a fragrant evening.

Part Five

HOW DO WE, TWO SINNERS, LEARN TO LIVE WITH EACH OTHER?

17

MARK AND JENNIFER:

THE COUPLE WHO

COULDN'T CONNECT

"How about tonight?" Mark plaintively asked.

Jennifer averted her eyes. She thought, *Get a life.* She felt trapped between Mark's eyes and her own lies. She could do what she had done a thousand times—let him take her and then drift to another world while he looked for something he could never find. She looked at him and wondered why his parents had never paid to straighten his teeth. "Sure, honey. Give me about a week."

Jennifer laughed and started to clean up the dishes. She knew Mark wouldn't have the slightest idea what to do with her remark. Before she could finish cleaning up the kitchen, he would be in a stew. She never had to do much to get him angry. And once he was angry, he would either retreat like a hurt puppy or bark like a chained mutt. His bark was always worse than his bite. She still wondered why his parents bought boats and vacation houses, and traveled to places they could not even pronounce, yet never fixed his teeth.

Jennifer was used to life working the way she wanted it to. She had grown up in the home of two working parents. Her mother was a real estate agent who owned her own agency. Her father was an accountant who had dabbled in real estate and eventually given up his practice to manage his growing kingdom. Jennifer was used to the finer things, and she did not barter with fools, though she wondered how she ended up with Mark.

Mark was a good guy, sort of. He was friendly, hardworking, and undemanding. He spent most of his free time working in the yard, doing odd jobs for his parents, or pouring out his complaints to his mother. He was a boy in a man's body. But he tried hard and wanted sex only a few times a month.

Jennifer had liked his boyishness. He had seemed fresh and innocent. Her mother had mocked his mannerisms, voice, and awkward efforts to ingratiate himself to her. And when her mother mocked him, Jennifer knew he was her man. Here was a man who offended her mother but served her with a dutiful eagerness that tickled her. She had never intended to marry him. She had never intended to do anything other than be successful.

And successful she was. She had never liked to work hard, but she was classy, effortlessly elegant, pretty, and confident. In college she had been the rush chairwoman for her sorority. She had made decisions about who would get in and who would live a life marked by their exclusion from the most elite women on campus.

She had often dreamed of a large house, a few unobtrusive children, and a husband who ranked high—very high—on the social register. The only problem was that men like that were arrogant, demanding, and somehow had not learned their place in the food chain. She wanted to be served, not to be the hood ornament for some man's shallow ego.

Jennifer had dated Mark through college. After college, she had moved to a nearby city and studied fine arts at a graduate school. She was a gifted painter, but her painting had required more attention and effort than she had wanted to expend. Mark had moved to the same city and eventually found a job selling baked goods. He had worked hard and made a decent salary. Eventually, he had asked Jennifer to marry him. She was bored, tired with school, aimless. She had said yes. Years later she could not recall where, when, or how Mark had asked her or why she had said yes. It had just happened.

Kids came. Mark and Jennifer had bought a house. They bought furniture, moved it around, relocated it to the base-ment, and started the process again. Jennifer liked furniture— she liked making Mark move it to different places in the house. Life had no real unhappiness. Jennifer had money, power, and control over her world; Mark had a director for his life.

But God had different plans for both Mark and Jennifer. A neighbor invited Jennifer to a women's Bible study. She thought the idea of studying the Bible was quaint, but it was something to do, and it provided free baby-sitting. Besides, many women from the art guild attended the Bible study. It was a natural move to go from sorority to church.

Jennifer studied the Bible and chatted with the attractive, powerful women for months. Then one day during the large meeting, a guest speaker invited the women to come forward to receive Christ as their personal Lord and Savior. Jennifer did. She didn't feel deep sorrow for her sin. She knew she was mean at times, but overall she had done nothing worse than anyone else in the room. In many ways, becoming a Christian that day reminded her of the secret ceremony she had led many initiates through after being selected to join the sorority.

Jennifer wanted to know God better. She was intrigued by the Bible, but she was careful not to agree with all the political or personal convictions of the somewhat conservative women with whom she met. She was an artist—a force in and of herself. But she was glad to take the necessary steps to join the church.

And, of course, Mark went along with her choice. He had grown up in a religious home that did not take religion too seriously. What was important was being good, or at least not getting caught when one was not. Boys were supposed to sow their wild oats. Girls, good girls, were supposed to do so only when they traveled far from home. And then they had only to make sure that they did not get pregnant.

Mark and Jennifer's marriage was a commercial success. Mark worked hard at a middle-income job, and Jennifer's parents provided the money needed to buy a larger, more ostentatious house. Mark's parents provided an emotional nesting place for him when he was discouraged and angry at Jennifer.

Their marriage was also a social success. They were attractive and convivial. In their new church, they hosted small-group Bible studies, worked in the nursery, and hobnobbed with the bright and the beautiful. Jennifer learned how to frame gossip in terms of prayer or spiritual concern. She made her way up in the women's ministry and was soon teaching studies that required no more of her than memorizing what was supposed to go in the blanks.

She was intrigued by spiritual matters. It was a new language, but it gave her a sense that something bigger and more untamed had made a claim on her life. It also gave her a new arena for exercising her joy in directing and managing the lives of others.

Mark talked business and sports. He smiled and shook hands with the acumen of a businessman. He was opinionated in matters of money and local politics; in all other concerns he was inoffensive and inert.

Mark and Jennifer were normal, faithful followers of the American-Religious-Yuppie-Evangelical way. But God had other plans.

THE TALK. One Sunday morning when Mark and Jennifer arrived at their Sunday school class, they were met by a new teacher. An older man was substituting for the regular teacher, who was sick that morning. It was an illness arranged by God from the foundation of the earth.

The older man was a respected community icon. He was an orthopedic surgeon, a crusty curmudgeon who had seen the insides of more people in that community than most counselors had. He wore hunting and fishing clothes to church. He drove a four-wheel-drive vehicle when it was gauche.

That morning his wife, Cassandra, introduced him.

Cassandra: "I am honored to introduce my husband, Bing, to you. We have been married for thirty-five years. We have four kids and twelve grandkids. Two of our sons are in the ministry. One of our daughters is the wife of a missionary surgeon. Our other daughter is about to graduate from a Christian college, and she is unsure of her future.

"I tell you this to let you know we have the pedigree of success. Few could look at our lives and say anything other than that we have done something right. And we are here for the next three weeks to dispel that myth. I introduce my husband to you as my best friend, my companion, and my lover. But that was not always the case.

"For the first two years of our marriage, I thought I was going to lose my mind. I saw a psychiatrist for medication to cope with my depression. I survived it, and then I spent the next thirty years enduring and hating Bing. He was and

271

still can be an awful, despicable, arrogant, harsh man. But in the last three years, something has happened to us. I can't explain it, but that something is a broken heart. My husband has begun to deal with his heart—with me, our children, and God. I love my husband. He is a godly man."

She sat down. The class sat in stunned silence. Most of the people in the class had attended the church for years. They had never before heard anyone say that she had hated her husband. No one had ever before said something as honestly and directly as Cassandra had.

Bing ambled to the podium and took off his reading glasses. He looked like a bird of prey squinting at his next meal.

Bing: "Let me tell you about orthopedic surgery. When I went into the field, orthopedic surgery was a notch above butchery. It required people who knew they knew everything, had no fear, and liked the sight of blood. We were the hackers, the fly-boys who went in at tree level and strafed the enemy on their level—not the kind that knew fear or at least admitted to being timid or unsure. Yes, Cassie is right. I was and still am at times cocky, confident, and utterly in control."

The class was intensely attentive. They were listening to a vintage John Wayne; except this guy had not acted it out in the movies—he had lived it. The men were engrossed; the women were respectfully demure.

Bing: "If I had died three years ago, I would have claimed to have done nearly everything I wanted, reached most of my goals, and lived a happy life. Then for some awful reason, I agreed to see a counselor with my wife. She was going through a hard period, and I thought to myself, *What can it hurt?* I had no idea what I was in for or how much it could hurt. Let me tell you the two things I discovered about marriage—about men and women."

He paused. The class was deathly quiet. The intensity of his gravelly voice and the surrealistic honesty made it seem as if they were watching a 1940s black-and-white movie.

Bing: "Men are cowards, and women are controllers. It is one of the hardest pieces of data I ever learned about myself or about my wife. I hate conflict; I am deeply afraid of being honest with my wife. Cassie has been a quiet, supportive wife. But I had never faced the reality that when I ignored people, I had left her to make decisions, enforce rules, and single-handedly supply life for the real needs of my family.

"I thought I was the provider. I was the workhorse, but I was not the heart of my family. And in my cowardly absence, Cassie grew to be a pretty good behind-the-scenes manipulator to keep her world working.

"What I want to talk about over the next three weeks is how men try to find some ground that will keep them from having to deal with the thorns and thistles of life. Men work to compensate. If that doesn't work, they will escape. If they are caught, they often will turn violent when they are put into a corner. It isn't a pretty picture. Then to make sure the women do not feel slighted, Cassie will talk about how women—even quiet, deferential wives—control their husbands. Should be fun, huh?

"Let's pray and begin."

Mark sat in inarticulate terror. He felt a chill run up and down his back. This older man sounded so much like his father. They were cut out of the same post-Depression, World War II mold. But unlike his father, Bing was kind of appealing. He spoke with too much confidence. But he said words that broke the code of silence—the basis of fellowship among men: No one was ever supposed to admit that all men are cowards. He had broken the oath of testosterone and had not died. Mark felt cold panic.

Jennifer was enraged. She could not explain why she felt such fury. She actually had felt warm toward Bing. But she could feel her body tense with unmitigated rage. She clutched the side of her chair in order not to bolt out of the room. Then her mind began to drift away. Slowly, unnoticed by anyone else in the room, she began to look at Bing's shiny head and how it held the glow from the fluorescent lights. Soon she was daydreaming about being a young girl lost in the arms of a strong man. It was not her daddy. He was never strong. He had never held her. He had never made the sad spot in her go away.

It was going to be a long hour.

18

RE-ENTERING EDEN:

STRUGGLING AGAINST

LONELINESS AND VIOLENCE

Marriages suffer under the freight of the Fall. We struggle with sin in every dimension of every relationship, but in marriage we struggle with it more intensely and with more potential for damage.

Are marriages hopeless because of sin? Absolutely not. Where the greatest sin arises, the greatest grace can surface. Forgiveness rises to its zenith when sin seems to place a stranglehold on intimacy. Marriages are the crucible not only for sin to be exposed but also for forgiveness to restore relationship and intensify our hope of heaven.

Redemption does not come, however, without a war. Mark and Jennifer are in a battle of fear and pride. Jennifer has had her way in most occasions. She is verbal, opinionated, and contemptuous; equally, she is an empty woman who has seldom had anyone strong enough to deal with her tragic ways of covering over her hurt. Mark is a nice but ineffective guy who leans on Jennifer's strength and sophistication. He doubts his capacity to deal with the chaos of life, so he withdraws and snipes at Jennifer from behind a rock at a safe distance. He is unhappy, but he blames his wife for their lonely existence. Far more, he blames her but does not even acknowledge what is wrong in their marriage.

MARRIAGES ARE THE CRUCIBLE NOT ONLY FOR SIN TO BE EXPOSED BUT ALSO FOR FORGIVENESS TO RESTORE RELATIONSHIP AND INTENSIFY OUR HOPE OF HEAVEN.

Mark and Jennifer's marriage has devolved into daily skirmishes that seem to justify a refusal to move toward the other in love. Failure is used as a weapon to wound the other. Eventually, Mark and Jennifer separate into two worlds that are superficially united by common activities like attending church.

What is required for this couple is more than a few tips on how to improve their marriage, increase communication, or work toward conflict resolution. They need to see their option in life: they can choose either to live by pretense and self-righteousness or to be broken by their sin and surrender to the gospel. How must they grapple with this choice? They must comprehend the importance of the Curse.

CONFLICT: CONSEQUENCE OF THE CURSE

All the deceit, rebellion, and shallowness in the relationship between Mark and Jennifer spring from Adam and Eve's rebellion against God. Their sin resulted in unimaginable tragedy for them and for all their countless descendants. Every tear that has ever been shed is due to their treason. Every moment of violence, death, divorce, and harm is the direct result of their choice to turn from the truth of God to trust in the deceit of evil.

THEY CAN CHOOSE EITHER TO LIVE BY
PRETENSE AND SELF-RIGHTEOUSNESS
OR TO BE BROKEN BY THEIR SIN
AND SURRENDER TO THE GOSPEL.

Now the serpent was more crafty than any of the wild animals the Lord God had made. He said to the woman, "Did God really say, 'You must not eat from any tree in the garden'?"

The woman said to the serpent, "We may eat fruit from the trees in the garden, but God did say, 'You must not eat fruit from the tree that is in the middle of the garden, and you must not touch it, or you will die.'"

"You will not surely die," the serpent said to the woman. "For God knows that when you eat of it your eyes will be opened, and you will be like God, knowing good and evil."

When the woman saw that the fruit of the tree was good for food and pleasing to the eye, and also desirable for gaining wisdom, she took some and ate it. She also gave some to her husband, who was with her, and he ate it. Then the eyes of both of them were opened, and they realized they were naked; so they sewed fig leaves together and made coverings for themselves. GENESIS 3:1-7

Eve's willingness to believe the lies of the serpent and Adam's silence and acquiescence to her request disrupted the harmonious relationship they had enjoyed with the Creator in the Garden. Before the Fall, Adam and Eve could meet God anywhere, anytime. After the Fall, this intimate divine-human relationship was severed by sin.

But it was not only our relationship with God that was broken at that time. All relationships were broken. To show this, we have only to observe the fury Adam vented.

> Then the man and his wife heard the sound of the Lord God as he was walking in the garden in the cool of the day, and they hid from the Lord God among the trees of the garden. But the Lord God called to the man, "Where are you?"
>
> He answered, "I heard you in the garden, and I was afraid because I was naked; so I hid."
>
> And he said, "Who told you that you were naked? Have you eaten from the tree that I commanded you not to eat from?"
>
> The man said, "The woman you put here with me—she gave me some fruit from the tree, and I ate it." GENESIS 3:8-12

Adam was violent. He spoke vicious words against God for creating Eve. Then he turned his contempt against Eve for having given him the fruit. In a barely whispered admission, he acknowledged in a passive way that he did eat the fruit. When Adam's sin was exposed, he used his violent contempt to defend himself. Man was meant to be a bold, creative artist who plunges into the unformed mystery of life and shapes it to a greater vision of beauty. At the Fall he became a cowardly, violent protector of nothing more than himself. Intimacy and openness were replaced by hiding and hatred.

The hiding and hatred may not be obvious flight or snarling fury. Mark is a nice guy. He may be somewhat ineffectual, but he is likable. His boyish demeanor and obvious efforts to avoid conflict and ingratiate himself reveal the tracks of hiding. He does not want to enter relationship courageously and boldly for the sake of doing good.

MAN WAS MEANT TO BE A BOLD, CREATIVE ARTIST WHO PLUNGES INTO THE UNFORMED MYSTERY OF LIFE AND SHAPES IT TO A GREATER VISION OF BEAUTY.

But the Fall did not merely affect relationships. The fallout of sin also affected the internal life of the man and the woman.

After they sinned, they felt shame as they stood before one another naked. Their relationship was marred, and for the first time since the creation of Eve, loneliness reigned.

The text tells us that Adam and Eve were stricken with overwhelming self-consciousness. In an instant, both realized they were naked and ugly. The ugliness could not have been an instantaneous change of outward appearance, a sudden decaying of the flesh. Instead, it reveals that the inner ugliness was seen in terms of physical nakedness. And from that moment, the inner world became seized by the horrible awareness of shame, fear, and intractable loneliness. Adam was divided not only from God and his wife, but even from himself.

Jennifer is a tragic example of a person who has hardened herself to her inner world. Her confidence and personal power have enabled her to escape the vital war of the soul. She does not appear to be divided from herself; but her charisma, confidence, and control over others indicate not an absence of conflict but a war of such force that she must flee the inner world with even greater fury.

They fled from each other rather than embracing one another.

It is significant that the tragic division in Mark and Jennifer's relationship is narrated in sexual terms. Like Adam and Eve, they could no longer be naked without feeling shame. They fled from each other rather than embracing one another. They no longer enjoyed the intimacy and innocence of pure pleasure and communion. Implied are distance and loneliness. Eve, the bearer of new life and relationship, was cast away by her husband's violence. In her desperate effort to redeem her own soul, she turned not against God or her husband but against the one who had tempted her. She was not only ashamed but also lonely.

> Then the Lord God said to the woman, "What is this you have done?"
> The woman said, "The serpent deceived me, and I ate."
> The Lord God made garments of skin for Adam and his wife and clothed them. And the Lord God said, "The man has now become like one of us, knowing good and evil. He must not be allowed to reach out his hand and take also from the tree of life and eat, and live forever." So the Lord God banished him from the Garden of Eden to work the ground from which he had been taken. After he drove the man out, he placed on the east side of the Garden of Eden

cherubim and a flaming sword flashing back and forth to guard the way to the tree of life. GENESIS 3:13, 21-24

In God's grace, he provided Adam and Eve with clothes to cover themselves. But the account of the Fall reminds us that we will never experience the kind of intimacy, passion, and union that God intended for husbands and wives.

Our souls are wired for what we will never enjoy until Eden is restored in the new heaven and earth. We are built with a distant memory of Eden. We are built with a heart that knows eternity (Eccl. 3:11). But we are earthbound, caught in what is now a tension between the spirit God breathed into us and the dust from which he formed us.

THE ACCOUNT OF THE FALL REMINDS US THAT WE WILL NEVER EXPERIENCE THE KIND OF INTIMACY, PASSION, AND UNION THAT GOD INTENDED FOR HUSBANDS AND WIVES.

A war rages inside us. And the war spills into our marriages. What is the internal war that stains all marriages? It is the war of violence and loneliness. We see the dimensions of this war in the curses pronounced against Adam and Eve.

SOUL BATTLE: LONELINESS AND VIOLENCE
The Struggle with Loneliness: Facing Emptiness
God pronounces a series of curses, first on the serpent, then on Eve, and finally on Adam. This order reflects the sequence in which the sin occurred: the serpent persuaded Eve to eat the fruit, then Eve convinced Adam.

To the woman he said,
"I will greatly increase your pains in childbearing;
with pain you will give birth to children.
Your desire will be for your husband,
and he will rule over you." GENESIS 3:16

God's words to Eve have a special bearing on the relationship between men and women. The fruit of relational and sexual intercourse would be attended by pain. The curse for a woman is directed against the area where she is uniquely built for joy: receiving and offering life in relationship. She will experience pain in childbirth and an internal struggle in relationship with her husband.

If the pain is exclusively physical, then it is mystifying. Presumably then, a woman who avoided bearing children and hormonally eradicated menses could escape the Curse. But that is not the case. While the pain is physical, the Curse implies that her unique calling as the ruler of relationship will be fraught with pain, therefore with loneliness. This is seen more clearly in the second portion of the Curse.

THE CURSE IMPLIES THAT HER UNIQUE CALLING AS THE RULER OF RELATIONSHIP WILL BE FRAUGHT WITH PAIN, THEREFORE WITH LONELINESS.

The curse of Eve ends with a statement that is difficult to understand in detail. "Her desire" could mean that the woman so wants a man that she ends up being ruled or pushed around by him. Or "her desire" could refer to a woman's desire to rule a man (based on the use of the same rather rare Hebrew word in Gen. 4:7). A woman's desire to rule a man is frustrated when that man ends up ruling her.

Both of these scenarios are true in experience, and both may be intended by the text. At the very least, we can say that this verse underscores the struggle with emptiness in the heart of a woman. She will live with unrequited desire, and her unfulfilled emptiness will put her in conflict with her husband. He will "rule" over her. The word "rule" does not imply appropriate dominion or caring, loving leadership. Instead, it implies violence and subjection. Eve and her gender will battle with an emptiness or loneliness that seems to compel control. She will labor not to give life but to absorb life into her empty soul in order to find relief from the Curse.

If her heart is instructed by the Curse, she will continue to offer relationship in freedom and joy, tempered by compassionate sorrow and strength.

Jennifer filled her emptiness with the frivolity of power—connections to gossip, organizational control, and ruling her husband. Even though Jennifer hid behind her cynicism and mockery, she, like every woman, still felt a hollowness that could not be filled by her furtive efforts to find relief. Jennifer simply cannot escape the Curse.

Not surprisingly, Eve will try to fill her emptiness with her "natural" inclination toward relationship. Consequently, her fleshly pattern will be to seduce and then bind a man with the power of her words. She will defend herself through verbal assaults—from nagging, to gossip, to vitriol. As the giver of relationship, she will become the stingy and manipulative dispenser of relationship. Where she was once to receive and surround her husband in sexual union, often she devolves into the one who withholds relationship and distances herself in busyness.

A woman is to be broken by the Curse. If she flees from loneliness or attempts to master it through more obvious control, she will become more obtuse and thick of heart rather than supple and elegant in humility. If her heart is instructed by the Curse, she will continue to offer relationship in freedom and joy, tempered by compassionate sorrow and strength. To flee from the Curse is to distort biblical femininity.

The Struggle with Futility: Facing Violence

For a man, the Curse is directed against the fruit of his engagement with the soil. He will bear pain and futility in attempting to subdue and rule the world.

> To Adam he said, "Because you listened to your wife and ate from the tree about which I commanded you, 'You must not eat of it,'
> "Cursed is the ground because of you;
> through painful toil you will eat of it
> all the days of your life.
> It will produce thorns and thistles for you,
> and you will eat the plants of the field.
> By the sweat of your brow
> you will eat your food
> until you return to the ground,
> since from it you were taken;
> for dust you are
> and to dust you will return." GENESIS 3:17-19

The soil—that is, all of life—will be filled with thorns and thistles that will haunt a man with frustration and failure. The curse for a man is directed against the area where he is uniquely built for joy: engaging and bringing forth fruit in tending the Garden.

The man will experience pain in a different form of labor. If the pain is exclusively physical, then it is mystifying. Presumably then, a man who avoided farming or gardening might be able to avoid the Curse. But this is not the case. The pain is soil-oriented, but the Curse implies that his unique calling as the ruler of the earth will be fraught with frustration, therefore with futility.

THE CURSE IMPLIES THAT HIS UNIQUE CALLING AS THE RULER OF THE EARTH WILL BE FRAUGHT WITH FRUSTRATION, THEREFORE WITH FUTILITY.

A woman typically struggles more with relationship, whereas a man struggles more with competence. Is he up to the task of succeeding in his next presentation, next job interview, next household chore, or next sexual encounter? The nagging fear is that he is not "enough" for the demands of life. Therefore, he finds an area in which he has sufficient success to gain a confidence that he can master the weeds that might arise. And then he avoids most other "fields."

The area in which most men feel the sting of futility and incompetence is deep, personal relationship. It is the area of tenderness, talk, dialogue, and give-and-take. Many men tip the hat to personal intercourse and then flee to the area of their competence. When trapped in relationship, it is far easier either to turn mute or, if pressed against the wall, to turn violent. Violence is a way of warning an adversary: "Don't tread on me. Don't expose my fear or shame."

As the one who is to create order out of chaos and enhance beauty, the man limits his engagement with the earth to a narrow and self-protective field rather than venturing into the area that requires the greatest courage. Whereas God created him to move toward and enter his wife in sexual union, often he devolves into the one who demands pleasure and distracts himself in his work or play.

IF HIS HEART IS INSTRUCTED
BY THE CURSE, HE WILL CONTINUE
TO SHAPE RELATIONSHIP IN
FREEDOM AND JOY, TEMPERED
BY COMPASSIONATE SORROW
AND TENDERNESS.

A man that is frustrated by futility turns not only to pleasure and work but also to violence. To attack—to wound another person, animal, or even an inanimate object in vengeance—restores a sense of power and equanimity to a man's unsettled soul. Violence, whether physical or emotional, perversely counterfeits the joy that is to be gained by being a servant and by offering his life for the sake of glory. Once the counterfeit is gained, he can then succumb to passive and detached quiescence that is a substitute for true rest. For many men, this is found in the vicarious experience of watching a favorite sports team "pound" an opposing, hated rival.

Tragically, for some men, vicarious violence is not enough,

and they resort to beating, raping, or emotionally scourging their wives, dating partners, and children. Immoral violence is a surety against the Curse. But a real man does not escape the Curse; instead, he embraces it.

A man is to be broken by the Curse. If he flees from futility or attempts to master it through narrow competence, he will become more obtuse and thick of heart rather than strong and honorable in humility. If his heart is instructed by the Curse, he will continue to shape relationship in freedom and joy, tempered by compassionate sorrow and tenderness. To flee from the Curse is to distort biblical masculinity.

THE WAR BETWEEN THE SEXES

Mark and Jennifer were in a war, not only the war of battling a fallen world, but also a war against each other. They were engaged in a war between the sexes.

What is the basis of the war between the sexes? It is ultimately, of course, the war between God and his adversary, Satan. We ought never to be naïve. The deepest struggles of life will occur in the most primary relationship affected by the Fall: marriage. No one on earth will have more potential to do harm or to do good than your spouse. Consequently, no relationship will be imbued with more desire and danger than your marriage. No wonder most couples soon settle down into a distant, parallel existence in which the pain and the joy are kept at a minimum.

What are we to do with this fact? We must never be naïve enough to think of marriage as a safe harbor from the Fall. If a man sees his wife as the one who will sustain him and keep him from the thorns and thistles, then he will hate her to the degree she asks him to be a man. If a woman sees her husband as someone who will take away the pain and disappointment of relationship, then she will despise him for inviting her to bear the pain of childbirth and involvement with others.

If that is true, then is marriage hopeless, destined for unresolved tension and pain?

Absolutely not. Our marriages are the ground for change. It is the place where exposure of our need for the gospel is most profound; therefore, it is the relationship where depravity is best exposed and where our dignity is best lived out. Marriage is the battleground of sin and the place where the Cross is revealed as the only hope for life and joy. In the midst of the Curse, God promises that redemption will come as the seed of the woman crushes the head of the serpent.

MARRIAGE IS THE BATTLEGROUND OF SIN AND THE PLACE WHERE THE CROSS IS REVEALED AS THE ONLY HOPE FOR LIFE AND JOY.

Marriage is the ground for growing glory in each heart as the Curse paradoxically breaks us and draws us to seek God. The curse is a friend that drives us to the hope of redemption. Marriage is the sweet wine and rich meat that heralds the final day and the wedding feast of the Lamb.

Summary for marriage: Our spouses are to grow in desperation for redemption under the weight of their unique curse. We are called to struggle with the Fall and to live in anticipation of the new creation. Our only option in living together as sinners is to survive with pretense or to surrender to the gospel.

QUESTIONS FOR REFLECTION AND CONVERSATION
1. How has the curse of the Fall had impact on your marriage? Be specific.
2. In what ways does your marriage ignore the Curse, attempt to escape the Curse, or surrender to the Curse?

3. In what ways and in what circumstances does your spouse most expose your inadequacies, failures, and sin?
4. As a man, how do you avoid futility and violence? As a woman, how do you avoid conflict and loneliness?
5. What fruits have you seen in your marriage as the result of being broken by your sin?

LIVING BEYOND THE FALL

Adam and Eve are the ancestors of us all. However, our individualistic culture finds it hard to figure out why we are blamed for something that Adam and Eve did. How can we be held responsible for something that took place millennia ago? Even more to the point, how can their punishment be applied to us today? If we had been in the Garden, perhaps we would have acted differently!

It is precisely at this point that the Bible tells us we are wrong. The point of the story of the Fall in Genesis 3 is that Adam and Eve are our representatives. That is, if we had been in the Garden, we would have acted just as Adam and Eve did. We would have eaten the fruit of the tree of the knowledge of good and evil. After all, we are sinners, every single one of us, as we will see from later exploration of various passages in Romans. Even more, deep down we all *know* that we are sinners. Our consciences tell us constantly that we are not living up to God's expectations for our lives.

We may try to soften the blow by telling ourselves that we are basically good people and slip up only occasionally. However, the Bible corrects our misunderstanding. We are not basically good people who occasionally mess up; we are essentially evil people who occasionally do "good" things, usually for the wrong reasons.

THE NATURE OF SIN

The reason why we can so often delude ourselves into thinking we are basically good people is that we do not appreciate what sin is. For one thing, we often believe that sin involves only actions. We think we can sin in our minds while preserving a high level of propriety. In other words, we can look good but be bad.

SIN INVOLVES NOT ONLY WHAT WE DO BUT ALSO WHAT WE THINK AND FEEL.

Sin involves not only what we *do* but also what we *think* and *feel.* Sin is an attitude that puts ourselves, not God and his will, as the most important thing in the world. At its root, sin is pride and rebellion against God. This pride will lead to actions that we call sinful, but sometimes our sin is hidden.

Albert Schweitzer is known for his sacrificial deeds on behalf of the people of Africa. However, while he was doing these admittedly wonderful things under the auspices of the church, he was also writing theological essays that showered shame on Jesus. In his writings, read mostly by other theologians and church leaders, Schweitzer argued that the Jesus of history was a deluded man who came to believe that he was the Messiah. Schweitzer's actions were noble and "Christian," but his writings, which give us a window into his soul, indicate that his heart was in rebellion against his Messiah. His kind deeds, therefore, were just a slap in the face of God.

Further, we can delude ourselves by quantifying sin. That is, we all know we occasionally slip and do a little something wrong, but most of the time we do the right thing. Surely God should not mind if we occasionally err. After all, we are only human, and to err is human.

THE FIRST SIN OCCURRED WITHIN THE CONTEXT OF MARRIAGE.

Once again, we misunderstand the significance of our sin. Adam and Eve probably said to themselves as they bit down on the fruit of the tree of the knowledge of good and evil, *It's just a small thing. What harm can it do? We are not hurting anyone as far as we can see.*

As we will see from later reflection on James 2:8-11, in God's eyes the least little sin is as major as the most gross sin. To put it starkly, yelling at my spouse for no good reason other than my own frustration and anger deserves hell as much as if I were to kill her. Both actions reveal the heart as murderous and rebellious.

It is important to note that the first sin occurred within the context of marriage. Eve ate the fruit first, but her dialogue with the serpent took place with Adam next to her. When Eve had finished, she handed the fruit to her husband, and he ate it without an argument.

We have observed in part 1 of this book that marriage brings together two glorious people created in the image of God. Through the lens provided by Genesis 3, we also clearly see that these two creatures are also two rebellious sinners. Both of these truths—that human beings are glorious creatures of God as well as ugly sinners—need to be fully grasped as a man and a woman enter into the marriage relationship. These two truths give a husband and a wife the basis for expectation and hope as they act in the present, deal with the past, and look forward to their future together.

While other chapters in this book have hinted at the impact of sin on our marriages, this chapter will focus directly on sin with all of its ugliness. We can see how sin disrupts and occasionally tears marriages apart. We will see that marriage, which God created to dispel loneliness, can still be an arena where loneliness and futility are felt with great force. We will see how loneliness and relational impotency lead to desperate acts of lust and murder against our spouses as we expect from the relationship things that it is simply unable to give this side of heaven.

Specifically, we will see certain triggers that lead to conflicts and pain in the marriage relationship. These include sex, violence, limited time and money, and divided loyalties. These are the areas that trigger division in a marriage and that sometimes lead to divorce.

As we think of the impact that sin has on marriage, we will explore another important theological teaching about marriage. Marriage is not just a casual arrangement between two people who decide to get together for a while. Marriage is a covenant between two people, a covenant made in the presence of God.

But God does not leave his people to wallow in their sin.

Even within the context of the Curse at the time of the Fall, God gives a glimpse of the promise of redemption (Gen. 3:15). We will take a closer look at this promise and also a number of other passages that give us hope for our marriages. The Bible's message of hope in marriage will be fully outlined in the epilogue that completes this book.

THE PERVASIVENESS OF SIN

How pervasive is sin? Romans 3:23 reminds us that "All have sinned and fall short of the glory of God." No one is an exception. No one can say, "I am not a sinner."

But what is sin? Sin is the refusal to trust God. Sin is the heart energy that moves to find life in gods of our own making. The essence of all sin is a slap in the face of God. When we rely on anything but God for sustenance, strength, and beauty, then we have turned from him to worship the creature and not the Creator.

SIN IS THE REFUSAL TO TRUST GOD.

In other words, we go against God's will for our lives as it is stated in the Bible. We can all discover the will of God by reading the Bible, which outlines the commands and principles by which we should live our lives. But we show ourselves to be sinners by not caring about God's will and by not following it when we do know it.

Now, we need to be clear to what we are referring when we speak of God's will. The expression is used loosely in contemporary Christianity.

Sin is rebellion against God and disobedience to how he tells us to act. Sin is not a matter of choosing the right profession or the right spouse. Sheila feels attracted to both Mark and Lou. They are also showing interest in her. Both of them are sincere

Christians. Now she has to make a choice between them. Which relationship will she pursue? The Bible does not answer that question for her. In the final analysis, she can marry either one of them. She needs to make her choice based on other considerations. But she does not sin if she marries Lou and not Mark; she does not sin if she marries Mark and not Lou.

But let's say Sheila marries Mark. Then a year later she grows dissatisfied with him. She meets Lou again and feels the old attraction growing within her. She decides to divorce Mark; she begins sneaking off and sleeping with Lou. Sheila is sinning at this point because she is rebelling against God's clear teaching about adultery and also about divorce.

But, of course, sin is not always this blatant. Sometimes the murder and adultery are matters of the heart. We will explore these dark recesses of our soul as we continue.

But before leaving the Romans passage, we need to see that Paul goes further to talk about the consequences of our sin. He points out that because of our sin, we fall short of God's glory. The verb "fall short" also could be translated in a way that indicates that we are deficient or even lack God's glory.

We have already seen that we were created in the image of God. Human beings reflect God's glory. However, we now realize that since the Fall that glory is diminished because of sin. We are not creatures who brightly shine with God's glory; instead, we are God's glorious creatures who are marred by our sin. In that sense, our sin robs us of humanness; when we sin, we become subhuman. Therefore, our marriages will always reflect some dimensions that still cry for redemption.

We must enter our marriage relationships with our eyes wide open. That beautiful bride and that handsome groom are two creatures who, left to their natural tendencies, care only for themselves. They are sinners, and their union will result in not only an increase in sin but also an increase in desire for redemption.

Now that we have a better understanding of what sin is, let's go back to the Garden of Eden by way of Romans 5. In this passage Paul interprets the impact of Adam's sin. Here we find out for sure that Adam's sin infects us. "Therefore, just as sin entered the world through one man, and death through sin, and in this way death came to all men, because all sinned—for before the law was given, sin was in the world. But sin is not taken into account when there is no law. Nevertheless, death reigned from the time of Adam to the time of Moses, even over those who did not sin by breaking a command, as did Adam, who was a pattern of the one to come" (Rom. 5:12-14).

Why does Adam's sin infect us? God set it up that way. Adam, as the first person, represents all of us. His actions would be our actions if we were in the same situation. The fall into sin demonstrates that our tendencies are rebellious.

And this is important as we think of all men and women as sinners. We are born sinners, not because we do something evil as we are leaving the womb, but because we are born with an attitude that is rebellious toward God. Speaking metaphorically, rebellion is in our blood.

We are creatures who, apart from God's grace, want anything and anyone except the true God to be our god. As Paul says at the very beginning of the book of Romans, "They exchanged the truth of God for a lie, and worshiped and served created things rather than the Creator—who is forever praised. Amen" (Rom. 1:25).

John Calvin rightly described human beings when he called the mind "a factory that continually makes idols." Ultimately, we make ourselves into our own gods. We do not want the true God to be our God because he is the only one who can utterly command our allegiance. We are his creatures, totally dependent on him for everything, and we simply do not like it.

When Adam and Eve ate the fruit from the tree of the knowledge of good and evil, they were putting not only the serpent but also themselves in place of God. They were saying that God's understanding of the tree was wrong and that they could do whatever they liked.

The consequences of the Fall showed Adam and Eve just how wrong they were. As Paul says, because of Adam's sin, all men and women die. Before they sinned, death was not the ultimate end of human life. Now it is the one thing we can count on in life. Everyone dies. Why? Because Adam and Eve, our representatives, did what any one of us would have done in their place: they spat in God's face and expected him to do nothing.

The end of the passage, though, hints that this is not the end of the story. Paul says that Adam "was a pattern of the one to come" (Rom. 5:14). We will continue this passage at the conclusion of this section, but, as we will see, as one man brought sin and death into the world, so one man brings salvation and life.

> What shall we conclude then? Are we any better? Not at all!
> We have already made the charge that Jews and Gentiles
> alike are all under sin. As it is written:
> "There is no one righteous, not even one;
> there is no one who understands,
> no one who seeks God.
> All have turned away,
> they have together become worthless;
> there is no one who does good,
> not even one."
> "Their throats are open graves;
> their tongues practice deceit."
> "The poison of vipers is on their lips."
> "Their mouths are full of cursing and bitterness."
> "Their feet are swift to shed blood;
> ruin and misery mark their ways,
> and the way of peace they do not know."

"There is no fear of God before their eyes."

Now we know that whatever the law says, it says to those who are under the law, so that every mouth may be silenced and the whole world held accountable to God. Therefore no one will be declared righteous in his sight by observing the law; rather, through the law we become conscious of sin.

ROMANS 3:9-20

Paul seems to be both redundant and despairing. He always harps on sin! Perhaps he does that because we have an incredible tendency to deny the truth. The problem in our marriages is seldom viewed as the log in our own eye. We see somewhat accurately the problem in others, but we do not see the weight of our own sin as the fundamental issue that must be dealt with in all relational problems.

We are really not so bad, we like to say to ourselves. Paul would shake his head with a sad laugh and tell us how little we know ourselves.

WE DO NOT SEE THE WEIGHT OF OUR OWN SIN AS THE FUNDAMENTAL ISSUE THAT MUST BE DEALT WITH IN ALL RELATIONAL PROBLEMS.

Everyone, everywhere, without exception, is a sinner. And more than that, everyone is totally sinful. That does not mean that our every action is equally wicked or that our every thought is evil or even that our every emotion is perverse. But it does mean that nothing is free from the impact of our sin, not our intellect, feelings, choices, or actions.

After all, what is the ultimate standard that God puts before us and by which he evaluates our performance? "Be perfect, therefore, as your heavenly Father is perfect" (Matt. 5:48; see also Lev. 19:2; Deut. 18:13).

If we can read this verse without our jaws dropping out of their sockets, then we are not honest with ourselves. Jesus here tells us that our thoughts, actions, emotions, and choices need to be those of the Lord God of the universe.

Impossible? Yes. It is impossible for creatures whose fundamental attitude toward God is one of rebellion and ingratitude. But God did not create us to be sinners; he created us to be his glorious creatures. In other words, even though we were created finite, if it were not for our rebellion, we could be perfect. But since we do sin and continue to offend God with our whole person, this standard is not attainable.

BUT GOD DID NOT CREATE US TO BE SINNERS; HE CREATED US TO BE HIS GLORIOUS CREATURES.

We are sinners. Why does Paul keep telling us this? Only because of our tendency to deny the truth? No. It is his heart's desire to drive us to the solution, which is not ourselves, but another. "If you really keep the royal law found in Scripture, 'Love your neighbor as yourself,' you are doing right. But if you show favoritism, you sin and are convicted by the law as lawbreakers. For whoever keeps the whole law and yet stumbles at just one point is guilty of breaking all of it. For he who said, 'Do not commit adultery,' also said, 'Do not murder.' If you do not commit adultery but do commit murder, you have become a lawbreaker" (James 2:8-11).

If by now we still have any hope of extricating ourselves from the label "sinner," James will now rip away all of our illusions. He tells us just how deep our sin runs; he calls us

300

"lawbreakers." We commit crimes against God, and while we would minimize our offenses, James says that we all deserve the death penalty.[1]

James points out that the law of God is a unity and that by breaking one law, we have broken the entire law. But how is this the case?

Take the example of Lou and Sheila. When Lou was sleeping with Sheila, he was doing much more than breaking the seventh commandment, which forbids sex outside of marriage. He was also guilty of coveting his neighbor's wife (tenth commandment). He also broke the commandment not to steal (eighth commandment). Adultery always involves lying and deceit (ninth commandment). And since adultery is an offense against God and a placing of one's own desires above those of God, Lou was also guilty of idolatry (first commandment). We could go on, but the point is well made: To break any law is to break them all.

ODDLY, IT WILL BE THE WOUNDS OF MARRIAGE THAT MAY PROPEL EACH PARTNER TO LOOK TO GOD IN THE MIDST OF THEIR HEARTACHE.

We now see just how deep our guilt lies. But how many people are desperate for mercy? How many marriages jointly propel both spouses to hunger for forgiveness? Sadly, many couples function with the relational and spiritual detachment of Jennifer and Mark. Mark was raised in a religious home and was a "good" boy, then a "good" man. Jennifer was mostly indifferent to God until she attended a Bible study. But her appraisal of sin was that too much fuss was made about nothing.

Even if couples take sin more seriously on a conceptual

level, it is rare for them to see and face sin deeply enough for them to seek God and to struggle to comprehend his grace for their lives.

Oddly, it will be the wounds of marriage that may propel each partner to look to God in the midst of their heartache.

HEARTACHES OF MARRIAGE
Loneliness/Futility

Ecclesiastes 7:26-29 gives voice to a relational loneliness that leads to a feeling of futility, a feeling shared by many people who marry in order to find companionship and end up disillusioned because they feel lonely, depressed, abused, and more confused than before.

While it is true that marriage can be a shield against loneliness, it can also become a weapon that provokes the greatest loneliness in life. Because marriage, more than any other relationship, reflects God's involvement with us and bears more potential to draw our hearts to heaven, it can more readily give us a taste of hell.

> *I find more bitter than death*
> *the woman who is a snare,*
> *whose heart is a trap*
> *and whose hands are chains.*
> *The man who pleases God will escape her,*
> *but the sinner she will ensnare.*
> *"Look," says the Teacher, "this is what I have discovered:*
> *"Adding one thing to another to discover the scheme of*
> *   things—*
> *while I was still searching*
> *but not finding—*
> *I found one upright man among a thousand,*
> *but not one upright woman among them all.*
> *This only have I found:*

God made mankind upright,
but men have gone in search of many schemes."
ECCLESIASTES 7:26-29

The point to be remembered is that after sin entered the world, the loneliness that Adam felt before the Fall returned. Only this time the loneliness was not a benign sigh but a heartrending cry. Marriages after the Garden of Eden are not the final solution, the Promised Land that will restore Eden.

Does that mean we should avoid marriage? No, though it is interesting that Paul encourages people who are called not to be married to rejoice, because he knows marriage is going to bring troubles and heartaches that will distract from service to God (1 Cor. 7:32-35). But marriage can be a wonderful avenue for intimate relationship when we no longer demand that our marriages restore us to the bliss of Eden.

MARRIAGE CAN BE A WONDERFUL AVENUE FOR INTIMATE RELATIONSHIP WHEN WE NO LONGER DEMAND THAT OUR MARRIAGES RESTORE US TO THE BLISS OF EDEN.

Even the Teacher in Ecclesiastes recognizes the benefits of relationship when he says, "If two lie down together, they will keep warm. But how can one keep warm alone?" (Eccles. 4:11; see also vss. 7-12).

Thinking of marriage as the re-entry into Eden leads to a feeling of futility or meaninglessness that can express itself in anger and frustration. When we feel slighted or unfulfilled by our spouse, it can fuel the lust and violence of our hearts in ways that increase the heartache.

Murder

Anger murders relationship. Anger is the response to a real or perceived attack, but it meets the challenge by pushing harder in return. The result is increased loneliness and a sense of futility.

But anger may not be directed against the object of attack. It may be redirected, and those who feel the force of anger most strongly are those who are standing nearby. No one stands closer than a spouse, and so often our spouses become the object of our anger and hatred.

Anger is a demand for immediate vengeance. It is a desire to make someone pay for the emptiness, the unfairness, the cruelty of life. Anger says, "If I suffer, then you will suffer too. If I get kicked by life, then I will kick someone who is weaker and smaller in my attempt to bear the rage I feel toward the strong."

> You have heard that it was said to the people long ago, "Do not murder, and anyone who murders will be subject to judgment." But I tell you that anyone who is angry with his brother will be subject to judgment. Again, anyone who says to his brother, "Raca," is answerable to the Sanhedrin. But anyone who says, "You fool!" will be in danger of the fire of hell.
>
> Therefore, if you are offering your gift at the altar and there remember that your brother has something against you, leave your gift there in front of the altar. First go and be reconciled to your brother; then come and offer your gift.
>
> Settle matters quickly with your adversary who is taking you to court. Do it while you are still with him on the way, or he may hand you over to the judge, and the judge may hand you over to the officer, and you may be thrown into prison. I tell you the truth, you will not get out until you have paid the last penny. MATTHEW 5:21-26

Anger played a major role in Mark and Jennifer's sense of loneliness. Mark wanted sex from her, but she refused. Mark's response was to become frustrated and angry. But he was a boy in a man's body, so his anger was pitifully impotent.

But in this case, it took two to tango. Jennifer herself had a simmering rage toward life, and she was in the power position in the relationship. She had something Mark wanted, and she took a perverse pleasure in denying him sex or any kind of intimacy.

Their encounter with Bing and Cassandra had the potential to change their lives because Bing and Cassandra were an older Mark and Jennifer, though in this case it was the husband who had been in the power position, while his wife had felt the hot rage of frustration. Bing and Cassandra had struggled to face and address their murderous tendencies with one another. They did so with hearts that longed to know the grace of God and to extend that grace to one another.

Lust

Lust and murder are the twisted passions that respond to the futility brought on by loneliness in relationships.

> You have heard that it was said, "Do not commit adultery." But I tell you that anyone who looks at a woman lustfully has already committed adultery with her in his heart. If your right eye causes you to sin, gouge it out and throw it away. It is better for you to lose one part of your body than for your whole body to be thrown into hell. And if your right hand causes you to sin, cut if off and throw it away. It is better for you to lose one part of your body than for your whole body to go into hell. MATTHEW 5:27-30

Jesus here shows that the seventh commandment is more than a prohibition of a certain behavior. Before adultery is a

305

specific deed, it is the energy of the heart. It is desire gone awry, a ravenous demand to be full.

But lust can be more than sexual. We can lust for material possessions, food, or status. Desire in and of itself is not evil, but when it is uncontrolled and assumes prominence in our life, then it threatens to consume us.

A gossip lusts for data. The craving for tidbits of information about others is not much different from the lust of the glutton who lives for food. Lust is so compulsive that the glutton cannot stop eating, even if it leads to death. The same is true for the one who craves information, power, prestige, or new possessions.

Jennifer wanted her desires filled and had a callous disregard for Mark and anything or anyone who stood in her way. She wanted to be among the elite, and she even used the church for her ends.

A strong, successful man might have enhanced her chances to move in socially prominent circles, but the downside would have been a man whom she could not control. So she fell into marriage with Mark, a weak man who frustrated her desires but did not stand in the way of her lust to control. The result was that she lashed out with murderous anger.

But we can go further in exploring sin's effects on marriage by looking at tension areas that husbands and wives face after they have been married for a while. We call these areas triggers, because they can expose the underlying conflicts between husbands and wives.

TRIGGERS TO CONFLICT
Sex
As we have seen in earlier chapters, sexuality is a wondrous expression of union within marriage. Couples experience an intimacy of unequaled proportions when they embrace with tenderness and passion.

But sex can also be a minefield of disaster within a marriage. Sin can eat away all the beauty that God intended for a sexual relationship. The Bible in its teaching and in its stories reveals three primary areas of sex gone awry:

1. adultery, which is sex outside the bounds of marriage
2. deadening of desire, which is an unwarranted denial of sexuality within marriage
3. perversion, which like adultery is sexuality outside of the bounds of marriage but has an additional vicious dimension to it

---

SIN CAN EAT AWAY
ALL THE BEAUTY THAT GOD INTENDED
FOR A SEXUAL RELATIONSHIP.

ADULTERY. The past forty years have witnessed the most amazing roller-coaster ride in attitudes toward sex outside of marriage. In the fifties, promiscuity and adultery occasioned public scandal, even though such things were carried on behind closed doors with great frequency. The sexual revolution of the sixties and seventies called into question traditional morality. Sex was good, clean fun, within or outside of the bonds of marriage. The eighties and nineties have seen the rise of a new attitude toward sex in our society. The AIDS epidemic has been like a sudden rain at a picnic. Sex, especially outside of a monogamous relationship, has taken on a never-before-thought-of danger.

This new fear has not caused a reversion to the fifties and before, but it no longer permits the free-and-easy attitude that was the dubious success of the sexual revolution.

The Bible's message is clear no matter what the age. Sex is the prerogative and joy of marriage and marriage alone.

> Marriage should be honored by all, and the marriage bed kept pure, for God will judge the adulterer and all the sexually immoral. HEBREWS 13:4

> If a man is found sleeping with another man's wife, both the man who slept with her and the woman must die. You must purge the evil from Israel. DEUTERONOMY 22:22

Why does the Bible confine sex to marriage? Is it a killjoy book, hating any human pleasure? No. Sex is reserved for marriage because God, the one who created sex for human enjoyment, knows that sex is more than a physical act. Sex is a physical reflection of what takes place on the level of the human soul. It intimately unites two bodies as a reflection of the union of two human souls. This level of union and vulnerability can be entrusted only to people who are committed to each other for the duration of life. Sex draws to the surface a deep potential for loneliness and impotency—less physical and far more relational. And those great dangers—loneliness and failure—require a safety net of durable quality, or one will never risk the depths of the heart in the relationship.

SEX IS A PHYSICAL REFLECTION OF WHAT TAKES PLACE ON THE LEVEL OF THE HUMAN SOUL.

Then why do so many people suffer the temptation and, further, the tragic consequences of adultery? Adultery is like the worship of false gods. It allows for the passion that God intended without bowing the knee to the one whom we are called to love. Adultery is not merely sex with the wrong person; it is union with someone who will never require us to face our sinfulness or draw forth our glory so that we are more and more in awe of God. It is intimacy without commitment, flight from the struggle of intimacy without ever facing our part in the loss.

ADULTERY IS NOT MERELY SEX
WITH THE WRONG PERSON;
IT IS UNION WITH SOMEONE WHO
WILL NEVER REQUIRE US
TO FACE OUR SINFULNESS OR
DRAW FORTH OUR GLORY
SO THAT WE ARE MORE AND MORE
IN AWE OF GOD.

Adultery, though, is a temptation that has lured many into marital destruction. As we will see below, its devastating power is so great that it is one of the rare justifications for divorce. God hates divorce, but he allows it in the case of adultery.

Thus, the Bible has laws against wanton sexuality (Deut. 22:22) and also warns against it through story (David and Bathsheba in 2 Samuel), wisdom saying (Prov. 2:12-19), and bald statement (Heb. 13:4).

> Wisdom will save you from the ways of wicked men,
> from men whose words are perverse,
> who leave the straight paths
> to walk in dark ways,
> who delight in doing wrong
> and rejoice in the perverseness of evil,

whose paths are crooked
and who are devious in their ways.
It will save you also from the adulteress,
from the wayward wife with her seductive words,
who has left the partner of her youth
and ignored the covenant she made before God.
For her house leads down to death
and her paths to the spirits of the dead.
None who go to her return
or attain the paths of life. PROVERBS 2:12-19

One evening David got up from his bed and walked
around on the roof of the palace. From the roof he saw a
woman bathing. The woman was very beautiful, and
David sent someone to find out about her. The man said,
"Isn't this Bathsheba, the daughter of Eliam and the wife of
Uriah the Hittite?" Then David sent messengers to get her.
She came to him, and he slept with her. (She had purified
herself from her uncleanness.) Then she went back home.
The woman conceived and sent word to David, saying, "I
am pregnant." 2 SAMUEL 11:2-5

David's sexual escapade with Bathsheba sends its destructive shock waves through the rest of his life. The book of 2 Samuel is very clear that the sin with Bathsheba led directly to all the harem intrigue and sibling fighting that so devastated the last part of David's otherwise successful reign. Soon after the episode recorded in the passage listed above, we learn that Amnon, David's son, seduces David's daughter Tamar. In revenge Tamar's brother Absalom kills Amnon and eventually goes to war against David. At the end of David's life, yet another son, Adonijah, tries to take the throne, only to be thwarted by David and then killed by Solomon.

Adultery triggers trouble that often dissolves marriages.

DEATH OF DESIRE.   A second evidence of sex gone awry is the absence of sexual desire. Paul addresses this concern quite strongly in his letter to the Corinthians.

> Now for the matters you wrote about: It is good for a
> man not to marry. But since there is so much immorality,
> each man should have his own wife, and each woman
> her own husband. The husband should fulfill his marital
> duty to his wife, and likewise the wife to her husband.
> The wife's body does not belong to her alone but also to
> her husband. In the same way, the husband's body does
> not belong to him alone but also to his wife. Do not
> deprive each other except by mutual consent and for a
> time, so that you may devote yourselves to prayer. Then
> come together again so that Satan will not tempt you
> because of your lack of self-control. I say this as a
> concession, not as a command. I wish that all men were
> as I am. But each man has his own gift from God; one
> has this gift, another has that. 1 CORINTHIANS 7:1-7

In the preceding part of his letter, Paul warned the Corinthians about sexual immorality, and at least some husbands and wives among the early Christian community may have overinterpreted Paul's concerns, thinking that sex itself is bad or unimportant, even in marriage.

IN MARITAL SEXUALITY WE GIFT OUR SPOUSES WITH OUR BODIES' POWER TO BRING PLEASURE TO THEM.

Paul sets up a profound and wonderful paradox for marital sexuality. As marriage partners, we do not own our own bodies; we become slaves to our spouses. But it is an excep-

311

tionally odd slavery in that I own my wife's body, but she also owns mine. Therefore, I have no right to demand sex or withhold sex from my wife. Because I do not own my own body, I have no right to exert my will on my spouse. In marital sexuality we gift our spouses with our bodies' power to bring pleasure to them. And giving pleasure to our spouses will bring relational and physical pleasure to us.

Paul knows that sex is an important and crucial expression of marital union. It is a gift that God gave his creatures for their enjoyment and pleasure. So for married couples to give up sex as a spiritual exercise for long periods of time was unnatural and would play into Satan's hands.

SEX IS AT THE CENTER OF A GROWING AND VIBRANT LOVE.

An absence of sexual desire can mean more than baldly denying sex to our spouses. It is possible to engage in a sexuality so passionless that, even though a husband and wife are having intercourse on a regular basis, their union is marked by a routine that bleeds into indifference. A man who cares only for his own satisfaction may not tenderly and passionately bring his wife to the point where she can have an orgasm. Or a wife who knows it is her "duty" to have sex with her husband might show little emotional or physical involvement. Both husband and wife should think of sex as a means of expressing their love to each other by working for each other's pleasure. Over time, couples can learn by talking about sex together and by exploring what gives pleasure to the other. Certainly no one enjoys perfect sex throughout their marriage. Our sinfulness and selfishness emerge to keep us from the type of intimate vulnerability involved in the sexual act.

But Paul reminds us that sex is not an optional part of marriage. Sex is not an afterthought. Sex is at the center of a growing and vibrant love.

PERVERSION.   We see a third evidence of sex gone awry in sexual perversions. Transvestism, bestiality, incest, and homosexuality are a few of the other sexual sins that the Bible recognizes and condemns. They are by definition sexual acts outside of biblically sanctioned marriage.

> A woman must not wear men's clothing, nor a man wear women's clothing, for the Lord your God detests anyone who does this. DEUTERONOMY 22:5

> "Cursed is the man who sleeps with his father's wife, for he dishonors his father's bed."
> Then all the people shall say, "Amen!"
> "Cursed is the man who has sexual relations with any animal."
> Then all the people shall say, "Amen!"
> "Cursed is the man who sleeps with his sister, the daughter of his father or the daughter of his mother."
> Then all the people shall say, "Amen!"
> DEUTERONOMY 27:20-22

> Because of this, God gave them over to shameful lusts. Even their women exchanged natural relations for unnatural ones. In the same way the men also abandoned natural relations with women and were inflamed with lust for one another. Men committed indecent acts with other men, and received in themselves the due penalty for their perversion. ROMANS 1:26-27

Sexual perversion is always a violent assault against the beauty of God's design for sexual pleasure and intimacy. Even Freud understood perversion to involve a desire to denigrate, demean, and violate rather than simply an alternate means of finding sexual release.

Sadly, many Christian homes have been torn apart by perversion. The perversion may seem as harmless and innocuous as chronic masturbation and the use of pornography, or the perversion may take the vilest forms of sexual abuse and assault. At any level, all perversions are not merely a misguided means to find release but far more a dark means of making someone pay. For example, the man who is more aroused by pornography than he is by his wife has made it clear that she is not the desire of his heart, nothing but an object of his uncontrolled desire, and as dispensable as his recent magazine. No woman can flower into glory if her husband sees sex as nothing more than his divine right and prerogative to feel good about himself. Perversion is not only an act, but it is also a violent demand that makes the spouse feel cheapened and used.

NO WOMAN CAN FLOWER INTO
GLORY IF HER HUSBAND
SEES SEX AS NOTHING MORE THAN
HIS DIVINE RIGHT AND PREROGATIVE
TO FEEL GOOD ABOUT HIMSELF.

Violence

A second trigger to conflict in marriage is violence. Loneliness and futility can ignite a rage that leads to violence—sexual, physical, or emotional. Sexual violence is not unique to our society. The biblical record indicates that violent sex invaded the lives and homes of people from all levels of society.

But if out in the country a man happens to meet a girl pledged to be married and rapes her, only the man who has done this shall die. Do nothing to the girl; she has committed no sin deserving death. DEUTERONOMY 22:25-26

"Send everyone out of here," Amnon said. So everyone left him. Then Amnon said to Tamar, "Bring the food here into my bedroom so I may eat from your hand." And Tamar took the bread she had prepared and brought it to her brother Amnon in his bedroom. But when she took it to him to eat, he grabbed her and said, "Come to bed with me, my sister."

"Don't, my brother!" she said to him. "Don't force me. Such a thing should not be done in Israel! Don't do this wicked thing. What about me? Where could I get rid of my disgrace? And what about you? You would be like one of the wicked fools in Israel. Please speak to the king; he will not keep me from being married to you." But he refused to listen to her, and since he was stronger than she, he raped her. 2 SAMUEL 13:9-14

Our age has become increasingly sensitive to matters of violence within the home. The statistics are staggering. It is estimated that at least one out of every three women is sexually abused by the time she reaches the age of eighteen. If the definition of abuse is broadened to include forms of interaction that do not include physical touch, such as exhibitionism, then the figure jumps to one in two women.[2]

Physical and sexual assault are also tragically present in marriage. More and more incidents of physical abuse and marital rape are coming to the surface. Even more prevalent are emotionally abusive homes in which family members are violated with demeaning, shaming words.

The data seem to indicate that abuse in marriage is a growing concern. As we have said before, no one knows, sees, and feels the impact of our sin more than our spouses do. Sometimes when our loneliness or our failure to succeed is exposed in our marriages, we develop a rage that desires to blind and silence our spouses. At that point, it is a great temptation to deprive our spouses of their glory when we feel deprived of our own. In those cases, verbal abuse is likely to occur. For people who feel profound shame or who have a history of physical or sexual abuse, that rage may escalate to even more abusive actions. All physical and sexual abuse in a marriage is a grave sign of degradation that must be dealt with both legally (it is a crime) and spiritually (with church discipline).

It is never loving merely to allow an abusive spouse to continue doing harm without intervention and consequences. If an abusive spouse merely says, "I am sorry; forgive me" and gets his or her family to "forgive" and return to a so-called normal life, then it is almost certain violence will occur again. It is crucial that everyone in the family pursue boldly loving the abuser to call forth brokenness and redemption.[3]

Limited Time and Money

A third trigger to marital conflict is the area of limited resources. We are finite creatures with finite resources. Time and money are the two resources that most expose our limits, our failures, and even our impending death. Consequently, few fights over time priorities or money are really about the commodity; instead, the conflict is about what time and money "mean." And we are most resistant to trusting God with our money and time because both expose our deepest vulnerabilities and our core inability to manage our lives as we desire. These passages from Ecclesiastes reflect on the relative value of money.

> Whoever loves money never has money enough;
> whoever loves wealth is never satisfied with his income.
> This too is meaningless. ECCLESIASTES 5:10

I have seen something else under the sun:
The race is not to the swift
or the battle to the strong,
nor does food come to the wise
or wealth to the brilliant
or favor to the learned;
but time and chance happen to them all.
Moreover, no man knows when his hour will come:
As fish are caught in a cruel net,
or birds are taken in a snare,
so men are trapped by evil times
that fall unexpectedly upon them. ECCLESIASTES 9:11-12

In our society money and time represent power—the ability to do things and to influence people. How a husband and wife manage their time and money demonstrates where they put their priorities. As husbands and wives we have many options for how we will spend these resources of power and control, but we do not always agree.

Does the budget include education or vacations? Do we buy a new washer or get season tickets for the football team? Do we have enough money for a new dress, or will that put our budget over the limit? These and other decisions become the occasion for conflict in marriage. Money is the medium of power. More often than not, the issue is not money, but power. The battle is not about who is most trustworthy or whose heart most deeply desires to sacrifice for the other but about who controls the most palpable means of setting the family agenda.

Time becomes a commodity of contention as well. Should a wife work, requiring her husband to take care of the kids after he gets home from his job? Is the husband spending too much time with his colleagues and neglecting his wife?

These conflicts over time and money cloud the real issue: Are we willing to sacrifice for the good and the glory of the other? Quarrels over money and time usually reflect a demand to "own" our life rather than to serve the other with our wealth and existence. The typical fight over who ought to pick up the kids usually is about whose time is more valuable, who works the hardest, and who is least appreciated. It is not wrong to alternate chores or divvy up responsibilities, but the hurtful interactions usually reflect drawing battle lines over more petty matters.

Divided Loyalties

Not only do we fight over money and time, but the real issue is the hint of betrayal. We value money or time more than our spouse. We are more committed to something or someone else than we are to our beloved. The hint of a divided loyalty always brings tension and heartbreak to the surface. King Solomon is a good example of the tragedy of divided loyalty.

> King Solomon, however, loved many foreign women besides Pharaoh's daughter—Moabites, Ammonites, Edomites, Sidonians and Hittites. They were from nations about which the Lord had told the Israelites, "You must not intermarry with them, because they will surely turn your hearts after their gods." Nevertheless, Solomon held fast to them in love. He had seven hundred wives of royal birth and three hundred concubines, and his wives led him astray. As Solomon grew old, his wives turned his heart after other gods, and his heart was not fully devoted to the Lord his God, as the heart of David his father had been. He followed Ashtoreth the goddess of the Sidonians, and Molech the detestable god of the Ammonites. So Solomon did evil in the eyes of the Lord; he did not follow the Lord completely, as David his father had done. 1 KINGS 11:1-6

Solomon was given wisdom from God. He has gone down in biblical history as the wisest of all kings of Israel. Indeed, his name is virtually synonymous with godly wisdom. However, Solomon married women who did not join him in his worship of the true God, and they dragged him away from his first love. As a result, Solomon worshiped other gods. The consequences of his actions were extensive; after his death the kingdom of Israel was divided into two parts.

Paul addresses the issue of divided loyalty in the New Testament. He warns that intimate relationships must have Christ in common or they will fail. Marriage brings enough trouble, but when the troubles come to two people who disagree at the most fundamental and crucial points of life, then disaster will follow.

> Do not be yoked together with unbelievers. For what do righteousness and wickedness have in common? Or what fellowship can light have with darkness? What harmony is there between Christ and Belial? What does a believer have in common with an unbeliever? What agreement is there between the temple of God and idols? For we are the temple of the living God. As God has said: "I will live with them and walk among them, and I will be their God, and they will be my people." 2 CORINTHIANS 6:14-16

The Bible clearly states that to marry a non-Christian is to court disaster. It is the worst kind of divided loyalty. How can true oneness and intimacy develop when one spouse worships God and the other spouse turns a cold shoulder toward the Lord?

It is instructive to note, however, that Paul was not primarily concerned with marriage in this passage. He is saying: "Wise up. Don't hook your horse to just any wagon. Be sure the people with whom you join hands have a common core commitment to God, or you will run into profound disaster." For that matter, it is unwise to marry people who merely profess to love Christ. We must test that faith. Do they have a heart for repentance? Do they long to serve God? Do they bear the same yoke in service, worship, and life? If not, then it is wise to wait and watch and talk until you can find a person who will share that yoke.

Paul has still further advice to people who become Christians after they are married or to Christians who realize that they have made a fundamental mistake in marrying a non-Christian (see later discussion).

Two other types of divided loyalties become the arena for conflict in marriage: arguments over in-laws and over children.

Parents of a married couple represent the most intimate ties of the past. When trouble comes or security is needed, some spouses feel an innate pull back to the womb of the past. This divided loyalty can retard the growth toward union in a married couple. The command to leave, weave, and cleave is crucial.

On the other side of the generational progression stand children. When a child is born, both parents should love and care for that child more than any other human being—except their spouse. That exception is often forgotten in the light of the excitement of the birth of a baby. Children become a promise of hope for the future. When the present seems dull or unhappy, children can represent possibilities for the future.

It is dangerous for husbands and wives to devote their lives to their children at the expense of their own marriage relationship. The irony is that by neglecting the marriage bond, parents can end up hurting their children.

Our loyalties as husbands and wives must be kept in balance. After our relationship to God, our marriage relationship must command our deepest commitment. While our relationships to our parents and children are important, they must not eclipse our primary devotion to our spouses. To allow any other relationship to crowd out that love is potentially deadly.

DIVISION LEADING TO DIVORCE
Marriage as a Covenant

No matter how sincerely it is said, "Until death do us part" rings hollow in today's society, where approximately 50 percent of marriages end in divorce. Christian marriages are not immune. Against this trend stands God's clear pronouncement, "I hate divorce."

> Another thing you do: You flood the Lord's altar with tears. You weep and wail because he no longer pays attention to your offerings or accepts them with pleasure from your hands. You ask, "Why?" It is because the Lord is acting as the witness between you and the wife of your youth, because you have broken faith with her, though she is your partner, the wife of your marriage covenant.
>
> Has not the Lord made them one? In flesh and spirit they are his. And why one? Because he was seeking godly offspring. So guard yourself in your spirit, and do not break faith with the wife of your youth.
>
> "I hate divorce," says the Lord God of Israel, "and I hate a man's covering himself with violence as well as with his garment," says the Lord Almighty.
>
> So guard yourself in your spirit, and do not break faith.
>
> MALACHI 2:13-16

No divorce is pleasing to God. No divorce makes him happy. Divorce rips apart a union that has been sealed before God with words and acts of commitment. A husband and wife have left their parents in order to weave a new family and cleave in a one-flesh union. To "tear asunder what God has put together" is like being drawn and quartered, and emotionally that is what divorce feels like. Amicable separations either are a fiction or are the end of an incredibly superficial relationship.

God hates divorce.

Malachi calls marriage a covenant, and divorce is a breaking of this covenant. A covenant is a relationship of the deepest union. A covenant unites two people or groups in a relationship where they depend on each other for their very survival. In a covenant people commit themselves to each other and take oaths. Their reputation, indeed often their very life,

MARRIAGE IS A COVENANT, AND DIVORCE IS A BREAKING OF THIS COVENANT.

depends on whether or not they keep these commitments.

Whether the covenant is a political treaty (Gen. 21:27), or the relationship between God and the people of Israel (Exod. 19–24), between Christ and the church, or between a husband and wife, to be unfaithful to a covenant relationship is the ultimate treachery. Breaking a covenant betrays the people who have made themselves vulnerable by entering into a relationship; it betrays the people with whom you have the closest relationship.

MARRIAGES ARE NOT GOING TO BE EASY. THEY INVOLVE LABOR AND STRUGGLE.

A divorce for convenience is an essentially cowardly and selfish act. Life is not easy. Marriages are not going to be easy. They involve labor and struggle. To divorce for reasons of incompatibility or to seek personal fulfillment or simply to start life all over again is like deserting during warfare.

The New Testament shares this perspective on marriage.

Paul says the following to the church: "A wife must not separate from her husband. But if she does, she must remain unmarried or else be reconciled to her husband. And a husband must not divorce his wife" (1 Cor. 7:10-11).

In examining Jesus' teachings about divorce, we will see that he holds marriage in the highest regard. Nonetheless, he teaches that in certain circumstances the offended person can (and perhaps should) seek a divorce.

> Some Pharisees came to him to test him. They asked, "Is it lawful for a man to divorce his wife for any and every reason?"
>
> "Haven't you read," he replied, "that at the beginning the Creator 'made them male and female,' and said, 'For this reason a man will leave his father and mother and be united to his wife, and the two will become one flesh'? So they are no longer two, but one. Therefore what God has joined together, let man not separate."
>
> "Why then," they asked, "did Moses command that a man give his wife a certificate of divorce and send her away?"
>
> Jesus replied, "Moses permitted you to divorce your wives because your hearts were hard. But it was not this way from the beginning. I tell you that anyone who divorces his wife, except for marital unfaithfulness, and marries another woman commits adultery."
>
> The disciples said to him, "If this is the situation between a husband and wife, it is better not to marry."
>
> Jesus replied, "Not everyone can accept this word, but only those to whom it has been given. For some are eunuchs because they were born that way; others were made that way by men; and others have renounced marriage because of the kingdom of heaven. The one who can accept this should accept it." MATTHEW 19:3-12

As Malachi 2 teaches, God hates divorce. However, by the time of Jesus, debates over the issue raged among interpreters of the

Hebrew Bible. One school of thought followed Rabbi Shammai, who believed that divorce was allowed only if a wife was unfaithful. Another important school followed Rabbi Hillel, who argued that a man could divorce a woman for the least little reason. They were debating the interpretation of Deuteronomy 24:1, which said, "If a man marries a woman who becomes displeasing to him because he finds something indecent about her, and he writes her a certificate of divorce . . ." The issue was the rather ambiguous phrase "becomes displeasing to him."

When the Pharisees approached Jesus to ask him about divorce, they were trying to catch him up in this debate. The parallel account in Mark puts the question more bluntly, "Is it lawful for a man to divorce his wife?" (Mark 10:2). The way the discussion is shaped in the gospel of Mark also lets us see that these Pharisees are trying to get Jesus in trouble with the leading local political authority, Herod Antipas, who had just divorced his wife in order to marry Herodias.

But even though the Jewish experts in the law tried countless times to get Jesus in trouble with their questions, he turned the tables on them by using each opportunity to teach the truth about the Old Testament, giving guidance to the church about how to act in ways that please God.

Jesus responds to their question by telling them to read Deuteronomy 24 in light of Genesis 1 and 2. Marriage was created for a lifetime union between one man and one woman. Moses in Deuteronomy 24 regulated the practice of his own day. As Robert Gundry says, "Later permission to divorce arose only in a set of instructions to check haste in divorce, the loaning of wives, and similar abuses by prohibiting resumption of the initial marriage."[4]

Jesus, who is God himself, informs the Pharisees that this loose understanding of marriage and divorce will no longer be tolerated. Divorce is not permitted—unless the marriage is broken by some action on the part of the offending person.

Jesus mentions "marital unfaithfulness," and Paul in 1 Corinthians 7 specifies the case of desertion by an unbelieving spouse. These are the two instances where divorce is permitted.

> To the rest I say this (I, not the Lord): If any brother has a wife who is not a believer and she is willing to live with him, he must not divorce her. And if a woman has a husband who is not a believer and he is willing to live with her, she must not divorce him. For the unbelieving husband has been sanctified through his wife, and the unbelieving wife has been sanctified through her believing husband. Otherwise your children would be unclean, but as it is, they are holy.
>
> But if the unbeliever leaves, let him do so. A believing man or woman is not bound in such circumstances; God has called us to live in peace. How do you know, wife, whether you will save your husband? Or, how do you know, husband, whether you will save your wife? 1 CORINTHIANS 7:12-16

MARITAL UNFAITHFULNESS. Marriage is a one-flesh covenant. This profound commitment is sealed by words and acts. At the time of the wedding, a bride and groom speak words that proclaim a lifelong devotion and commitment. Then certain actions, most notably sexual intercourse, become symbolic acts that further express this commitment of union.

MARITAL UNFAITHFULNESS BETRAYS THE RELATIONSHIP BY TAKING THIS SPECIAL ACT, INTERCOURSE, AND SHARING IT WITH OTHERS.

Marital unfaithfulness betrays the relationship by taking this special act, intercourse, and sharing it with others. It breaks the commitment by rebellion and betrayal. Even though it may not be the spoken intention of the adulterers to abandon their spouses, the very act accomplishes the divorce.

The betrayal is called *porneia*. It is a word that can best be translated *sexual immorality*. It certainly includes adultery, but it also includes any other sexual sin that violates the covenant of love. For example, it includes homosexuality, perversion, bestiality, incest, sexual abuse, or assault. It is the joining with any other being or object for sexual pleasure that defrauds our spouses of trust.

In other words, when a woman finds out that her husband has been sleeping with another woman, she in essence discovers that her husband has divorced her. He has deserted his vows, and now she can legitimately leave the relationship through divorce.

UNBELIEVING SPOUSES.   Paul raises another exception to the prohibition of divorce, but once again it is a reaction to the breaking of the covenant by the offending person. As we have already observed, Paul warns Christians not to marry unbelievers. It is not a good idea to enter into life's most intimate relationship with someone who does not share our deepest beliefs and hopes.

However, Paul also recognizes that this is not a perfect world and that some Christians will find themselves married to unbelievers. Note that Paul does not say whether or not they are happily married. His comments to follow are not dependent on the happiness of the Christian. In essence, Paul tells Christians, "Stay with your unbelieving spouses; don't abandon them because good things can come out of the relationship. But if the unbelieving spouse chooses to leave, then consider yourself out of the relationship."

Once again, it is the offending person who has broken the covenant relationship, not the person who is left behind. But Paul encourages such people that they may legitimately and with God's blessing leave the relationship and by implication remarry with the blessing of God.

Now, life is not always cut-and-dried. Applying these biblical passages to real situations sometimes involves hard thinking, prayer, and the advice of church leaders.

For one thing, since even the most mature Christians are sinful and the strongest marriages struggle, the spouse whose partner has left or been unfaithful will likely experience guilt. After all, only people who have not explored their own hearts will find no fault with themselves. Nonetheless, while separation and divorce must be a time for personal meditation and growth, people must not lose sight of who committed the ultimate act of betrayal, adultery, or desertion.

Second, what does it mean to be deserted by an unbeliever? Does this verse apply only to atheists and agnostics who pack up and move out? We would suggest not.

IT IS IMPORTANT, EVEN BEFORE
MARRIAGE CRISES ARISE, TO BE IN
CHRISTIAN COMMUNITY WHERE THE
WISDOM AND ENCOURAGEMENT
OF FELLOW BELIEVERS
ARE AVAILABLE TO HELP.

In the first place, people may proclaim Christ as their Lord with their mouths but reject him with their actions. Such would be the case of a so-called Christian man who keeps physically abusing his wife and/or children. His very actions demonstrate that he is not a Christian and has deserted his family. With that in mind, a woman can legitimately seek separation, if not divorce, from her husband.

But—and this is crucial—such decisions were not meant to be made alone. It is important, even before marriage crises arise, to be in Christian community where the wisdom and encouragement of fellow believers are available to help. It is crucial to be in a good church, before, but especially when a tragedy hits. Divorce may be necessary and permitted by Scripture, but it is never easy and often excruciatingly painful. Support is essential.

HOPE OF REDEMPTION

The Bible is a realistic book. It does not sugarcoat life. It does not always present positive thoughts. The world is a difficult, evil place, and life does not always live up to our expectations.

Divorce is not the only consequence of a difficult marriage. Many marriages that stay together are unhappy relationships. They do not even have to be abusive; they may simply be cold, distant relationships that provide no compassion or support in the battle of daily life.

Marriage may be difficult, but divorce should not be the quick answer. Divorce is a last resort under certain fairly restricted conditions.

But what should we do about a difficult marriage? And even if we are not in a marriage that is perpetually difficult, we all experience the annoyances and frustrations of living closely with another person for life.

HOPE COMES IN BROKENNESS.

Where is the hope for even those glimpses of joy that God gives us while we are still here on earth? It seems paradoxical, but hope comes in brokenness. It comes with forgiveness and a desire to cancel debt and to love boldly. Hope comes through grace, which gives us a taste of the glory to come. We will explore that coming glory in the epilogue, but now we will take a brief look at biblical hope for contemporary marriages.

Marital Brokenness

We began our exploration of sin with Romans, and we now return to that book to find hope. When we read Romans 5:12-14, we learned that sin came into the world through the act of one man, Adam. He was our representative in the Garden of Eden, and when he sinned, we all were guilty. The one can stand for the many, and as that section of Scripture ended, it characterized Adam as "a pattern of the one to come."

That one is Jesus Christ. But it has to be recognized immediately that the comparison between Adam and Christ is a comparison of opposites. In the words of the theologian John Murray, "There is analogy but analogy in respect of what is completely antithetical."[5]

> But the gift is not like the trespass. For if the many died by the trespass of the one man, how much more did God's grace and the gift that came by the grace of the one man, Jesus Christ, overflow to the many! Again, the gift of God is not like the result of the one man's sin: The judgment followed one sin and brought condemnation, but the gift followed many trespasses and brought justification. For if, by the trespass of the one man, death reigned through that one man, how much more will those who receive God's abundant provision of grace and of the gift of righteousness reign in life through the one man, Jesus Christ.
>
> Consequently, just as the result of one trespass was condemnation for all men, so also the result of one act of righteousness was justification that brings life for all men. For just as through the disobedience of the one man the many were made sinners, so also through the obedience of the one man the many will be made righteous. ROMANS 5:15-19

The similarity between the two is that their actions have an impact on those to whom they are related. Through Adam's sin came death and condemnation. But through Christ's righteous act came grace and life.

JESUS CHRIST IS THE ONLY FIRM FOUNDATION FOR A SUCCESSFUL MARRIAGE.

Just as Adam's act branded us rightly as sinners, so Christ's act brands those who are united to him as righteous. But who are those who are united to him? Who are those who know the gift of God's grace as a result of Christ's great act of sacrifice? They are Christians, those who turn to Jesus for help. They know they are sinners who have no other place to go than to the Savior.

Jesus Christ is the only firm foundation for a successful marriage. Marriage unites two selfish sinners. Left to their own resources, their marriage would devolve into divorce, which is the marital equivalent of death.

THE ONLY SOURCE FOR HOPE AND JOY IN MARRIAGE IS IN THE GOSPEL.

Even apart from faith, a grace, which theologians call *common grace,* restrains people from acting as sinfully as we are, which is the only reason why any non-Christian marriages stay together. But the only source for hope and joy in marriage is in Jesus Christ.

Jesus Christ made the ultimate sacrifice and died for our sins on the cross. The gospel is the story of an abundant and overwhelming forgiveness in light of horrid sin. His forgiveness saves us from our guilt and sin and also gives us meaning in our lives right now as well as giving us the promise of eternal life with him forever.

The gospel also gives us a pattern for living in relationships in a sinful world. Christ's example demonstrates that we must be people who know our own sin as we also forgive the sins of others.

The Log in Your Eye

> Do not judge, or you too will be judged. For in the same way you judge others, you will be judged, and with the measure you use, it will be measured to you. Why do you look at the speck of sawdust in your brother's eye and pay no attention to the plank in your own eye? How can you say to your brother, "Let me take the speck out of your eye," when all the time there is a plank in your own eye? You hypocrite, first take the plank out of your own eye, and then you will see clearly to remove the speck from your brother's eye.
>
> MATTHEW 7:1-5

Contrary to popular opinion, this passage does not completely and absolutely forbid judging other people. If it did teach that, it would contradict a number of other passages that not only give permission but also encourage Christians to help each other discover and deal with sin in their lives (Luke 17:3; Gal. 6:1; 1 Tim. 5:20). What it does prohibit is a proud judgment, a judgment that does not allow me to recognize the sin in my own life, a proud judgment that allows me to use my wife's sin to crush her rather than build her up.

Marriage will provide many, many occasions to act on this verse. From the time I get up in the morning until the time I go to sleep (and sometimes during sleep), I have the potential for real and imagined offense.

It is right and good for my wife and me to deal gently and compassionately with each other's faults. Together we can help each other grow into maturity in the faith.

I MUST KNOW THAT MY SIN IS GREATER THAN MY WIFE'S SIN.

But I must know that my sin is greater than my wife's sin. Only then can I approach her with an attitude that will win her to Christ rather than drive her away from me and possibly from the faith.

Unremitting Forgiveness

> If your brother sins, rebuke him, and if he repents, forgive him. If he sins against you seven times in a day, and seven times comes back to you and says, "I repent," forgive him.
> LUKE 17:3-4

These verses show us that, though we must first recognize our own sins, my wife and I still should tenderly expose each other's faults. Such exposure can be frightening and painful; that is why we must exercise great care and consideration. After all, we are uncovering something ugly.

The object of such exposure is not ridicule or hurt but restoration and strengthening of relationship. Jesus here teaches that our forgiveness should be unending toward those who come to us broken and sorry for their offenses.

Marriage thrusts two people into a lifelong intimate relationship where this type of repetitive offense can flourish. Husbands and wives will feel tempted to say, "Enough is enough!"

Jesus, by using the number seven, which stands for completion, tells his disciples that our forgiveness never ends. There is never a point where we can say, "That's it. I'm leaving!"

Forgiveness Fuels Love

People are under the false impression that many faults or sins can only destroy a marriage. And they can, unless we adopt a forgiving attitude that stems from the recognition that my faults are greater than my spouse's.

JESUS IS THE ONE WHO GIVES US
THE GRACE THAT ALLOWS US
TO ACKNOWLEDGE OUR OWN SINS
AND ALSO TO FORGIVE THE SINS
OF OUR SPOUSES.

But the surprising truth is that forgiveness enhances love. In other words, if my wife can live with me in spite of my faults, she must really care about me! Even when I offend her, she still stays with me and helps and encourages me. That is deep and abiding love.

> Then he turned toward the woman and said to Simon, "Do you see this woman? I came into your house. You did not give me any water for my feet, but she wet my feet with her tears and wiped them with her hair. You did not give me a kiss, but this woman, from the time I entered, has not stopped kissing my feet. You did not put oil on my head, but she has poured perfume on my feet. Therefore, I tell you, her many sins have been forgiven—for she loved much. But he who has been forgiven little loves little."
> LUKE 7:44-47

Knowing my faults and sharing them with my spouse is not a sign of weakness. It is a step toward strength. That vulnerability produces confidence in our relationship.

What hope is there for the marriage of two sinners in a fallen world? Jesus Christ is the hope that brings joy in the present and certainty about the future. Jesus is the one who gives us the grace that allows us to acknowledge our own sins and also to forgive the sins of our spouses.

The lifestyle of repentance and forgiveness gives us hope for joy in the present. It also looks beyond to something greater. The gospel opens our eyes to the Marriage that every one of us desires.

QUESTIONS FOR REFLECTION AND CONVERSATION

1. What is sin? How does sin mar your marriage relationship? What are the subtle ways sin affects your marriage?
2. Do you consider yourself a basically good person? Do you think you are totally bad, with no good qualities? How does the Bible describe you? What would keep you from seeing the copresence of sin and glory in most of what you do?
3. Are all sins the same or are some worse than others? How does God see sin?
4. In what ways do you rebel? How does your rebellion or pride hinder your marriage relationship?
5. Why is it important to acknowledge that you are a sinner in order to make a marriage grow?
6. How can someone be married and lonely? How are you lonely in your marriage?
7. What are the "triggers" that lead to anger, frustration, and lust in your marriage relationship?
8. Everyone struggles with limited time and resources in life and marriage. Where are the tension points in your relationship? How are you coping with them?

9. Where are the divided loyalties in your life? What other relationships are putting a roadblock in the way of a better marriage?

10. On what grounds do you think divorce is allowed? Do you and your spouse share the same views? Would you contemplate divorce on any other grounds?

11. As you approach your spouse, do you acknowledge your own brokenness?

12. Do you have a forgiving heart toward your spouse?

13. How has your marriage changed your spouse in negative ways? What in your relationship has caused your spouse to feel more distant from God?

14. How has your marriage changed your spouse in positive ways? What in your relationship has caused your spouse to feel closer to God?

15. How has God used your spouse to change you? In what ways has your spouse helped you move closer to God?

MARK AND JENNIFER
BECOME INTIMATE ALLIES
AGAINST EACH OTHER'S SIN

The Sunday school class ended. The thirty couples sat quietly long after Bing had finished. A few moved to get on their jackets and pick up the discarded cups that littered the floor. It was a somber crowd. A few stalwarts joked with Bing, but even their banter felt hollow and contrived.

Mark felt genuine fear. He could not get the word *coward* out of his mind. He reflected on how hard it was to ask Jennifer for a check at the beginning of the week to have money for lunch. She wanted him to pack his lunch; it was cheaper. He hated to be the only employee who did not roll over to Fred's Diner—a greasy, all-male establishment that women did not enter due to the leers of the regulars or at least the probability of dysentery.

And Mark would need to ask for the check today. He was afraid Jennifer might have listened to Bing. If so, then she would be even more surly and cranky. She might make him grovel before she wrote a check for half of what he wanted. He felt like such a little boy.

He need not have worried. Jennifer was not cranky; she was not even attuned to the nausea she felt. She had tuned out Bing's comments well before even a few phrases passed through her detached consciousness. She was thinking about how she wanted to open the bottle of Cabernet she hid under the sink. It would take away her upset stomach and soothe an ache she could not name.

She put on her coat and began to walk alone out of the room. Mark tagged along behind, chatting with a few folks as he kept his eye on Jennifer. She started to walk out the door instead of turning down the hallway to get the kids. He pulled away from a conversation and ran up to Jennifer. "Did you want me to get the babes?"

"Yeah, I'll meet you at the car."

Mark was surprised. Usually she got the kids. She received their overtures of joy, and he usually stood in the background holding their coats. It seemed odd to be the one to receive their hugs. It felt good.

The ride home was uncharacteristically subdued. It was as if a cloud of unknowing divided them. They were both lost in the kind of thought that is an attempt to avoid thinking. The day hurried by.

So did the week. All that Bing had talked about fell by the wayside due to the normal busyness of life.

The only change was the way Jennifer had written out the check for Mark's lunch money. She had done it with an absentminded friendliness. She had even asked how much he wanted. He had asked for half of what he desired and was furious when it appeared he could have asked for twice the amount and gotten it easily.

Soon Sunday morning stared them in the face like a rainy November morning in which only those who were paid to be religious ventured out in the dreariness. But both Jennifer and Mark dressed without a word or without a thought of missing their Sunday school class.

An awkward stillness shrouded the classroom as people took their seats and barely acknowledged one another. The same men who had tried to break the silence with playful banter sat looking out the window with sullen indifference. Cassandra, Bing's wife, rose to start the class.

Cassandra: "Welcome back, folks. I imagine a few of you were offended or at least taken aback last time by Bing's remarks. Men, you can relax. I am going to talk about women today."

The women in the room smiled politely, and their husbands glowed with relief. What they did not realize was that Cassandra was not telling the whole truth. She could not talk about her failures without implicating Bing, any more than he could talk about his cowardice without implicating her.

Cassandra: "Let me talk about a woman's view of sex. Let it be said first of all, I love sex, but not for the same reason Bing does. I love an orgasm, but for me it is the dessert, not the main course. Bing sees an orgasm as the hors d'oeuvre, salad, main course, and dessert. He may even see it as someone else paying the bill."

The women were now smiling in unison, and the men were grinning like boys who got caught trying to bring a frog into class.

Cassandra: "Men want sex; women want connection. Men think connection is sex; women think sex is a way for men

339

to avoid connecting. It's sad, but both are right. I found that it was nearly impossible for Bing to understand that he could not ignore me or mistreat me and then two hours later expect that I would want sex. Bing seemed to be confused that I would withhold something so basic, natural, and good from him simply because he had not done something perfectly."

Bing: "Yeah. I thought she was just making me pay. If I wasn't a good boy, then I wouldn't get dessert. If I did something right, then I would feel rewarded. I felt so controlled. Cassandra seemed to be in charge. I worked and handled problems, but if I didn't say the right thing, I was in the doghouse."

Cassandra: "I want to follow up on Bing's remark about me being controlling. I don't look as if I am in control. I am a quiet, deferential woman who is as manipulative and as bossy as any domineering, fear-provoking woman. . . ."

Cassandra and Bing spoke for forty-five minutes. They talked about in-laws and sex—the two areas that had most deeply affected their marriage. Their stories regaled the class. Cassandra told about how Bing had refused to call to get directions to a restaurant. He made her do it, so then when they got lost, he could blame her. And Cassandra admitted that she had never really listened to the street names because she felt it was Bing's responsibility to check out a map if they got lost.

At one point, Cassandra began to cry when Bing brought up how that pattern had created tragic tension with his oldest daughter. Bing would never make decisions, but he also would not let Cassandra make decisions. Decisions about dating, driving, or clothes were postponed until Janet, their daughter, chose to rebel out of a refusal to wait.

The class went on a roller-coaster ride of humor and pathos.

Soon most of the people saw the patterns of cowardice and control as personal and not just an unsettling concept.

Jennifer playfully poked Mark in the ribs when Bing talked about the way men ask for money from their wives. Mark was stunned. She had poked him before but never with a gentle nudge. He looked at her, expecting her eyes to be full of condescending mockery; her expression was playful and kind. A strange sequence followed: he pointed his finger at her and frowned. He had never dared call her bluff. If he had, he would have paid in full with interest from countless other small debts incurred over years.

Instead, she lowered her eyes and said in a whisper: "I know. We have a lot to talk about." Mark turned away from her, turning her words over in his mind.

The drive home was neither distant nor normal. For the first time, Mark felt as if Jennifer was inviting him to start the conversation. The conversation did not begin in bold confidence or articulate repentance. But for one of the first times, Mark felt as if they were both involved in a dialogue.

Mark: "Jen, I know we've got a lot to talk—"

Jennifer: "Yeah, we do."

Mark: "Jen, don't interrupt. This is not easy for me."

Jennifer: "What am I supposed to do? Pave the way for you?"

Mark: "Look! Your sarcasm is just what—"

Jennifer: "No. You look. I am sick and tired of having someone with life experience tell me what to think. And I am sick and tired of you telling me that you're unhappy."

Mark: "I never said I'm unhappy."

Jennifer: "Well, you ought to be if you think you are a coward."

Mark: "You're twisting things and—"

Jennifer: "Oh, grow up. I don't know what you thought you were getting into when you married me, but I knew it was not going to be any picnic to go on this joyride with you."

Mark turned away. He was making a left-hand turn, and he looked away long enough not only to make the turn but also to indicate he was no longer interested in sparring with her. He felt his heart sink. He had felt hope. He had noticed Jennifer laugh during the class, and at one point it seemed as if she had almost cried. He had so hoped she would give up her testy, biting sarcasm and admit she was a shrew. The word *coward* was nowhere in his mind as he sighed and quietly drove on, sulking in his self-righteousness.

Before Mark had finished the turn, Jennifer had put her elbow on the car door and then had put her cheek on her hand with a lazy nonchalance. She was his superior, and she hated him for it. Her heart flirted with saying she was sorry, but he would have to come after her before she would admit to even partial wrong. She could feel her heart grow hard by degrees, and she put up no fight to end his silence. She had won again. And she knew she desperately wanted him to fight, to scream, to engage.

The sunlight hit her directly in the face. She closed her eyes. She could feel the heat on her face and the salty tears growing under her eyelids. The warmth felt so good; the tears felt even better. She was surprised that the warm rain running down her cheeks felt good. It made her feel as if someday, maybe, someone else—someone other than she—might win instead.

Jennifer had no sense of what her husband was doing or feeling. She was cut off from all connection with him, caught up in the narrowing spiral of her dying desire. If she had turned, she would have seen a look that may have triggered terror. Mark was not glazed and focused on the road. He was not indulging in silent, violent contempt. His eyes were warm and full of sorrow.

Mark knew he was a coward. When he averted his eyes, he could feel both rage and fear boil up inside. In the past, he could justify his rage, ignore his fear, and concentrate on the sin of his shrewish wife. But he could no longer do that. He knew her nonchalance was a lie. She did care; she did desire. The Bible told him so.

He leaned over to her and put his hand on her shoulder and said, "Jenny, I'm afraid, but I won't let your sin or mine win this time. You can leave me, but I know you and I are meant for something better, frankly more glorious, than what either of us have ever known. When we get home, let's talk."

Jennifer turned from the window and looked at him. She was stunned. Never had he talked with her warmly, gently, and full of courage after she had eviscerated him. It all seemed like a dream, at first a nightmare of lost desire, and then a wild, lovely dream of waltzing over a waterfall made of sparkling clouds and cerulean sky. She could feel herself stiffen and her heart harden with her ancient habit of killing hope, but even to her surprise, she said, "OK. I agree. I don't want to end here."

Mark smiled. He knew, for the first time, she was a castle he could scale, a fortress he could surmount in time. He was not so foolish anymore to believe it would be done in a night, but he knew that nothing was more important than wooing the woman God had called to be his wife. He drove the next few blocks with a smile that would have shamed a Cheshire cat.

EPILOGUE

Marriage brings together two people who are created in the image of God. They individually and as a couple
reflect divine glory. Marriage is an awesome and wonderful
union that has great potential for joy and celebration.

The Bible, though, is a realistic book. It also describes us as
flawed, selfish creatures; we are sinners. When two sinners
come together, they do not become less selfish or less flawed;
they become more so. Marriage is a frightening prospect that
can be the arena for harm and pain.

Married people do not function in a moral vacuum either.
God created the world good. It is an incredibly beautiful place,
but, like human beings, the entire world has felt the effects of

the Fall. We are not surprised, then, to find the world a hostile and dangerous place to live.

Married people confront life as a battle. As intimate allies, they push back the chaos. With the power of God, marriage is an awesome calling and at times a delightful prelude of heaven. But no matter what joy or what sense of meaning is found in marriage, it is always involved in a war. At times marriage itself is part of the war.

MARRIED PEOPLE CONFRONT LIFE AS A BATTLE. AS INTIMATE ALLIES, THEY PUSH BACK THE CHAOS.

Some readers may be repelled by such a picture of the Christian life. "Isn't Christ supposed to fill my life with joy?" "Doesn't he promise me success after success?"

The answer to these questions is a resounding yes, but sometimes we define what we mean by joy and success in a way that Jesus never meant it. Life continues to be a struggle for Christians. We are not immediately transported outside of a fallen world when we are converted, and we are not transformed into perfect, sinless people.

The picture of marriage that we have presented in this book is not a pessimistic, negative one. It is wonderfully positive. And the exciting thing is that the picture of marriage in this book is positive without glossing over the disturbing nature of reality.

It is a relief to discover that no marriage is perfect. Some people worry that their marriages are the only ones that struggle. It seems that all their Christian friends have such flawless unions; it makes them wonder what is wrong with them.

Also, once we see that no marriage is perfect, we can see

where the real joy is found. As we commented in the last section, joy can be experienced as we discover our sin and offer each other forgiveness. A successful marriage is one in which two broken and forgiving people stay committed to one another in a sacrificial relationship in the face of life's chaos. We are intimate allies in the war. We rejoice together in our victories and cry together as we encounter setbacks. But even in the setbacks, we can have joy because we know that the final victory is ours. We look forward to the ultimate Wedding, which our own weddings only faintly reflect.

A SUCCESSFUL MARRIAGE IS ONE
IN WHICH TWO BROKEN
AND FORGIVING PEOPLE STAY
COMMITTED TO ONE ANOTHER
IN A SACRIFICIAL RELATIONSHIP IN
THE FACE OF LIFE'S CHAOS.

True intimacy comes about only when a husband and wife are willing to be broken and to bless one another with forgiveness. Our marriages ought to provide the context for seeing our own sin and for changing. The Christian life within the context of marriage is a forward-moving path. As time goes on in a marriage that operates on the principle of brokenness and forgiveness, the marriage will get stronger and stronger.

The preceding paragraphs have summarized the important principles from the five main sections of the book.

1. Marriage unites two creatures who bear the image of
   God. As husbands and wives, we both reflect God's glory.
   We are called to delight in and to enhance one another's
   already-present glory to the glory of God.

2. Our spouses are joint heirs and rulers over creation. Together husbands and wives are to create order and beauty out of chaos and form in one another an even clearer picture of God, the divine ruler.
3. Men and women are equal but unique reflections of God. A strong man will awaken the strong tenderness of his wife. A tender woman will draw forth the tender strength of her husband. We are allies, not enemies or strangers.
4. We long for the delight of union. Our alliance is intimate. We need to put aside anything that blocks the possibility of our one-flesh relationship.
5. Sin affects our marriages. Marriages exist in a dangerous, sinful world. Our marriages themselves are constantly challenged by the offenses we commit against our spouses. Our marriages must be characterized by brokenness and the willingness to forgive.

However, we have not exhausted the Bible's rich teaching about marriage. Indeed, if we stopped here, we would fail to provide the understanding needed to give our marriages strength in the midst of the struggle.

Our marriages have meaning and joy in the present, thanks to the grace of Jesus Christ. But as we conclude this book, we look to the future. The hope of the future grounds our present glimpses of grace.

The Bible speaks of marriage from Genesis 1 to the end of the book of Revelation. In the previous pages we have taken a topical approach centered on five crucial teachings from Genesis 1–3. We will conclude our meditation on the Bible's vision of marriage by exploring God's design for marriage and sexuality as it unfolds in the narrative of the Scriptures. As we do this, we will have a glimpse at an incredible mystery. Our marriage reflects another marriage. God speaks of our relationship with him as a marriage. It is amazing, but our relationship with God is so intimate that it can be understood only in light of the passion that is to be shared within a marriage union.

OUR RELATIONSHIP WITH GOD IS SO INTIMATE THAT IT CAN BE UNDERSTOOD ONLY IN LIGHT OF THE PASSION THAT IS TO BE SHARED WITHIN A MARRIAGE UNION.

As we survey the Scriptures, we will return to a number of passages that are familiar to us from earlier study, but we will be looking at them from a different perspective.

Genesis 1–2: Creation of Marriage and Sexuality

God created everything "good," including relationship. In the Garden of Eden three beings were knit into a deep, intimate relationship—Adam, Eve, and God.

Although we cannot fathom the depths of the mystery, God desires relationship. If not, then why would he have bothered to create the cosmos? Why would he have bothered to create Adam, then Eve?

Adam and God enjoyed a wonderful relationship from the start, but God noted a loneliness in his creature. Adam was created from the dust of the earth and from the breath of God; thus he related to the creatures of the earth as well as to God himself. But something was still lacking, and that something was a creature who was his peer, someone who was his equal.

God created Eve, a creature who captured Adam's heart

right from the beginning and set him singing: "This is now bone of my bones and flesh of my flesh; she shall be called 'woman,' for she was taken out of man" (Gen. 2:23).

The relationship between Adam and Eve was deep and satisfying. They could stand before one another, naked and completely vulnerable to one another, and feel absolutely no shame or guilt. They could give and receive love and affection. They were two similar, though not identical, creatures who could fully enjoy their union into one.

ALTHOUGH WE CANNOT FATHOM THE DEPTHS OF THE MYSTERY, GOD DESIRES RELATIONSHIP.

But this was not all. They also experienced union with God. Adam and Eve also knew God with a profound intimacy. The depth of this relationship is characterized in the Bible as "walking in the Garden" (Gen. 3:8). The relationship was carefree and fulfilling.

So as human history dawned, the relationship between a man and a woman—as well as the relationship between humans and God—was deep, intimate, and satisfying. The human-human relationship between the sexes as well as the divine-human relationship were characterized by an openness to receive love and a passion to pursue it:

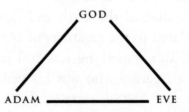

Although the word *marriage* is not used in Genesis 1–2, we see in these chapters its beginnings. Adam and Eve are the first husband and wife. But more than that, as we will see, God likens his relationship with his people to a marriage as well. Thus, God, Adam, and Eve experience perfect and joyful union.

Genesis 3: Trouble in the Garden of Relationship

In light of the ecstasy of relationship described above, a question immediately confronts us. Why choose evil? Why choose to disobey God in a way that threatens this bliss?

Theologians have asked this question for centuries. Where did evil come from? Certainly the serpent lures Eve and Adam to their fateful decision, but where did the serpent come from? The Bible chooses not to answer this question in detail. But we do learn from Genesis 3 that human evil resulted from a choice, a choice to follow evil rather than God's good.

WE DO KNOW THAT GOD CREATED
ADAM AND EVE AS HUMAN BEINGS
WHO WERE CAPABLE OF MAKING
A CHOICE EITHER FOR HIM
OR AGAINST HIM.

We do know that God created Adam and Eve as human beings who were capable of making a choice either for him or against him. Why Eve foolishly and wickedly chose wrong rather than good and thus enslaved human choice to evil from that moment on is hidden in mystery but perhaps reflected in our own evil hearts.

This choice had immediate and devastating effects on relationships. In a word, loneliness re-entered human experience, but this time the loneliness was like a jagged shard. Before Eve was created, Adam felt a lack that could be called loneliness, but then he knew that God was intimately involved with him. After the fall into sin, loneliness packed a double force. Adam knew what it was like to know Eve intimately, but because of sin that intimacy was no longer possible.

Loneliness is intensified by loss, a loss intensified by fear and shame. This loss of intimacy is narrated in sexual terms. No longer could Adam and Eve exist in the Garden together naked and feel no shame. Now barriers, both physical and emotional, blocked easy relation between the man and the woman.

Not only were Eve and Adam lost to each other, but they also lost God's intimate presence. No longer could Adam and Eve enjoy simple walks in the Garden with their God. After the Fall, the divine-human relationship experienced a breach that required Adam and Eve and all human beings since to acknowledge their sin before moving close to God again.

Men and women felt pain and distance in their most personal relationships. Adam and Eve remained married, and they remained children of God, but alienation characterized both of these intimate relationships:

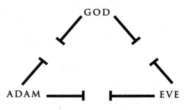

Song of Songs: Sexuality Redeemed
In the Garden God loved Adam and Eve and related to them with the most profound intimacy. Their sin was a betrayal of the most severe magnitude. It erected a relational barrier that resulted in their ejection from the Garden.

But God did not completely abandon the objects of his love. He neither killed them on the spot nor left them to make it on their own. Rather, he reached out to them with grace by giving them clothing. Even more significantly, he opened to them a way of redemption, a path by which they might enjoy relationship with him once again.

The restoration of relationship between God and his human creatures also opens up the possibility for renewal of the relationship between man and woman. The Song of Songs poetically presents the vision of a redeemed sexuality.

Throughout the preceding chapters, we have looked at different sections of the Song of Songs. Now we will place the whole book in the context of the Bible's continuing message about divine-human and man-woman relationships.

The Song of Songs is a return to the Garden. The woman and the man find themselves once again in a garden setting, and, just as Adam and Eve were before the Fall, they are naked and feel no shame. Rather, they revel in one another's bodies, extolling the beauty of their spouse. Using the most erotic and playful language, they take full joy in their physical attributes. The Song of Songs confirms that God gave married couples sexual pleasure as a gift that they are encouraged to enjoy to the fullest.

Nonetheless, as we read the Song, we get the feeling that more is coming. The man and woman experience bliss but not uninterrupted joy in the Song of Songs. Intimacy is not constant; obstacles still break the bond. Perhaps most notable is the episode in chapter 5. In an erotically provocative scene, the man comes to his beloved's door seeking entry into her room. She puts him off, and by the time she gets to the door, he has disappeared into the night. Aroused, she sets off in pursuit, but she is blocked by the night guards, who abuse her.

The Song of Songs is not recounting a real historical event or telling us about actual people. It is not even a narrative. It is a lyric that sings of love in the period after the Fall but before the consummation of history when Jesus Christ returns a second time. The account in the Song reminds us that our marriages have potential for love and true intimacy between spouses, but our love will be marred by sin and the Curse. Total intimacy is not possible this side of the Second Coming.

The Song of Songs does more than speak of human love. At the time of the ancient church and until recently, it was believed that the Song sings only of the relationship of the church and Christ. While this interpretation is wrongly blind to the human eroticism of the Song, it does preserve a true insight into the deeper meaning of the Song.

The Song is not an allegory but a metaphor for the relationship between Christ and Christians. The Song read in light of Ephesians 5:21-33 is a poem extolling the sensual, passionate intimacy that we can enjoy with God through the redemption supplied by Jesus Christ.

Hosea and Gomer:
A Human Parable of Divine Pursuit

The Song of Songs tells us that we can have glimpses of the Garden even now. We can find joy in marriage and have relationship with God today. It also warns us that we will find rocks in the Garden, not only in human marriage but also in our relationship with God. Hosea's marriage to Gomer, described in Hosea 1–3, typifies both problems.

Hosea's prophecy opens with God's command to the prophet to marry a woman of dubious sexual behavior. The prophet gives no indication that this is a parable; he seems to be reflecting on his actual marriage to a real woman. What is a little unclear is whether Gomer was promiscuous at the time of the wedding or whether she became so afterward. While scholars debate this issue, it makes little difference for our purpose. In either case it is quite clear that the marriage of the prophet and the adulteress represents the relationship between God and his sinful people, Israel.

We see again the close connection between marriage and the divine-human relationship. They are closely tied together, so that adultery can symbolize idolatry. Marriage is a mirror reflection of our relationship with God. To cheat on a spouse is like cheating on God. They both involve betrayal of an intimate, exclusive relationship. To break one's relationship with God or a spouse is to break a covenant, as we have discussed before.

TO CHEAT ON A SPOUSE IS LIKE CHEATING ON GOD.

At the time of Hosea's ministry the people of Israel had become complacent toward God. They began to worship false gods, especially the hated god of the Canaanites, Baal (Hos. 2:17). In the midst of this false worship, God commanded Hosea, "Go, take to yourself an adulterous wife and children of unfaithfulness, because the land is guilty of the vilest adultery in departing from the Lord" (Hos. 1:2). Hosea then married Gomer, with whom he had three children, Jezreel, Lo-Ruhamah, and Lo-Ammi. The first name reminded everyone of Jehu and the massacre at the valley of Jezreel. The names of the second two meant "No compassion" and "Not my people," indicating that God was going to abandon his people and no longer love them. These three names obviously pointed to the coming judgment, a judgment that was realized when Assyria devastated the ten northern tribes and when Babylon exiled the southern tribes nearly fifty years later.

Just as Hosea's wife was unfaithful to him, so the people of God had "slept around" with other gods. Hosea's marriage and children were shocking, a real community scandal. Although the scandal caused Hosea real pain, God used it to show Israel just how bad they were.

The words at the beginning of the second chapter were addressed to both Gomer and the people of Israel. These words give the tone of the whole chapter:

> Rebuke your mother, rebuke her,
> for she is not my wife,
> and I am not her husband.
> Let her remove the adulterous look from her face
> and the unfaithfulness from between her breasts.
> Otherwise I will strip her naked
> and make her as bare as on the day she was born;
> I will make her like a desert,
> turn her into a parched land,
> and slay her with thirst. HOSEA 2:2-3

Although the book of Hosea was addressed primarily to the Old Testament people, its message must penetrate our hearts as well. As Christians, we are married to God. He is our spouse. We share with God the kind of intimate relationship that a husband and wife share. Indeed, if anything, our relationship to God must be deeper, truer, more intimate and profound.

AS CHRISTIANS, WE ARE MARRIED TO GOD. HE IS OUR SPOUSE.

When we neglect God or turn our backs on him, we are spitting in the eye of our lover. And the amazing message of Hosea is that this lover, though he judges and purifies his bride, does not completely abandon her. Israel is not cast off as a whole; God loves his people even though they are sinners. He abandons them to a taste of absence in order to restore them to relationship. Such is the intention of God's second command to Hosea concerning his wife, "Go, show your love to your wife again, though she is loved by another and is an adulteress. Love her as the Lord loves the Israelites, though they turn to other gods and love the sacred raisin cakes" (Hos. 3:1).

WHEN WE NEGLECT GOD OR TURN OUR BACKS ON HIM, WE ARE SPITTING IN THE EYE OF OUR LOVER.

God pursues us with a holy love for the sake of winning his bride. He is willing to endure shame, heartache, and frustration in order to regain his love. This paradigm implies that our marriages are the testing ground for God to win us to himself. Our marriages are basic training for the one Marriage that will not disappoint.

Revelation 19:1-9: The Final Wedding

Hosea and the author of the Song of Songs are not alone in seeing that human marriage with its wonders and dangers is a fitting mirror of our relationship with God. We are built for deep, satisfying relationships reflecting the kind of relationship that exists within the Godhead himself—Father, Son, and Holy Spirit. Relationship is at the core of existence.

We are not meant to feel distant from each other or from God. Such loneliness exists in marriage and in worship as the result of sin and a fallen world. It is not surprising, then, to see that one of the pictures the Bible gives us of the future is a great wedding feast, ushering in a marriage that restores and surpasses the intimacy of the Garden.

After this I heard what sounded like the roar of a great
multitude in heaven shouting: "Hallelujah! Salvation and
glory and power belong to our God, for true and just are
his judgments. He has condemned the great prostitute
who corrupted the earth by her adulteries. He has avenged
on her the blood of his servants."

And again they shouted: "Hallelujah! The smoke from
her goes up for ever and ever."

The twenty-four elders and the four living creatures fell
down and worshiped God, who was seated on the throne.
And they cried: "Amen, Hallelujah!"

Then a voice came from the throne, saying: "Praise our
God, all you his servants, you who fear him, both small
and great!"

Then I heard what sounded like a great multitude, like
the roar of rushing waters and like loud peals of thunder,
shouting: "Hallelujah! For our Lord God Almighty reigns.
Let us rejoice and be glad and give him glory! For the
wedding of the Lamb has come, and his bride has made
herself ready. Fine linen, bright and clean, was given her
to wear." (Fine linen stands for the righteous acts of the
saints.)

Then the angel said to me, "Write: 'Blessed are those who
are invited to the wedding supper of the Lamb!'" And he
added, "These are the true words of God." REVELATION 19:1-9

This hymn to God may be split into two related parts; they
are the negative and positive sides of the same final act. First
God destroys the whore, and then he marries the bride. Even
the end of all history, like the beginning in the Garden, is
conceptualized in light of marriage and adultery.

From the previous scriptural meditations we know that the
prostitute stands for all those forces, human and spiritual, that
stand against God. She has rebelled against God and has
exploited others. So God does away with her.

But all of this is in preparation for the great wedding ceremony, the marriage of the Lamb, who is Jesus, to his bride, the church. The heavenly realities of Ephesians 5:25-33 will come to their ultimate realization when Jesus returns and brings his people to himself. The intimate relationship experienced briefly in the Garden will be restored. The desired communion between God and his human creatures will be reestablished, never to be broken again. We will be married to God himself.

GOD DESTROYS THE WHORE, AND THEN HE MARRIES THE BRIDE.

But what of human marriage? What will happen to the relationships that we have with our spouses right now?

Luke 20:27-40: The End of Marriage, the Beginning of Heavenly Bliss

Some of the Sadducees, who say there is no resurrection, came to Jesus with a question. "Teacher," they said, "Moses wrote for us that if a man's brother dies and leaves a wife but no children, the man must marry the widow and have children for his brother. Now there were seven brothers. The first one married a woman and died childless. The second and then the third married her, and in the same way the seven died, leaving no children. Finally, the woman died too. Now then, at the resurrection whose wife will she be, since the seven were married to her?"

Jesus replied, "The people of this age marry and are given in marriage. But those who are considered worthy of taking part in that age and in the resurrection from the dead will neither marry nor be given in marriage, and they can no longer die; for they are like the angels. They are God's

359

children, since they are children of the resurrection. But in the account of the bush, even Moses showed that the dead rise, for he calls the Lord 'the God of Abraham, and the God of Isaac, and the God of Jacob.' He is not the God of the dead, but of the living, for to him all are alive."

Some of the teachers of the law responded, "Well said, teacher!" And no one dared to ask him any more questions.

LUKE 20:27-40

There is no marriage in heaven. Jesus' pronouncement here causes diverse reactions in people. People who enjoy their spouses may feel disappointed if they think that Jesus meant that they will not experience the same kind of deep relationship they presently enjoy. Those who struggle in their marriage may greet this information as gospel—that is, liberating news of hope.

First, we must acknowledge that we really know so little about heaven and the afterlife. We do know it is wonderful, but why it is so wonderful is not detailed. Its reality will exceed anything that we can imagine presently.

HEAVEN WILL NOT BE DULL; IT WILL BE A PLACE OF THE MOST INTENSE AND FULFILLED PASSIONS.

Second, Jesus' words here raise as many questions as they answer about marriage in heaven. After all, the question presented to him was not really about the nature of marriage. Some Sadducees wanted to make him look silly. They did not believe in the afterlife. They merely wanted to ask Jesus a question that would make his position seem ridiculous. They asked him about a woman who had remarried a number of times after each one of her husbands had died.

360

Jesus, as always, saw through their ruse and cut right to the point. He made one thing very clear in response to their absurd issue: In heaven there is no marriage as we know it now. But what we often miss is that Jesus does not discuss the nature of relationship between his creatures in heaven.

EACH MOMENT OF MARRIAGE IS AN ANTICIPATION OF THAT MOMENT WHEN WE WILL WALK DOWN THE AISLE TO THE LAMB'S WAITING EMBRACE.

This denial of marriage and the absence of anything in its place has conjured in the minds of many people a picture of heaven as a sterile, somber place with no desire, no passion, no arousal. Once again, we need to remind ourselves that the Bible intentionally minimizes discussion of life in heaven. But we think it is fair to say that, at least using human language, heaven will not be dull; it will be a place of the most intense and fulfilled passions. We agree with the insightful comment of Lewis Smedes, "Many readers of Jesus' words have thought he meant that there can be no sexuality in heaven; that there can be no males and females relating to each other in the many-colored nuances of their sexual differences. But why should we add so dismal a prospect to Jesus' promise? What the Lord tells us is that in God's kingdom the limits and discipline of the marriage structure will be transcended. On earth most of us have time, energy, and dedication enough for only one other in committed union; in heaven we will be capable of intimacy unbounded. And the intimacy could be sexual even if it were not physical."[1]

Marriage as an institution, if not a particular relationship, can now give us a taste of heavenly realities. It is a lens that enables us to peer into our depraved demands and into our anticipated full redemption when we are drawn into the wonder of the marriage ceremony of the Lamb. Each moment of marriage is an anticipation of that moment when we will walk down the aisle to the Lamb's waiting embrace. It is also the anticipation of the day when we will enjoy the most profound, the most intimate, the most sensual (remember we will have heavenly bodies), the ultimately satisfying relationships. Our union with God will ignite and solidify our relationships with one another. Truly, male and female will be one flesh again.

NOTES

CHAPTER 7: Shaping Beauty and Order out of Chaos

1. Wendell Berry, *What Are People For?* (San Francisco: North Point Press, 1990), 90.
2. R. N. Longenecker, *Galatians* (Dallas: Word, 1990), 226.

CHAPTER 10: Re-entering Eden: Leaving, Weaving, Cleaving, and Becoming One Flesh

1. J. G. Wenham, *Genesis* (Dallas: Word, 1987), 69.
2. Carol Gilligan, *In a Different Voice* (Cambridge, Mass.: Harvard University Press, 1982), 160.
3. Ibid., 160–3.
4. Diana E. H. Russell, *The Secret Trauma: Incest in the Lives of Girls and Women* (New York: Basic Books, 1986), 307–11.
5. For more information about perversion and men, read Patrick Carnes, *Contrary to Love* (Minneapolis: CompCare Publishers, 1989), 122–31; and Patrick Carnes, *Don't Call It Love: Recovery from Sexual Addiction* (New York: Bantam, 1991).
6. Dana Crowley Jack, *Silencing the Self: Women and Depression* (Cambridge, Mass.: Harvard University Press, 1991), 1.

CHAPTER 11: Submitting to Each Other in Love

1. Author's translation.
2. Peter Craigie, *Psalms 1–50* (Dallas: Word, 1983), 340.
3. Even though the primary focus of several of these passages is the church, they still have relevance for family life. There is a profound relationship between the family and the church. Nonetheless, some of the principles here have specific application for church life, but not for the relationship between men and women in the broader society. An instance of a misunderstanding of this distinction is when modern Christians use this passage to argue that women can have only a restricted role in modern society, that they must stay home and tend the children while their husbands go out to work in society. While these passages may teach that women are restricted from certain roles within the church, they do not speak to women's participation in various professions and careers outside of the home. Since this is a book about marriage and not about the church, we will not address such issues as whether women can be ordained as pastors or officers in the church.
4. Peter Davids, *1 Peter*, New International Commentary of the New Testament (Grand Rapids: Eerdmans, 1990), 115.

CHAPTER 15: Glorying in Sexuality and Sensuality

1. Stanton and Brenna Jones, *How and When to Tell Your Kids about Sex* (Colorado Springs: NavPress, 1993).

2. Mike Mason, *The Mystery of Marriage* (Portland, Ore.: Multnomah Press, 1985), 123–4.

3. We will not treat the Song as a whole, however. The Song of Songs is not a narrative with a plot. The endless debates over whether the Song is a drama which tells a story about Solomon and his Egyptian princess or whether it is about Solomon, a peasant girl, and her shepherd boyfriend are all wrongheaded. It is the Song of Songs—that is, the book is a collection of love poems which extol the gift of human love and sexuality which God has given to his creatures. Later we will expand on the idea that the Song is a picture of sexuality redeemed.

4. Gordon Fee, *The First Epistle to the Corinthians,* New International Commentary of the New Testament (Grand Rapids: Eerdmans, 1987), 640.

CHAPTER 19: Living beyond the Fall

1. The context for this passage is the problem of showing favoritism toward rich visitors to church while snubbing the poor. By doing so, James is saying that the Christians to whom he is writing are breaking the royal law, given by God the King, which states "Love your neighbor as yourself." This reference draws us back to Matthew 22:34-40, where Jesus summarized the entire law under two headings: "Love the Lord your God with all your heart and with all your soul and with all your mind," and "Love your neighbor as yourself." In this way, Jesus summarized the Ten Commandments, since the first four concern how best to love God and the last six direct us in our relationship to other people. James cites only the second half because that is the issue at hand, Christians showing favoritism in church. We can just hear the recipients of the letter saying to themselves, *Give us a break. This isn't so bad. It's not as if we were killing anyone.* Here James says, "You're wrong. You are killing someone. By your hate, you are breaking the commandment that forbids murder. You hate the poor, and thus you have broken the sixth commandment."

2. Diana E. H. Russell, *The Secret Trauma: Incest in the Lives of Girls and Women* (New York: Basic Books, 1986).

3. Dan Allender and Tremper Longman III, *Bold Love* (Colorado Springs: NavPress, 1992).

4. Robert Gundry, *Matthew,* 2d ed. (Grand Rapids: Eerdmans, 1994), 380.

5. John Murray, *Romans* (Grand Rapids: Eerdmans, 1959), 179.

EPILOGUE

1. Lewis B. Smedes, *Sex for Christians* (Grand Rapids: Eerdmans, 1994), 27.